The Art & Business of Professional Trading

FIRST PRINCIPLES, MENTAL MODELS, AND
THE MATHEMATICS OF EDGE

RYAN WRIGHT

WILEY

This edition first published 2026
© John Wiley & Sons Ltd

All rights reserved, including rights for text and data mining and training of artificial intelligence technologies or similar technologies. No part of this publication may be reproduced, stored in a retrieval system, or transmitted, in any form or by any means, electronic, mechanical, photocopying, recording or otherwise, except as permitted by law. Advice on how to obtain permission to reuse material from this title is available at http://www.wiley.com/go/permissions.

The right of Ryan Wright to be identified as the author of this work has been asserted in accordance with law.

Registered Offices
John Wiley & Sons, Inc., 111 River Street, Hoboken, NJ 07030, USA
John Wiley & Sons Ltd, New Era House, 8 Oldlands Way, Bognor Regis, West Sussex, PO22 9NQ, UK

For details of our global editorial offices, customer services, and more information about Wiley products visit us at www.wiley.com.

The manufacturer's authorized representative according to the EU General Product Safety Regulation is Wiley-VCH GmbH, Boschstr. 12, 69469 Weinheim, Germany, e-mail: Product_Safety@wiley.com.

Wiley also publishes its books in a variety of electronic formats and by print-on-demand. Some content that appears in standard print versions of this book may not be available in other formats.

Trademarks: Wiley and the Wiley logo are trademarks or registered trademarks of John Wiley & Sons, Inc. and/or its affiliates in the United States and other countries and may not be used without written permission. All other trademarks are the property of their respective owners. John Wiley & Sons, Inc. is not associated with any product or vendor mentioned in this book.

Limit of Liability/Disclaimer of Warranty: While the publisher and the authors have used their best efforts in preparing this work, including a review of the content of the work, neither the publisher nor the authors make any representations or warranties with respect to the accuracy or completeness of the contents of this work and specifically disclaim all warranties, including without limitation any implied warranties of merchantability or fitness for a particular purpose. No warranty may be created or extended by sales representatives, written sales materials or promotional statements for this work. The fact that an organization, website, or product is referred to in this work as a citation and/or potential source of further information does not mean that the publisher and authors endorse the information or services the organization, website, or product may provide or recommendations it may make. This work is sold with the understanding that the publisher is not engaged in rendering professional services. The advice and strategies contained herein may not be suitable for your situation. You should consult with a specialist where appropriate. Further, readers should be aware that websites listed in this work may have changed or disappeared between when this work was written and when it is read. Neither the publisher nor authors shall be liable for any loss of profit or any other commercial damages, including but not limited to special, incidental, consequential, or other damages.

Library of Congress Control Number: 2026936343

Print ISBN: 9781394391745
ePub ISBN: 9781394391752
ePDF ISBN: 9781394390953

Cover Design: Antonio Stojceski
Cover Image: bull - Hans Eiskonen/Unsplash
Author Photo: Courtesy of the Author

Typesetting: Set in 11/13pt NewBaskervilleStd by Lumina Datamatics

Printed and bound by CPI Group (UK) Ltd, Croydon CR0 4YY

C9781394391745_160326

To the trader who survives.

Contents

Acknowledgments — vii
About the Author — ix

Introduction — 1

PART I: First Principles — 7

Chapter 1: The Invisible Opponent — 9

Chapter 2: Process Over Outcome — 23

Chapter 3: Adverse Selection — 37

Chapter 4: The Mirage of Certainty — 51

Chapter 5: Probabilistic Thinking and Expectancy — 67

Chapter 6: The Operator's Equation — 79

PART II: Mental Models — 95

Chapter 7: Where Edge Comes From — 97

Chapter 8: Structural Discipline — 115

Chapter 9: Position Sizing — 129

| Chapter 10: | Risk Definition | 149 |
| Chapter 11: | Decomposition | 163 |

PART III: The Professional's Edge — 177

Chapter 12:	Second-order Thinking	179
Chapter 13:	Mathematics of Survival	193
Chapter 14:	Regime Awareness	205
Chapter 15:	Operating System	221

PART IV: The Business of Trading — 227

| Chapter 16: | Tactical Protocols | 229 |
| Chapter 17: | Building a Professional Future | 241 |

| Glossary | 255 |
| Index | 261 |

Acknowledgments

Trading is a solitary endeavor, but the refinement of edge is a collective process.

My gratitude to Larry Lau for the commitment and the hours. To Carlos Salas for the strategic counsel. And to the team at ARB Trading Group for the infrastructure that makes institutional-grade execution accessible to those who have earned it.

> To Lance Breitstein: A Market Wizard and a builder. It is a privilege to execute alongside you. Your presence in the firm is proof that excellence attracts excellence.
>
> To Peter Brandt: Thank you for the dialogue. Your longevity in this arena—five decades of survival and performance—is the standard we all aspire to. When you speak of process, the words carry the weight of compounded experience.
>
> To the team at Raen Trading: You are the proof that exceptional results are generated by rigorous process, not pedigree. This book is the manual for what we are building. Every chapter reflects conversations we've had, mistakes we've corrected, and principles we've forged together.

Intellectually, I stand on the shoulders of giants. *Fooled by Randomness* by Nassim Nicholas Taleb was the pivot point that shifted my perspective from amateur to professional. Before that book, I thought trading was about prediction. After it, I understood that trading is about survival under uncertainty. That single insight reframed everything.

I must also acknowledge the foundational work of Brent Donnelly, whose *Alpha Trader* and *The Art of Currency Trading* set the standard for practical trading education. Agustín Lebrón's *The Laws of Trading* gave me the language of edge. Rishi Narang's *Inside the Black Box* opened the door to systematic thinking. Adam Grimes showed what rigorous technical analysis actually looks like. Robert Carver's work on position sizing and leverage crystallized the mathematics of survival. Each of these authors contributed a piece of the puzzle.

To the many other authors and operators pushing the boundaries of this craft online—through Substack, through Twitter, through podcasts and Discord servers—thank you for making this an open-source profession. The barriers to entry for quality trading education have never been lower. That democratization matters.

Finally, to the invisible peers in the marketplace who make this the most challenging game in the world: Thank you for the competition. Every dollar I have made came from someone who lost it. Every edge I have found exists because someone else failed to see it. This is a brutal business, and the brutality is what makes success meaningful.

The market owes us nothing. We earn our place or we are removed.

Thank you for reading. Now go execute.

About the Author

Ryan Wright is the founder and CEO of Raen Trading, a principal trading firm established in 2024. Raen deploys systematic and discretionary strategies across global futures, equities, and energy markets, operating on institutional infrastructure through partnerships with Trading Technologies and ARB Trading Group. The firm attracts talent from major organizations, including Jane Street, Point72, Gelber Group, and DRW.

Wright placed his first trades in 2008 while serving in a helicopter squadron in the US Navy, pursuing his economics degree between deployments. After completing his service, he founded and sold a technology company—an exit that capitalized his full transition to professional trading. Prior to founding Raen, he served as a principal at a futures proprietary trading desk established in 2020 and spent the decade prior managing capital for ultra-high-net-worth individuals and family offices while refining the risk frameworks that now define his firm.

Beyond the trading desk, Wright oversees Raen Ventures and Sentinel, an institutional trading journal and performance intelligence platform built around quantitative risk metrics and applied AI. He also runs Raen's Global Talent Scouting Program, an open assessment system designed to identify exceptional trading talent regardless of background or pedigree.

Wright's approach incorporates neuroscience, cognitive behavioral psychology, and evolutionary psychology. He views trading as a performance discipline where biological impulses meet mathematical realities—where the ancient hardware of the human brain confronts the novel environment of modern markets. *The Art and Business of Professional Trading* bridges the gap between independent trading and institutional standards, providing the frameworks that Wright wishes someone had given him when he started.

He writes regularly on his Substack and can be found on Twitter sharing market observations, trading psychology insights, and the occasional dry observation about the absurdities of financial markets.

Connect with Ryan Wright:
Website: ryanwright.co
Substack: ryanswright.substack.com
X (Twitter): @baynkr
Raen Trading: raentrading.com

Introduction

The Missing Manual

The library of trading literature is split into two distinct and largely useless categories.

On one side sits what I call the pop psychology shelf. These are the bestsellers with dramatic covers and big promises. Books filled with platitudes about mindset, discipline, and visualization. They tell you to "master your emotions" and "plan your trade" without giving you a framework for actually doing so. Telling a trader to "be disciplined" without giving them a structural edge is like telling a soldier to "be brave" without giving them a weapon. Courage without capability is just a faster route to the graveyard.

On the other side, you have the academic tome. These are monuments to technical rigor, written by PhDs for PhDs. Four hundred pages on portfolio risk mathematics or option pricing derivation. For the quant at a hedge fund or the risk manager at a prime brokerage, they're essential. But for the independent trader trying to figure out whether to hold a position overnight, they are a map of a territory you will never visit. They describe the physics of the engine. They don't teach you how to drive the car.

This creates a void. And that void is exactly where the actual profession of trading lives.

The Gap

I wrote this book because it didn't exist when I needed it.

My path into trading wasn't linear. I started as a retail trader in 2008, during the financial crisis, and worked through principal trading firms and family offices. The education came through trial and expensive error. Along the way, I've worked with operators from Point72, Jane Street, and Susquehanna. Today, through Raen Trading, I back many of these traders, which means I see not just their results but the operating systems that produce them. What I've learned from watching them: their success isn't a function of IQ, passion, or predictive ability.

It's structure.

Professionals don't rely on willpower. They run an operating system—decision protocols, risk limits, feedback loops—that insulates them from their own biology. They treat trading as an engineering problem, and engineer their way out.

A Note on Method

Finance doesn't exist in a vacuum. Throughout these chapters, you might find yourself wondering why I'm opening a section on risk management with a story about the *Challenger* explosion or explaining market mechanics through the lens of buying a camera, or drawing lessons from fighter pilots and nuclear reactor operators.

This is deliberate. The best lessons come from cross-domain parallels—the same principles showing up in different fields. (And, frankly, because most pure finance textbooks are incredibly dry, and I refuse to write another one.) I've borrowed heavily from decision science, systems engineering, military strategy, and behavioral economics. If this book has any claim to usefulness, it's because it draws from fields where being wrong has immediate consequences. Pilots, surgeons, nuclear operators—people who can't afford to confuse confidence with competence. Neither can traders.

This isn't a "get rich quick" manual. If you're looking for a magic indicator or a secret pattern that'll make you wealthy by next quarter, put this down. You are the liquidity that the professionals are hunting. This book will not help you; it will only delay your inevitable education.

This is a guide to building a business that's robust to uncertainty, resistant to emotional error, and capable of extracting rent from a hostile market over the long term. Survival first. Prosperity second. You can't compound returns from the grave.

More than anything, this is a book about awareness. I won't teach you where to buy and where to sell. I won't hand you a paint-by-numbers system that worked in backtests. What I'll do is show you the blind spots—where your intuition betrays you, where the market's structure works against you, where your own biology becomes your opponent. The value isn't in the answers. It's in learning to see the questions you didn't know to ask.

What This Book Won't Do

Let me be direct about something that might frustrate you: I am not going to tell you what to buy or when to sell.

Deliberate choice, not evasion. Retail trading education is built on prescription—indicator settings, entry triggers, exact setups with precise rules. And almost all of it is useless, or worse, actively harmful. Not because the prescriptions are wrong, but because they create the illusion of certainty in a game that has none.

The approach I've taken instead is *via negativa*—the path of removal. Rather than telling you what to add to your process, I'm focused on stripping away the false certainties, the comfortable illusions, and the mental models that feel right but lead you off a cliff. Michelangelo supposedly said he sculpted *David* by removing everything that wasn't *David*. That's the approach—not handing you a statue, but helping you see what needs to be chipped away.

What remains is epistemology, not instruction. I want you to see the game for what it is: an environment of irreducible uncertainty. The feedback loops are noisy. Survivorship bias corrupts the historical record. Your pattern-recognition machinery will see signal in randomness. Once you understand this—really understand it, not just nod along—you can't un-see it.

This might feel nihilistic at first. When I read *Fooled by Randomness* for the first time, the whole thing felt **futile**. If everything is survivorship bias and lucky idiots, what's the point? But the disorientation fades. Strip away false certainties and you're left with what actually survives scrutiny. Instead of asking, "What should I do?" you learn to ask, "What should I avoid?" and "What can I actually know?" Those answers are more durable than any setup.

A Word on Scope

The original manuscript for this book ran to nearly 160,000 words. What you're holding is half that, distilled and compressed and in some places painfully condensed. Trading is interconnected—every concept touches every other—and the temptation to explain everything is real. I've resisted it. What remains is what I believe matters most. If certain ideas feel underdeveloped, they probably are, but a usable framework beats an encyclopedic one. The goal isn't comprehensiveness. It's clarity.

The Axioms

Before we begin, three operating assumptions.

> First, information is always incomplete. If you wait for clarity, you have already missed the move. The amateur sits paralyzed, waiting for "confirmation." The professional acts on partial information, sizes for uncertainty, and updates as data arrives. Clarity is a mirage that recedes as you approach it.
>
> Second, inaction is a position. Standing still feels safe. It isn't. Standing still is a bet that the environment will not change, that the status quo will persist. In markets, where the only constant is change, this is usually a losing wager. Every moment you're flat, you're betting you can't find a positive expectancy trade. Sometimes that's true. Often, it's just fear wearing the costume of prudence.
>
> Third and most important, prediction is fragile; structure is robust. The amateur obsesses over "what happens next," spending endless hours trying to forecast the market's next move. But prediction is a brittle strategy. Even if you're right 60% of the time (which would make you one of the best forecasters alive) you are still wrong 40% of the time. What happens during that 40%?

The professional doesn't optimize for the one path they expect. They size for the thousand paths they don't. They build portfolios and position sizes that survive being wrong because they know they will be wrong. Frequently, painfully, expensively wrong. The question isn't, "How do I avoid being wrong?" It's, "How do I survive being wrong long enough for my edge to manifest?"

This is what separates amateurs from professionals. We stop trying to eliminate uncertainty—that's impossible—and start engineering our survival within it.

What Follows

The book is organized into four parts.

Part I: Foundations covers the basics—the nature of the opponent you're facing, why process matters more than outcome, and the math behind professional decision-making.

Part II: Mental Models gives you the cognitive tools—where edge actually comes from, how to think about position sizing and risk, how to break complex situations into tractable problems.

Part III: The Professional's Edge covers what separates good traders from great ones—second-order thinking, survival mathematics, regime awareness, and the operating system that ties it all together.

Part IV: The Business of Trading addresses the practical reality of building a sustainable career. Edge means nothing if you can't execute it over years and decades.

Read it straight through, or skip to the chapters that address your most pressing problems. But skim the Foundations section even if you think you know it. The traders who struggle most are the ones who skipped the fundamentals, not the ones who lack advanced techniques.

Let's begin.

PART I
First Principles

CHAPTER 1

The Invisible Opponent

At 10:45 a.m. Eastern Time on August 1, 2007, something shifted in the electronic bloodstream of American finance.

No alarm sounded. No headline scrolled across Bloomberg terminals. The S&P 500 drifted sideways. Treasury yields held steady. Unremarkable.

Forty-five minutes later, deep inside quantitative trading desks from Greenwich to Chicago, P&L screens started flashing red. Positions that had been profitable for years started hemorrhaging money. Not gradually. Not explicably. Violently.

The positions were long/short equity portfolios—mathematically constructed, designed to be immune to market direction. They held hundreds of stocks simultaneously, long the statistically cheap, short the statistically expensive. They had been minting money since 1995. The firms running these strategies employed physics PhDs, spent hundreds of millions on infrastructure, ran risk models simulating 10,000 scenarios per second.

None of it mattered.

Between 10:45 and 11:30 a.m., a hidden trigger sparked a cascade. One large portfolio—likely facing margin calls from deteriorating subprime positions—started liquidating. The selling hit the exact stocks that every other quantitative fund owned. Prices moved. Other funds' risk limits triggered. More selling. More price impact. Within hours, strategies that had never experienced more than a 2% drawdown in their entire histories were down 5%, then 10%.

By Friday, August 10, the Goldman Sachs Global Equity Opportunities fund had lost more than 30% of its value. Renaissance Technologies reported losses of 8.7% in a week. Highbridge Statistical Opportunities was down 18%. David Viniar, Goldman's chief financial officer, would later tell reporters they were seeing "things that were 25-standard-deviation moves, several days in a row."

A quick aside: if market returns followed a normal distribution, a 25-standard-deviation event should occur once every 10^{135} years. The universe is about 10^{10} years old. According to their models, what just happened was impossible. It happened anyway.

This story illustrates who you're really fighting when you enter a market.

The traders at those desks were among the most sophisticated participants in financial history. They had information advantages, technological advantages, and mathematical advantages that retail traders cannot comprehend, let alone replicate. They had risk models that incorporated every historical crisis back to the Great Depression. They had execution algorithms that could slice orders into thousands of invisible pieces. They had co-located servers that reduced latency to microseconds.

They were destroyed not by being wrong about their positions, but by being on the same side of the same trades as participants they couldn't see. Their edge was real. Their models were sound. Their risk management was state-of-the-art. But they were competing against a counterparty they had failed to identify: each other.

The funds failed because they were blind to the nature of their opponent.

Who they are, what constraints they operate under, why they're trading against you—that's the foundation of everything that follows.

The Myth of the Democratic Market

Most people arrive at trading seduced by a dangerous narrative: markets aggregate information efficiently. Prices reflect collective wisdom. If you're rational, diligent, and hardworking, you can identify mispricings others have missed. Your intelligence and effort will be rewarded. The market is, in some fundamental sense, fair.

This narrative contains truth. It also contains a blindness that costs most traders everything they have.

The blindness: when you trade, you're not trading against "the market" as an abstract entity. You're trading against a specific participant—a human being, or more likely an algorithm, with specific information, specific constraints, specific motivations. If that participant has better information, faster access, different constraints, or has already positioned before you noticed an opportunity, your trade isn't an intelligent bet against inefficiency.

It is a transfer payment from you to them.

John Maynard Keynes understood this in 1936 when he compared financial markets to a beauty contest—not the kind where judges select the most attractive face, but a peculiar newspaper game of his era where readers chose the six faces they thought other readers would find most attractive. The prize went not to the person with the best aesthetic judgment, but to the person who best predicted the crowd's predictions.

"It is not a case of choosing those which, to the best of one's judgment, are really the prettiest," Keynes wrote, "nor even those which average opinion genuinely thinks the prettiest. We have reached the third degree where we devote our intelligences to anticipating what average opinion expects the average opinion to be."

Every trader who analyzes a chart is playing first-level thinking: what does this pattern suggest price will do? Every trader who asks, "what will other traders do when they see this chart?" is playing second-level. The game is won at the third level, anticipating what others expect others to expect. Most people don't even know it exists.

Winning requires understanding what other participants believe, what constraints they operate under, and what they'll do next. Understanding the metagame. Your analysis of the underlying asset matters only to the extent that it differs from and exceeds the analysis of the person on the other side of your trade.

The Arithmetic No One Teaches You

Forget the charts for a moment. Look at the math.

Trading is not just zero-sum. It is negative-sum.

Zero-sum means every dollar you make comes directly from another participant's pocket. For you to profit, someone else must lose. No company grows because you bought a contract from someone else. No productivity increases. No innovation happens. Just a transfer of capital from one account to another.

But the situation is worse than zero-sum because every trade carries costs that leak profit from the system entirely: commissions to brokers. Bid-ask spreads paid to market makers. Slippage from imperfect execution. Exchange fees. Data fees. Platform costs. Technology infrastructure. These costs are explicit and unavoidable.

The derivatives market is a pure zero-sum game before costs. Every dollar gained on one side of a contract is a dollar lost on the other side. After costs, it becomes negative-sum. The aggregate pool of trading profits, across all participants, is negative by the amount of total transaction costs. Money flows out of the trading ecosystem to intermediaries, exchanges, and infrastructure providers.

A clarification: this zero-sum framing applies to trading—speculating on price movements over short horizons. Long-term equity investing, where you hold companies that grow earnings and pay dividends, creates real value. But this is a book about trading, not investing. Every dollar you extract comes directly from another participant.

The math is simple: most traders must fail. Not as a moral statement. Not because they lack discipline or intelligence. As arithmetic.

If the total pool of trading profits is negative, then the average participant must lose. Some will win, capturing more than their share. But for every winner, there must be losers whose losses exceed the winners' gains by the amount extracted in costs.

The distribution of trading returns is heavily skewed. A small percentage of traders capture the vast majority of profits. Everyone else finances their success.

The question becomes: if the game is negative-sum, and you must take money from someone else to survive, who exactly is that "someone"?

The Marginal Participant

The marginal participant is, in my view, the single most important mental model for understanding price action.

Markets aren't set by consensus. They're set by the *marginal participant.*

When you lift an offer on the ES, you're not trading against "the market." You're trading against whoever is sitting on that offer—the marginal seller willing to accept that price right now.

The person or algorithm standing at the front of the line.

That price is now your entry price. The marginal participant set it.

The marginal participant is not a fixed category. It is a role that shifts depending on market conditions. And the nature of the marginal participant at any given moment determines whether you face an insurmountable opponent or a vulnerable counterparty.

Two Types of Marginal Participant

In normal conditions, the marginal participant is extraordinarily sophisticated.

In 1995, the marginal participant was often a human floor trader with a telephone—constrained by geography, information latency, human cognitive limits. The edges were obvious: faster information, better tools, basic pattern recognition.

Today? At its peak in 2009, high-frequency trading firms generated over 60% of US equity volume. The figure remains near 50%, and their presence in futures markets is at least as significant. These firms make decisions based on patterns humans cannot perceive. They execute thousands of orders across multiple markets simultaneously, in microseconds. They use co-located servers positioned right next to exchange matching engines. They employ hundreds of PhDs and spend billions on infrastructure.

Call this the *typical marginal participant*: patient, unconstrained, optimizing for profit. You can't outthink them on their terrain. You can't out-analyze them. You can't see what they see.

But there is a second type.

The *opportunity marginal participant* is not optimizing for profit. They're constrained by forces that override their economic rationality. They must trade—not because they want to, but because they have to: the mutual fund facing redemptions who must sell regardless of price. The hedge fund hitting margin limits. The corporate treasurer hedging currency exposure before quarter-end. The index fund buying on inclusion day regardless of valuation.

The typical marginal participant is sophisticated. The opportunity marginal participant is desperate.

This resolves the paradox: if the marginal participant is so sophisticated, how does anyone profit? The answer is that the identity of the marginal participant changes. In equilibrium, you face the algorithms and the PhD quants. But equilibrium breaks, regularly, and when it does, the marginal participant becomes someone whose constraints create predictable, exploitable behavior.

Professional edge doesn't come from being smarter than the HFTs. It comes from recognizing when the marginal participant has shifted from unconstrained optimizer to constrained seller. The game isn't "beat the algorithm." The game is "identify when the algorithm isn't your counterparty."

The Paradox of Efficient Markets

If the typical marginal participant is so strong, why does the market exist at all? Why doesn't the efficient money simply eat everything instantly?

Economists Sanford Grossman and Joseph Stiglitz formalized the answer in 1980. Stiglitz would later win the Nobel for this work.

The paradox: if markets were perfectly efficient—if prices fully reflected all available information—then no one would have incentive to gather information. Why spend money on research if the price already incorporates everything you could learn? But if no one gathers information, prices can't reflect it. The efficient market eats itself.

The resolution is elegant: markets exist in a state of dynamic equilibrium where they are efficient enough that most participants cannot profit from information gathering, but inefficient enough that the most skilled participants can still earn returns that compensate them for their efforts.

The returns earned by sophisticated investors are, in theory, compensation for information gathering and analysis. In practice, they also include profits extracted through structural advantages—co-location and speed—that offer zero benefit to price discovery.

Who pays? The traders without edge. The uninformed. The slow. The weak.

The Grossman-Stiglitz framework assumes participants are making voluntary, optimizing decisions. It doesn't account for the opportunity marginal participant, the forced trader whose constraints create inefficiencies that cannot be arbitraged away by speed alone.

When an index fund must buy on a specific day because index rules require it, that's not an information signal—it's mechanical flow. Price moves not because of new information about value, but because of the buying pressure itself. Patient, unconstrained traders can exploit this—not by being faster, but by providing liquidity when the opportunity marginal participant needs it most.

The market is efficient not in spite of competition, but because of it. Built on the bones of everyone who isn't sophisticated enough to compete—including those who must trade on someone else's schedule.

The Mechanics of Extraction

We saw this machinery bare its teeth in March 2020.

In the first week of that month, global markets experienced a historic liquidity crisis. COVID-19 was spreading. Governments were implementing lockdowns. Uncertainty was maximal.

Foreign central banks sold large amounts of US Treasury debt and borrowed nearly $500 billion from the Federal Reserve through currency swap facilities. Corporations drew down credit lines and liquidated investments to preserve cash. Mutual funds faced redemptions and were forced to sell assets regardless of price. Hedge funds faced margin calls and had to reduce exposure immediately.

Every one of these participants became a forced seller—someone who must trade regardless of price because their constraints demand it.

The marginal participant shifted. The typical marginal participant, patient capital seeking fair value, algorithms optimizing for edge, stepped back. They withdrew their bids. They waited. And into that vacuum rushed the opportunity marginal participant: desperate capital seeking survival.

When the marginal participant turns desperate, everything changes.

Support levels did not hold. They evaporated. Correlations that had been stable for years spiked toward one. Everything fell together because everyone was selling everything. Liquidity that seemed infinite disappeared. Bid-ask spreads that were measured in fractions of pennies blew out to full dollars.

Retail traders watching charts saw their technical patterns fail spectacularly. But the patterns hadn't failed—the patterns assumed a patient, rational marginal participant. That assumption was no longer true. The marginal participant had changed, and with it, the entire logic of price formation.

Bill Ackman recognized this shift. In late February 2020, he spent $27 million on credit default swaps—insurance contracts that pay out if corporate credit conditions deteriorate. He wasn't betting that specific companies would default. He wasn't predicting the virus or government policy. He was betting that the marginal participant would become forced, that credit spreads would widen as fear spread, that everyone trying to exit at once would create the conditions for his hedge to pay off.

By March 23, his $27 million position was worth $2.6 billion. Nearly 100× in less than a month. He exited the same day the Federal Reserve announced unlimited quantitative easing—the moment maximum fear began to subside, the moment the opportunity marginal participant began to recede, the typical marginal participant began to return.

Ackman wasn't predicting the virus. He was predicting the transformation of the marginal participant under stress. Edge doesn't require being smarter than the HFTs. It requires recognizing when the HFTs are no longer setting price.

He was playing the metagame.

The Quant Meltdown Revisited

Now we can return to August 2007.

Andrew Lo called it the "Unwind Hypothesis." The losses weren't caused by the strategies being wrong. They were caused by the strategies being right but crowded.

Over the preceding decade, profitability of quantitative equity strategies had declined steadily. In 1995, a simple contrarian strategy generated average daily returns of 1.38%. By 2006: 0.15%. The edge was being competed away.

To maintain returns as edge compressed, funds increased leverage. A strategy that once generated 10% annually unleveraged might need 4× or 8× leverage to hit the return targets investors demanded. Assets devoted to similar strategies grew from hundreds of millions to tens of billions.

The funds had become, unknowingly, each other's counterparties. They held similar positions. They used similar risk models. They had similar stop-loss triggers. They were all marginal participants in the same trade.

When one large fund began liquidating, it sold the exact positions that every other fund owned. Prices moved against all of them simultaneously. Risk limits triggered. More selling. More price impact. A cascade.

The losses over August 7–9, 2007, weren't from being wrong about valuations. They were from being on the same side of a crowded trade when one participant was forced to exit. The strategies had edge—real, demonstrable edge. But they all had the *same* edge. And that concentration created fragility.

The marginal participant, in those three days, wasn't a rational investor optimizing returns. It was an algorithm executing a liquidation order. The typical marginal participant had transformed into the opportunity marginal participant. The funds that blew up failed to recognize the shift.

Adverse Selection: The Hidden Tax

A specific mechanism underlies much of what we've discussed. It operates continuously, invisibly, extracting value from the uninformed. Adverse selection.

In 1970, economist George Akerlof published a paper titled "The Market for Lemons" that would eventually win him the Nobel Prize. (Three journals initially rejected it as "trivial.") We'll return to Akerlof's framework in much greater detail in Chapter 3. His insight was simple but devastating: when one party to a transaction has more information than the other, markets can break down entirely.

Akerlof used the example of used cars. A seller knows whether their car is a peach or a lemon. A buyer can't tell the difference. Because buyers can't distinguish quality, they offer a price reflecting average quality. Sellers of peaches withdraw. Only lemons remain. The market selects adversely.

In financial markets, adverse selection operates continuously. When you enter a trade, you are revealing information about your beliefs. You think the price is wrong. You think there is an opportunity. But so does the person taking the other side. And one of you is wrong.

The question is: why is your counterparty willing to trade with you?

If you're buying, you believe the price will rise. The seller implicitly believes the price will fall—or at least has better uses for the capital. One of you has superior information. If it's them, you're the lemon buyer, paying fair price for an inferior opportunity.

Market makers understand this intimately. When a large, informed order arrives, the market maker who fills it loses money.

They compensate by widening spreads, using algorithms that detect informed flow, adjusting prices to reflect the information content of trades.

Retail traders often trade against market makers who have already priced in the information content of their orders. The retail trader believes they have spotted a pattern. The market maker knows the pattern has already been exploited or was never real to begin with. The retail trader buys. The market maker sells. The retail trader pays the spread plus the adverse selection cost plus the information disadvantage.

This isn't conspiracy or manipulation—just the fundamental structure of competitive markets. The informed profit at the expense of the uninformed. The fast profit at the expense of the slow. The typical marginal participant is almost certainly better informed than you.

But the opportunity marginal participant is not trading on information at all. They are trading on constraint. And against a constrained counterparty, the information disadvantage disappears.

The Evolutionary Filter

This competitive pressure never stops. It intensifies.

Poorly informed traders lose money and are eliminated. They quit, or reduce position sizes to irrelevance as capital erodes. Informed traders win at their expense. The market is a sorting mechanism that ruthlessly removes weakness.

Every year, every market cycle, the weak are culled. Capital concentrates toward those who are better. The surviving participants are increasingly skilled, motivated, and well-funded.

The typical marginal participant of 2025 is incomparably more sophisticated than the marginal participant of 1995. They have better information, faster execution, more capital, superior analysis. The competitive standard is higher. The edge is smaller. The margin for error is tighter.

The bar for entry keeps rising. What worked five years ago may not work today. What works today may not work five years from now.

The Freedom Edge

So how does anyone survive?

Not by being smarter—the algorithms are smarter. Not by being faster—the co-located servers are faster. Not by having more information—the institutional desks have infinitely more.

The edge must come from somewhere else.

Return to August 2007. The quantitative funds were destroyed because they were all doing the same thing. They had edge, real edge, but they had no freedom. Their risk models mandated liquidation at certain thresholds. Their investors demanded certain return profiles. Their leverage ratios required volatility targets.

When one fund was forced to sell, they all became forced to sell. Their constraints were correlated even when their positions were diversified.

The traders who survived were those who had freedom the others lacked. They could hold through the drawdown because they were not leveraged to the same degree. They could buy when others were forced to sell because they had dry powder. They could wait because their investors were patient. They could sit out entirely because they were not trapped by the same risk limits.

Your edge, as a discretionary trader, can't come from pure analysis. The algorithms see patterns first. The professionals see them before the algorithms. You won't out-analyze them.

Your edge comes from identifying when the marginal participant is constrained. When they have to trade regardless of preference. When their constraints create predictable behavior. When their forced action creates opportunity for someone patient.

Build your strategy around their necessity, not your analysis. Your advantage comes from freedom they don't have. You can wait. You can sit out. You can trade the instruments they can't afford to care about. You can hold through drawdowns that would trigger their risk limits. You can be absent when the marginal participant is sophisticated and present only when they're desperate.

The Strategic Implication

If you're competing against the typical marginal participant, you will lose. Not because you're stupid—you're bringing a knife to a drone strike. The terrain is theirs. The rules favor them. The math is insurmountable.

But you're not always competing against them.

The professional's edge comes from identifying windows when the marginal participant shifts. Index reconstitutions forcing mechanical buying or selling. Month-end or quarter-end flows creating predictable pressure. Margin calls cascading through the system.

Sentiment reaching extremes that force capitulation. When the constrained must trade and the unconstrained can choose.

In those moments, you are not competing against sophistication. You are providing liquidity to desperation. You are the patient capital that the opportunity marginal participant needs.

This isn't a guarantee of profit. Forced flows can run further than you expect, and identifying the shift requires skill. But it reframes the game. You don't need to be faster than the HFT. You need to be more patient than the forced seller.

The question is not "How do I beat the algorithm?" The question is "Who is on the other side of my trade, and why are they trading?"

The Counterparty Question

Every trade you enter requires an opposing trade. That counterparty wasn't randomly selected.

If someone is willing to sell to you at a price you believe is a bargain: what do they know that you don't? If they're willing to buy at a price you believe is expensive, why? What information do they have? Or are they trading not on information, but on constraint?

The patterns you learned aren't wrong. They're incomplete. They assume the marginal participant is patient, rational, and playing the same game you are. When that assumption holds, the patterns work. When it doesn't—when the marginal participant shifts from patient to forced, from rational to desperate—the patterns become traps.

Understanding the marginal participant is understanding the engine of market competition. Why prices move when they move. Why your stops get hit at exactly the wrong time. Why technical analysis sometimes works brilliantly and sometimes fails catastrophically.

Markets aren't democratic. They're adversarial. The adversary isn't an abstraction—it's whoever is on the other side of your trade. A participant with their own information, their own constraints, their own motivations.

Your job isn't to analyze charts. Your job is to understand counterparties.

Your job isn't to predict prices. Your job is to identify when the marginal participant is weaker than you. And when you can't—when the marginal participant is a sophisticated algorithm with better information, faster execution, and more capital—your job is to stay out of their way entirely.

That's the first principle of survival in competitive markets.

Know your opponent. And if you can't identify who in the trade is the weaker party, the weaker party is you.

Notes

August 2007 Quant Meltdown. Khandani, Amir E., and Andrew W. Lo. "What Happened to the Quants in August 2007?" *Journal of Financial Markets* 14, no. 1 (2011): 1–46.

Keynes Beauty Contest. Keynes, John Maynard. *The General Theory of Employment, Interest, and Money.* London: Macmillan, 1936. Chapter 12.

Grossman-Stiglitz Paradox. Grossman, Sanford J., and Joseph E. Stiglitz. "On the Impossibility of Informationally Efficient Markets." *American Economic Review* 70, no. 3 (1980): 393–408.

The Market for Lemons. Akerlof, George A. "The Market for 'Lemons': Quality Uncertainty and the Market Mechanism." *Quarterly Journal of Economics* 84, no. 3 (1970): 488–500.

Bill Ackman's COVID Trade. Chung, Juliet. "Bill Ackman Scored $2.6 Billion with Hedges in 27 days." *Wall Street Journal*, March 25, 2020.

High-frequency Trading Market Share. Various sources including SEC reports and industry analyses. The 60% peak figure is from 2009; current estimates vary by market and measurement methodology.

CHAPTER 2

Process Over Outcome

Trading is a negative-sum game. That's structural hostility. But there's a second layer, and it's biological.

The Deterministic Trap

Human learning is built on a tight, causal feedback loop that has served our species for 200,000 years. If a prehistoric hunter touches a fire, he burns. The pain is immediate, localized, directly correlated to the error. The lesson is encoded instantly: Action A (touching fire) leads to Outcome B (pain). Do not repeat Action A.

This feedback loop—Action, Outcome, Learning—is the fundamental mechanism of skill acquisition. It's how a toddler learns to walk, how a musician learns guitar, how a surgeon learns to suture. In these deterministic domains, the quality of the result is a nearly perfect proxy for the quality of the decision. If the guitar sounds bad, your finger placement was wrong. If the bridge collapses, the engineer calculated the load incorrectly.

If you fail, you erred. If you succeed, you performed.

You've spent your entire life conditioned by this logic. You studied for exams and got the grades. You practiced the sport and won the game. Your brain expects the world to be fair—inputs equal outputs, and the outcome is the ultimate arbiter.

Then you enter the market.

The market is one of the few places on earth that breaks this evolutionary expectation. It's not designed to teach you—it's a mechanism for price discovery that often functions as a mechanism for confusion.

Trading isn't deterministic. It's a probabilistic domain wrapped in noise—hidden information, ragged distributions, nonlinear feedback. The link between decision and result isn't just loose; it's frequently severed entirely.

You can commit gross risk management negligence—overleveraging a hunch, ignoring a stop-loss, trading on a rumor from a group chat—and be rewarded with a windfall profit. You can execute a trade with flawless logic, perfect sizing, and a genuine mathematical edge, only to be stopped out by a geopolitical shock or a random liquidity void that had nothing to do with your thesis.

The result: the market will frequently train you to do the wrong thing. It spikes your dopamine when you're reckless and punishes you with cortisol when you're disciplined. If you bring your deterministic learning model into this environment—if you let your short-term P&L teach you how to trade—you're not learning. You're being groomed for failure.

The core challenge of professional trading isn't mastering technicals or macro. It's the epistemological crisis of having to ignore the most powerful signal your brain receives: the result.

This is the psychological counterpart to structural hostility. The market isn't just mathematically rigged against you—it's biologically rigged against you.

The Drift and the Noise

Susquehanna International Group—SIG—is one of the largest market makers on the planet, trading billions of dollars daily across equities, options, and derivatives. Their partners didn't come from the Ivy League economics departments you'd expect. They started as poker players—serious ones—who applied probabilistic thinking to trading. And today, SIG doesn't just play poker on Friday nights for fun; they use it as a mandatory filter for hiring and training.

Because poker teaches the one lesson that humans are wired to reject: you can do everything right and still lose.

Jerrod Ankenman, a mathematician and former professional poker player who became a quant at SIG, quantifies this with a specific statistic from Limit Hold'em.

In a heads-up game between a professional and a decent amateur, the pro's edge—expected profit per hand—might be 0.02 big bets. That's the signal. The tiny structural advantage that, over thousands of hands, compounds into a living.

However, the standard deviation—the luck factor, the random distribution of cards—on any single hand is roughly 2.5 big bets.

The noise (2.5) is 125 times larger than the signal (0.02).

This is the signal-to-noise ratio of a single trade. Variance swamps edge. If you judge your strategy based on 1 hand, or 10, or even 100, you're looking at 99% noise and 1% skill. You can't "A/B test" a strategy by playing it for a day. You'd need 100,000 hands to statistically prove the edge exists.

The following image visualizes this massive discrepancy between short-term noise and long-term signal in a probabilistic domain:

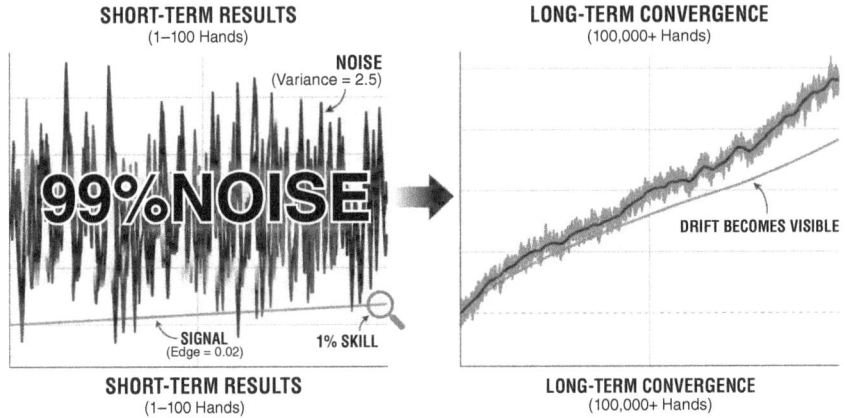

The noise (variance) is 125x larger than the signal (edge).
Short-term outcomes are dominated by randomness.

In trading, the ratio is often worse.

You execute a breakout trade on Crude Oil. Your entry is textbook—a reclaim of the prior day's high on expanding volume. Your stop is logical, placed below the structure that defines your thesis. Your target is based on a genuine inefficiency you have identified in the term structure. You have positive expectancy. You have what Ankenman would call "drift"—the slow, statistical pull of edge working in your favor over time.

Then, a geopolitical headline hits. Or a massive liquidation order from a blown-out hedge fund sweeps the book. Or the market just wanders randomly because liquidity is thin during the European lunch hour.

You take a loss.

Your brain, trapped in its ancestral feedback loop, screams: Bad Result = Bad Decision. Don't do that again.

Think about the poker player holding pocket aces who gets their money in pre-flop against an opponent holding 7-2 offsuit—statistically the worst hand in Hold'em—and loses when the board runs out 7-7-2. Did they make a mistake? Should they stop playing aces?

No. They put their money in good. They maximized their drift. The loss was just variance collecting its tax.

The lesson isn't "aces are dangerous." It's that single observations are meaningless in a game dominated by variance. The poker player who adjusts their strategy based on one bad beat isn't learning—they're degrading their edge by reacting to noise.

The same is true for you.

The Three-step Audit

If we can't trust our P&L to tell us whether we're trading well—at least not in the short term—how do we evaluate ourselves? If the result is noise, where's the truth?

The poker world developed a framework for exactly this problem. It breaks every trade (or hand) into three distinct phases.

The Ante

In poker, before you see a single card, you post an ante or a blind. A sunk cost. It forces action. Without it, the optimal strategy would be to wait for aces until the heat death of the universe. The ante forces you to play marginal hands, to take risks, to participate.

In trading, your ante is not just the commission. It is the fixed cost of readiness.

It is your data fees. It is your screens. It is the mental energy required to sit and stare at a tape that does nothing for four hours. It is the opportunity cost of the capital sitting in your account instead of compounding in an index fund. Every time you enter a trade, you pay the bid-ask spread. You start underwater. You must overcome that friction before you can profit.

Amateurs view the spread as an annoyance. Professionals view it as the vig—the price of admission. Your edge must exceed this ante, or you're slowly bleeding to death while feeling busy.

(More on this in Chapter 6.)

The Decision

This is the only thing you control.

In a poker hand, you have private information (your hole cards) and public information (the board, your opponent's betting patterns). Your job is to synthesize these into a decision that maximizes expected value under time pressure.

Two constraints: time pressure and incomplete information.

If you could pause the game, take the cards into a laboratory, run a solver, and analyze for a week, you'd play perfectly. You can't. You have 10 seconds. The clock is running. The market is moving. You must act now, or the opportunity evaporates.

This is why trading is hard. Not because the math is complex—a competent high schooler can calculate expected value. It's hard because you must do the math while your amygdala is screaming, while your P&L is flashing, while the market is printing bars that look like they're about to run away without you.

A good trade isn't "a trade that made money."

A good trade is a decision that's as close as possible to the decision you'd have made with infinite time and a supercomputer. If you approximate that decision and lose money, you traded well. If you deviate from that decision and make money, you traded poorly.

The Audit

Here's the crucial shift. You can't trust the P&L of a single trade, so you must trust the process review.

At SIG, traders don't just high-five over wins. They sit down and narrate the hand.

"I held jacks. The flop came queen-high, rainbow. Villain checked. I bet two-thirds pot. He raised. I folded."

A peer might respond: "Bad fold. Based on his range in that spot, he's bluffing 40% of the time. You have the odds to call."

Even if folding saved money that specific time—even if the opponent happened to have queens—the process was wrong. The fold left EV on the table. Over thousands of identical spots, that fold is a leak.

Conversely, if you call and lose, the peer might say: "Good call. Unlucky result. Do it again next time."

This is how you must treat your trading journal. Not a diary of your feelings. Not an accounting ledger of your fills. A forensic audit of your drift.

After every significant trade, three questions:

Did I adhere to my entry criteria? Was there genuine edge, or was I rationalizing?
Did I size appropriately for the setup and my conviction?
Did I exit because the thesis was invalidated, or because I was scared?

If the answer to all three is "yes, I followed the plan," and you still lost money—circle that trade in green. Winning decision, losing outcome. Pocket aces that got cracked. Drift overwhelmed by noise. Do it again next time.

If you broke your rules, chased a candle, oversized on tilt, and made $5,000? Circle it in red. Losing decision, winning outcome. That money isn't profit—it's a loan from the market gods. They will collect.

The worst thing that can happen to a bad process is that it gets rewarded—because then it gets repeated.

The Negative Skew Trap

The signal-to-noise problem explains why good traders lose on individual trades. There's a deeper trap—a structural trap—that explains why entire strategies can appear profitable for years before detonating.

This is the trap of negative skew.

Take the options seller who collects premiums in a low-volatility regime. They sell uncovered puts on an index, month after month, betting that the market will stay calm, that implied volatility will exceed realized volatility, that they can pocket the difference.

For three years, they win. Small, frequent checks. Their equity curve is a beautiful 45-degree line rising to the right. Sharpe ratio of 2.0 or 3.0—the kind of number that attracts capital allocations and speaking invitations. To the outside observer, they've solved the market. They write blog posts about "harvesting volatility premium." They confuse the absence of volatility with the absence of risk.

The market is feeding them dopamine. Win. Win. Win.

Then the tail event arrives.

(In a normal distribution, a six-sigma move should occur once every 1.4 million years. Markets don't follow normal distributions—they follow power laws. The tails are fat. Six-sigma moves happen every few years. The models say "impossible"; the market says "Tuesday.")

Volatility expands 300% in a single morning. Liquidity evaporates. The position moves against them by 10 standard deviations. Three years of profits wiped out in an hour—followed by the principal, followed by the firm's solvency.

Nassim Taleb has the perfect metaphor for this: the turkey before Thanksgiving. Fed every day. Confidence growing with each data point. On day 1,000, the turkey has overwhelming statistical evidence that humans are friendly.

Day 1,001 is Thanksgiving.

The outcome of the previous three years taught the option seller their process was sound. The outcome was a lie—noise masquerading as signal, right up until it became catastrophe.

Strategies that rely on being right most of the time but carry catastrophic tail risk function like a narcotic—constant validation while dynamite hides in the foundation. Strategies with positive skew—trend following, long volatility—often look like failure. You bleed slowly. You take small losses 60% or 70% of the time. Constant pain. But this pain is the premium you pay for the outlier trade that makes the decade.

The amateur looks at the option seller's smooth chart and says, "That's a good trader." The professional looks at the payout structure and asks, "Where's the tail risk hiding?"

The Probabilistic Reality

If you're serious about longevity in this business, you must accept a mathematical truth: your short-term P&L tells you almost nothing about your skill.

Take a strategy with 15% annualized return and 10% annualized volatility. World-class. The kind of risk-adjusted returns that sovereign wealth funds allocate billions to capture. What's the probability this strategy makes money on any given day?

About 54%.

That's your edge. That's what excellence looks like in practice. On any given Tuesday, your probability of winning is marginally better than a coin flip. Your daily P&L is a single draw from a distribution. Most draws cluster around the mean. You are obsessing over observations that are overwhelmingly likely to be noise.

Now examine the implications. If you check your P&L frequently—and most intraday traders do, obsessively—you are staring at a data stream that is approximately 95% noise and 5% signal. When you judge your performance based on a single day, or even a single week, you are not analyzing data. You are reading tea leaves.

A winning day doesn't mean you traded well. It means the draws landed in your favor. A losing day doesn't mean your edge is broken. It means you are experiencing the toll of variance. This is expected. This is normal. This is survivable—if you understand it.

But the human brain is a pattern-recognition machine built for the African savanna, not the Chicago Mercantile Exchange. We suffer from apophenia—the tendency to see meaningful patterns in random data. We see faces in clouds. Gamblers believe in "hot streaks." Traders see "regime shifts" in random price ticks. Conspiracies in coincidence. Structure where there's only noise.

When you stare at a losing P&L for three days straight, your amygdala screams that something is wrong. Fear triggers fight-or-flight. You convince yourself the market has changed, the setup is broken, you've lost your touch. You make decisions in a state of biochemical panic that would horrify your calm self.

This is where deterioration begins. You react to noise. Tighten stops. Tweak entry criteria. Abandon the system to chase a new hot sector or a new guru's setup. You're not tuning your strategy—you're curve-fitting it to noise. You are degrading the robustness of your process by chasing the ghosts of variance.

This phenomenon has a name in decision theory: resulting—judging the quality of a decision by its outcome. Annie Duke wrote an entire book about it. The lesson is simple but hard to internalize: in any domain with significant variance, short-term outcomes are a terrible teacher.

The Cognitive Architecture of Failure

Resulting isn't random. It's driven by specific, identifiable biases.

Attribution bias is the first culprit. Your brain constantly invents narratives to explain outcomes in ways that preserve your ego. In trading, this manifests as attribution asymmetry.

When you win, the internal monologue: "I read the flow perfectly. My thesis on the Fed was spot-on. I sized appropriately. I am a skilled operator." The brain assigns the outcome to internal competence.

When you lose? "The algorithms hunted my stop. The market maker widened the spread at exactly the wrong moment. The Fed surprised everyone. I got unlucky." External malevolence.

This is a perfect intellectual shield against learning. If every win validates your genius and every loss is a victimhood story, you never examine your own errors. Trapped in a loop of self-congratulation, slowly bleeding capital while blaming the dealer. The catastrophic consequence is that you systematically prune the behaviors that lead to losses, even when those behaviors have positive expected value.

Hindsight bias is the second trap—the "I knew it all along" effect. Once an event has occurred, it's neurologically impossible to accurately reconstruct your prior uncertainty.

After a market crash, the narrative crystallizes instantly. *Of course* the market crashed. The yield curve was inverted. Valuations were 30× earnings. The geopolitical situation was unstable. Obvious now.

Be honest: it wasn't obvious then. In the moment of decision, the yield curve had been inverted for 18 months while stocks rallied. Valuations were high but earnings were growing. The geopolitical situation was ambiguous, as it always is. Anyone who acted decisively on those "obvious" warning signals would have bled to death before the actual turn.

Hindsight bias erases uncertainty from the past. Makes the market appear deterministic and solvable. Creates the false belief that if you were just "smarter" or "more disciplined," you'd have seen it coming.

Black-and-white thinking is the third failure mode. Humans prefer all-or-nothing categories: 100% right or 100% wrong, good trade or bad trade, smart or stupid.

Trading doesn't operate in binary space. It operates in probability distributions. A trade can be perfectly constructed—high expected value, appropriate sizing, clean execution—and still lose money. That is not a failure. That is just the cost of doing business in a probabilistic domain.

The professional evaluates trades on process, not outcome. Did I have edge? Did I size correctly? Did I manage risk appropriately? Did I execute the plan? If yes, the trade was good—regardless of whether it made or lost money this time.

Why Intelligence Is Not Your Ally

At this point, you might be thinking: "These biases are real, but I'm smart. I can think my way around them."

Bad news. Intelligence isn't an antidote to bias—it's frequently an accelerant.

High-IQ individuals are often more susceptible to motivated reasoning, not less. If you're intelligent, you're exceptionally good at rationalizing. You have the cognitive horsepower to construct elaborate, sophisticated arguments to justify whatever your emotional brain wants.

A novice trader panic-sells at the market bottom and admits: "I got scared."

A sophisticated trader panic-sells at the bottom and writes a three-page memo explaining how "a structural shift in the volatility regime, combined with deteriorating credit conditions and a breakdown in cross-asset correlations, necessitates a tactical rotation into cash to preserve optionality for re-entry at more favorable levels."

The action is identical. The outcome is identical. But the intelligent trader has built a fortress around their delusion. They've insulated their ego from the error. They won't learn from this mistake because their intelligence has convinced them no mistake occurred—circumstances simply changed.

To see this, we need to revisit the most exhausted case study in finance: Long-Term Capital Management.

(Yes, every trading book cites LTCM. We revisit it because it's still the cleanest case study of intelligence accelerating ruin.)

In 1998, LTCM was staffed by intellectual titans: two Nobel Laureates (Myron Scholes and Robert Merton), plus some of the finest quant traders on earth. They'd constructed a mathematically rigorous framework for identifying mispricings between related securities and betting on convergence.

The thesis was sound. The mathematics elegant. The backtests stunning. On paper, LTCM was a machine for converting uncertainty into profit. They believed they'd quantified risk so precisely that they could leverage 25-to-1.

LTCM was also a monument to overconfidence. They'd confused luck—favorable market conditions that happened to reward their thesis—with structural law.

The cracks appeared months before the collapse. In May and June 1998, spreads started to widen inexplicably. The model said convergence; the market said divergence. Then Russia defaulted on its domestic debt. A tail event their models suggested was extraordinarily unlikely. The structure shattered. Markets went haywire. Correlations that had been stable for years broke down. Positions LTCM had deemed "hedged" moved together, in the wrong direction.

The fund hemorrhaged more than $4 billion in weeks. The Fed had to orchestrate a private bailout to prevent systemic collapse.

The lesson isn't leverage, or fragile models, or crowded trades—though all those apply. It's this: LTCM didn't fail because the traders were stupid. They failed because they were geniuses who couldn't imagine being wrong. Their intelligence let them construct an elaborate narrative in which their models were correct and any contrary evidence was "noise." When the market moved against them, they didn't cut risk. They doubled down.

Intelligence without humility is just a faster route to ruin.

The Institutional Solution: Architecture Over Willpower

If you can't trust your brain to naturally prioritize process over outcome (you can't), and you can't trust your intelligence to override your biases (you definitely can't), what remains?

Professional trading firms don't rely on their traders being stoic philosophers. They assume their traders are flawed humans with dopamine-addicted brains. They don't rely on willpower. They rely on architecture—external scaffolding that forces rational behavior even when you're emotionally compromised.

Precommitment: Ulysses Binding Himself

In Homer's *Odyssey*, Ulysses knew he wouldn't be able to resist the Sirens. He didn't try to "stay hard" or "trust his training." He acknowledged his future weakness and created a physical constraint—ordered his men to tie him to the mast.

You must tie yourself to the mast while the waters are calm.

Define your trade parameters—entry trigger, stop-loss, position size, profit target—before the market opens. Before the tape is moving. Before the P&L is flashing red or green.

When you're in a "cold" cognitive state, operating rationally, you're a competent risk manager. Once the position is live, you shift into a "hot" state—intoxicated by cortisol and adrenaline. You're no longer the decision-maker; you're the executor of the plan written by your rational self.

For intraday traders, this means having a morning plan. Brent Donnelly's "12-12" framework: twelve hours back (brief post-mortem—what worked, what broke, what you learned) and twelve hours forward (what's the plan for today? which products? what setups? what maximum risk? where are you flat no matter what?).

The plan sits in front of you. It is past-you, lashing present-you to the mast.

The Ex Ante Decision Journal

The Three-step Audit framework we discussed earlier requires a specific tool: the ex ante decision journal.

Most traders keep a journal that's merely accounting: "Bought ES at 6120, sold at 6145, made 25 handles." That's not a learning tool. It's bookkeeping.

The real power of journaling comes from writing things down before you enter the trade.

Before you put risk on, write down the thesis: Why am I entering this trade? What outcome would prove I'm wrong? What's my edge? How am I sizing relative to conviction? Be specific—"opening drive fade into overnight VWAP with 2:1 reward-to-risk," not "looks toppy."

After the trade, add a few lines: Did it work for the reason I expected? Did I stick to the plan? Did I exit at my predetermined level or deviate?

Six months later, you compare outcomes to journal entries. Did the market move in your favor for the reason you wrote down? If yes, that's potential skill—signal emerging from noise. If no—if you bought expecting a squeeze and it went up because of a surprise earnings leak—that's not a win. It's a lucky accident grafted onto a failed thesis. A professional marks that trade as a process failure, even though it printed money.

A loss burns the hand; a lucky win infects the mind. The journal makes lying to yourself harder.

The Pre-mortem

Optimism is the default for anyone entering a trade. You don't put risk on expecting to lose. Natural, but it creates a blind spot.

Run a pre-mortem before every significant position.

Assume it's tomorrow and the trade has been a disaster. You're sitting at your desk staring at your maximum loss. What happened?

Force your brain to construct the failure narrative in advance. Correlation break? Fed surprise? Misread order flow? Liquidity evaporate at the worst moment? By articulating failure modes before they occur, you break the illusion of inevitability. You might realize the "surprise" risk is actually a reasonable-probability event you were ignoring because it conflicted with your thesis.

(More on this in Chapter 12.)

The Probabilist's Vow

The transition from amateur to professional isn't technical. It's philosophical.

The amateur is a historian. They look at the chart, the account balance, the news, and rewrite the past to make themselves the hero. They judge the quality of the bet by where the ball landed on the roulette wheel. Slaves to the outcome.

The professional is a probabilist. They accept they're operating in a fog of incomplete information. They accept that the outcome of any single trade is largely noise. They care only about the integrity of the coin they're flipping.

They know that if the coin is weighted in their favor, and they manage risk so they can flip it thousands of times, the law of large numbers will eventually drown out the noise.

You must learn to feel a strange, counterintuitive emotion: pride in a losing trade that followed your rules, disgust at a winning trade that broke them.

When you can lose money and honestly say, "That was a good trade," you've finally broken the deterministic feedback loop. You're no longer letting short-term results train you.

You're playing a game where the odds are weighted in your favor, where you're sized appropriately for survival, where you understand the short-term scoreboard isn't your enemy—it's irrelevant noise to be endured while the math converges.

The market doesn't care about your feelings. But your feelings will determine whether you survive long enough for your edge to compound.

Process over outcome. Signal over noise. Drift over variance.
This is the vow.

Notes

Signal-to-noise in Poker. Ankenman, Jerrod, and Bill Chen. *The Mathematics of Poker.* ConJelCo, 2006. The definitive text on quantitative poker theory and its application to trading.

Resulting. Duke, Annie. *Thinking in Bets: Making Smarter Decisions When You Don't Have All the Facts.* Portfolio, 2018. The core text on decoupling process from outcome.

Negative Skew and Fat Tails. Taleb, Nassim Nicholas. *Fooled by Randomness: The Hidden Role of Chance in Life and in the Markets.* Random House, 2004. The turkey metaphor and the critique of naive empiricism.

LTCM Collapse. Lowenstein, Roger. *When Genius Failed: The Rise and Fall of Long-Term Capital Management.* Random House, 2000. The narrative account. For academic analysis, see Jorion, Philippe. "Risk Management Lessons from Long-Term Capital Management." *European Financial Management* 6, no. 3 (2000): 277–300.

Attribution Bias and Motivated Reasoning. Kunda, Ziva. "The Case for Motivated Reasoning." *Psychological Bulletin* 108, no. 3 (1990): 480–498.

Pre-mortem Technique. Klein, Gary. "Performing a Project Premortem." *Harvard Business Review,* September 2007.

12-12 Framework. Donnelly, Brent. *Alpha Trader: The Mindset, Methodology and Mathematics of Professional Trading.* Harriman House, 2021.

SIG Training and Poker. Background on Susquehanna's poker-based training is documented in various industry profiles and interviews. The firm's partners have publicly discussed their poker origins and the role of game theory in their trading philosophy.

CHAPTER

Adverse Selection

"The market is a place set apart where men can deceive each other."
—Anacharsis, sixth century BC

*T*rading is a negative-sum game. Your brain is wired to mislead you about whether you're trading well. Now the third layer: even when you think you've found an opportunity, the fact that it's available to you may be evidence that it isn't an opportunity at all.

The Broken Camera

It's almost midnight on a Tuesday in February. The house is silent, lit only by the blue glow of your monitor. You've been hunting for a Leica M10-R for three months.

For the uninitiated, a Leica is not merely a camera. It's a dense brick of brass and magnesium, hand-assembled in Wetzlar, Germany. A mechanical object of desire that costs more than a used Honda Civic. You know this market with the intimacy of an obsessive. You've scraped photography forums at sunrise, tracked eBay listings over lunch, refreshed classifieds during conference calls.

A clean one—unblemished sensor, calibrated rangefinder, original packaging—trades in a tight band between $5,200 and $5,600. You know the serial number ranges to avoid, the difference between a "motivated seller" (divorcee liquidating assets) and a "tire-kicker" (collector testing the waters). You've become, in your own estimation, an expert.

38 The Art & Business of Professional Trading

A new listing appears. "Buy It Now." $4,200. You lean forward.

The listing photographs are crisp, shot under studio lighting that suggests a professional seller. The description is meticulous: "Minor scuff on baseplate (see Figure 3.1), glass is perfect, shutter count 8,400, original box included." The seller has accumulated 100% positive feedback over five years. A near-pristine reputation.

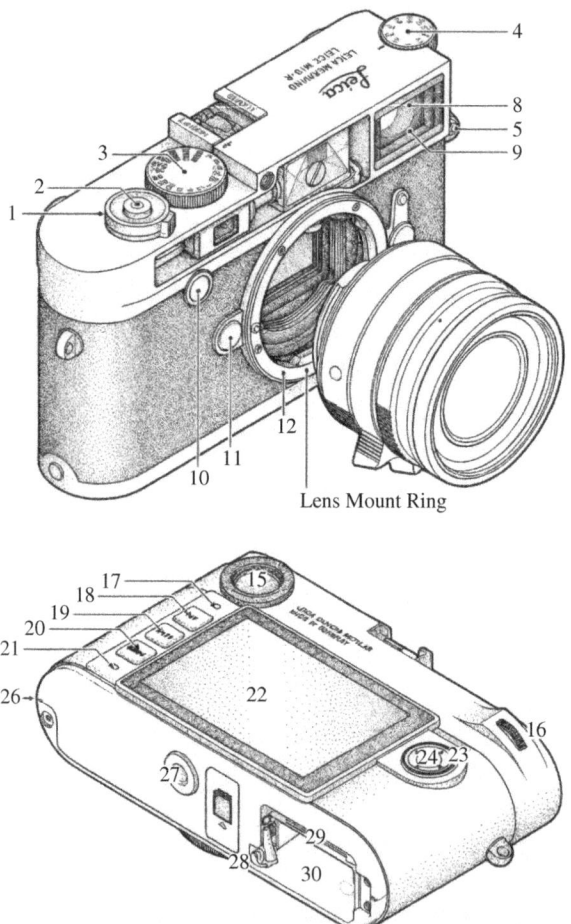

Figure 3.1 A clinical dissection of the Leica M10. While external features like the top plate or lens mount ring may appear pristine in a listing photograph, critical internal components—specifically the complex rangefinder mechanism—remain hidden from the buyer. This invisibility creates the information asymmetry necessary for adverse selection to occur.

Your pulse quickens. This is it. A mispricing. An anomaly. According to the efficient market hypothesis—that elegant academic fiction—this opportunity shouldn't exist. Information travels instantly; arbitrageurs should have closed this gap milliseconds after it opened. Yet here it is, glowing on your screen: $1,300 of instant equity. So obvious it feels like a gift. You could flip this camera tomorrow for a 30% profit. Or you could keep it, finally owning the tool you've coveted for years, having paid thousands less than fair value.

You click "Buy It Now" before you can talk yourself out of it. PayPal. Confirmed.

You sit back, dopamine flooding. You didn't merely purchase a camera. You beat the market. You were faster, more vigilant, better informed than every other buyer who missed this while sleeping or living their lives without the proper reverence for deals. You are the hunter who caught the prey. You fall asleep dreaming of street scenes in golden hour, portraits with that legendary Leica rendering.

Three days later, the package arrives. The camera is beautiful. Machined aluminum, heavy brass, the satisfying click of the shutter dial through its detents. You mount your 50mm Summilux, point it at your bookshelf, take a test shot. Load it into Lightroom, anticipating the pleasure of pixel-peeping.

You zoom to 100%.

The image is soft. Not motion-blurred, not obviously out of focus, just off. There's a haze where there should be crispness. You take another shot. Tripod, f/8, cable release, focus calibration chart taped to the wall. Same result. The plane of sharpest focus falls two inches behind your subject. You test three times, methodically, refusing to believe it. Same result each time. The rangefinder is miscalibrated.

Your stomach drops.

You search the serial number online and find a forum thread from 2021, buried in a Leica enthusiast community. A known manufacturing defect in a specific production run: a cam-follower issue causing the rangefinder to drift out of alignment. Progressive. Can't be fixed by any local shop. Requires a return to the Leica factory, a six-month waitlist, and a $1,400 repair bill.

The seller knew.

He had to know. The listing photos were taken in Live View—bypassing the defective rangefinder entirely. The "minor scuff on baseplate" was a distraction, a small, disclosed flaw to create the appearance of transparency while concealing the catastrophic one. The detailed description. The professional lighting. The impeccable feedback score. All of it was stagecraft.

The "impossible" price was not an error. Not a grieving widow ignorant of what she possessed. Not a lucky find. It was precision. The seller understood the repair cost, the market price of a functioning unit, and your psychology. He priced the camera at exactly the point where greed would overwhelm skepticism.

You thought you were the hunter.

You were the inventory disposal mechanism.

The Bioluminescent Lure

What happened in that auction is not unique. It's not bad luck. It's a biological constant governing every exchange of value in a competitive ecosystem.

Deep in the bathypelagic zone—roughly 2,000 meters down, where sunlight can't penetrate—swims the female Anglerfish.

In the crushing darkness, she's invisible. The only thing visible to her prey is a small, glowing sphere suspended in the water column. This is the esca, a bioluminescent lure dangling from a modified dorsal spine that arches over her mouth like a fishing pole.

To a smaller fish navigating the eternal black, this light is irresistible. It breaks the monotony of the void. In the deep ocean, light implies life. Implies food. Signals opportunity.

The prey sees a chance to eat and approaches. It's not stupid—it's acting rationally based on the information available.

But the signal is a lie.

The light is a mask for translucent, needle-like teeth angled inward—entry is easy, exit impossible. By the time the prey realizes the opportunity was a trap, the jaws have snapped shut.

That eBay listing wasn't a camera. It was the esca—a bioluminescent lure designed to extract capital from the uninformed.

This is adverse selection.

It's the most dangerous dynamic in financial markets. More lethal than volatility, more persistent than drawdowns, more subtle than fraud. Any "easy" meal you find in the market is likely a lure dangling above a predator's mouth.

When you sit at your trading desk, you're not in some clean, neutral marketplace. You're in the bathypelagic zone. Surrounded by entities—Goldman Sachs, Citadel, Renaissance Technologies, Jump Trading—that have evolved to strip calories from the water with ruthless efficiency. They're not "providing liquidity" out of altruism. They are the anglerfish. And that flashing green tick on your screen? That breakout pattern that looks so perfect?

That is the light.

The Market For Lemons

We want to believe liquid markets are different. "I trade the S&P 500, crude oil, the euro. These are the deepest, most efficient markets in the world. No monsters in the order book."

We want to believe the market is a supermarket—goods displayed at fair prices, take what you want. But it's not a supermarket. It's a used car lot in 1970.

To understand why you consistently buy the top and sell the bottom, we return to George Akerlof—we met his lemons framework briefly in Chapter 1, but now we need the full mechanism. In 1970, Akerlof was a young economist who wrote a paper titled "The Market for 'Lemons.'" It was rejected by three major journals. The reviewers dismissed it—two as trivial, one as simply wrong. Just a story about cars.

They were wrong. Two decades later, that "trivial" paper won Akerlof the Nobel Prize. It proved a devastating mathematical truth: information asymmetry doesn't just make markets inefficient. It destroys them.

Akerlof's logic was simple, but the implications are terrifying. Imagine a used car market. Two types of car exist: peaches (pristine, maintained religiously, oil changed every 3,000 miles, worth $20,000) and lemons (defective, transmissions that slip when hot, hairline cracks in the engine block, worth $10,000).

The critical friction—the asymmetry—is that the seller knows which car is which. He's lived with it. He knows the transmission slips. The buyer sees only "a car." He can't tell the difference until he buys it.

Watch what happens.

The buyer can't risk paying $20,000 for a lemon. Rationally, he offers an average price. If half the cars are peaches and half are lemons, he offers $15,000.

Now look at the incentives. The lemon owner holds a $10,000 car. He's offered $15,000. Windfall. He accepts instantly, dumps his toxic asset on the buyer. But the peach owner holds a $20,000 car.

He's offered $15,000. Insulted. Why take a $5,000 loss on a quality asset? He refuses. Drives his peach home.

The result is a death spiral. Good inventory leaves. Bad inventory rushes in. Average quality drops, forcing buyers to lower their bids ($12,000, then $10,000), driving out even the mediocre cars. Eventually the market collapses. It becomes a mechanism for selecting the worst outcomes. The only things left for sale are things nobody should buy.

This is not a parable about cars. It is a description of your order flow.

Every time you look at a price on your screen, you're the buyer in the used car lot. You're looking at a limit sell order—an offer to sell a contract at a specific price. Ask yourself: is this contract a peach or a lemon?

If the contract is a peach—about to go up on good news—why is the seller offering it to you? Why aren't they holding it? Why hasn't a smarter, faster professional already bought it?

If it's a lemon—about to drop on bad news—the seller is desperate to get out. They'll hit your bid instantly.

This leads to the fundamental rule of adverse selection: if you're filled easily, you're probably owning the lemon.

When you place a limit order and it sits unfilled while the market ticks higher, you're watching the peaches drive away. The sellers know value is rising. They won't sell to you. But when you place a limit order and—WHACK—you're filled instantly, price immediately ticks against you? That was the lemon owner dumping his inventory. You didn't "get a fill." You became the liquidity for someone else's exit.

The Limit Order Paradox

This dynamic plays out in real time on your platform, often in ways you don't notice until it's too late. The trap springs in milliseconds.

Imagine you're trading the E-mini S&P 500. Late 2025, market at 6,800.00. You're bullish. Bid 6,800.00, Ask 6,800.25.

You act like a disciplined professional. Refuse to pay the spread. Place a limit buy at 6,800.00. Join the queue on the bid. Wait.

This limit order is not a neutral tool. It's an option you've written to the market. You're saying: "I promise to buy at 6,800.00, regardless of what happens in the next five minutes."

Whether this is a good trade depends entirely on who takes you up on that offer.

Scenario A: The Noise Trader. A dentist in Omaha sells his portfolio because he read a scary headline. He hits your bid. You get filled. Fair value hasn't changed—the dentist just paid the spread to exit. You captured edge. You bought at the bid, and the market is still worth the offer. This is how market makers print money.

Scenario B: The Informed Trader. Bearish news hits the wire—surprise rate hike, geopolitical shock. Fair value of the S&P 500 instantly drops to 6,795.00. The HFTs see this in microseconds. They need to dump inventory. They see your limit order sitting at 6,800.00—a stale price. They hit your bid. SNAP. You're filled.

You think you got a great price. In reality, the HFTs cleared the book because your price was wrong. The market is now 6,795.00. You're underwater by five handles.

This is the adverse selection paradox:

When you're right (the market goes up), informed traders won't sell to you at your limit price. You sit on the bid and miss the move.

When you're wrong (the market is about to drop), informed traders rush to hit your bid. You get filled immediately, right before the loss.

Limit orders are passive risk. If you can't distinguish between the dentist and the HFT—if you can't read the flow to know when fair value is moving—your limit orders will systematically capture the downside while missing the upside. You'll be the liquidity of last resort for the smart money.

The Institutional Architecture

The problem runs deeper than individual trades. The structure of the market itself is tiered to ensure you receive the lowest quality flow.

In equities, this happens through dark pools and internalizers. Dark pools are private exchanges where institutions match large orders without revealing their intentions. Internalizers are wholesale market makers like Citadel or Virtu that pay brokers for the privilege of filling retail orders.

When a large institution wants to buy, it doesn't show its hand on the public exchange. It trades in private venues. If you're a retail trader on a zero-commission app, your order is routed to an internalizer. The internalizer looks at your order. If it thinks you're uninformed—random noise, no edge—it fills you itself and keeps the spread. If it thinks you're informed—you know something—it sends your order to the public exchange where it can move the price against you.

In futures, the mechanism is different but the result is the same. The central limit order book (CLOB) is the primary venue, but institutions still mask their intentions through block trades (large off-exchange transactions between institutions) and iceberg orders (algorithms that hide true size by showing only a small fraction at a time). The whales trade with each other "upstairs" via block desks, or hide their size using algorithms that show one lot at a time while holding thousands in reserve.

The lit market—the public order book on your DOM—isn't the liquidity of last resort the way it is in equities. Futures trade primarily on the CLOB; there's no internalization layer siphoning off the best flow before it reaches you. But institutions still mask their intentions. Block trades happen upstairs between counterparties you'll never see. Iceberg algorithms hide true size behind one-lot displays. And the fastest participants—HFTs with co-located servers—see and react to order flow before you can process it. The playing field is more level than equities, but speed still creates a hierarchy.

This is what academics call toxic flow. When you buy on the public exchange, you're often buying the exhaust of the institutional machine. Eating the leftovers. Can you find a gem in the trash? Yes. But the probabilities are stacked against you. You're betting you see value in something the most sophisticated players in the world looked at and said, "No thanks."

Trading Against Necessity: A Case Study

Adverse selection is even more unforgiving at macro scale. The most lethal form occurs when you trade against a counterparty who isn't playing for profit. They're playing for survival.

In November 2018, the natural gas market went insane. I use this example because it illustrates the difference between value—what the chart says—and structure—who is trapped.

NatGas had been grinding higher for months, but it hit a wall at $4.00. This wasn't just a psychological number. It was the value area high of the previous three years—the price level above which almost no historical volume had traded.

I was new to NatGas and studying the volume profile. We were trading into a low volume node—a zone of thin liquidity where prices typically reject hard. My yearly VWAP bands showed we were extended three standard deviations to the upside. The widowmaker spread was blowing out to historic levels.

Every metric in my institutional playbook screamed short.

The logic was sound: "Producers hedge at these levels. We're trading into a liquidity void. Mean reversion is the highest probability setup."

So I shorted. Sold December futures at $4.10, looking for a rotation back to VWAP at $3.60. I felt like a sniper. Fading a parabolic move into structural resistance.

I was destroyed.

On November 14, the price didn't reject. It accelerated.

The bid didn't just hold—it reloaded. I watched the DOM: every time a seller hit the bid, a larger buyer stepped in and absorbed it. This wasn't liquidation. This was initiation.

Price ripped through my resistance at $4.20. Then $4.50. Then, in a final violent squeeze, $4.93. An 18% move in a single session.

In futures, an 18% move against a leveraged short isn't a loss. It's a funeral. Option sellers who had sold "safe" deep-out-of-the-money calls were carried out on stretchers. One fund, OptionSellers.com, lost its entire client equity that week and had to send a now-infamous video explaining the wipeout.

I was right about value. Gas wasn't worth $4.93. It crashed back to $3.50 a few weeks later.

I was wrong about the counterparty.

Who was buying at $4.50, $4.80, $4.93? Not speculators chasing momentum. Utilities and short gamma blowups—traders who had sold options and were being forced to buy the underlying to hedge their exploding risk.

Think about a utility company in the Northeast during an early freeze. They have a regulatory mandate: the heat cannot turn off. If they run out of gas, the grid fails, people freeze, the utility loses its license.

When the tanks ran low, they entered the market.

Did they care about the value area high? No. Three standard deviations over VWAP? No. They were price insensitive. They had to buy. If gas was $5, they'd pay it. If it was $10, they'd pay it. The cost of gas was a rounding error compared to regulatory failure.

I was looking at a chart of fair value. They were looking at a chart of survival.

You cannot win a negotiation against someone who has no choice.

My error was adverse selection. I selected a trade where the counterparty—the utility—had infinite motivation to keep buying, and the other counterparty—the short gamma funds—was being force liquidated. I stepped in front of a freight train because my VWAP model said it was speeding.

The Winner's Curse

These traps lead to a concept in auction theory: the winner's curse. It formalizes something we've been circling throughout this chapter—the act of "winning" a trade may itself be evidence that you've lost.

Imagine an auction for an offshore oil drilling lease. The geological data is complex. Multiple energy firms employ teams of geologists and engineers to estimate the value of the reserves. Their estimates vary, forming a bell curve around the true, unknown value

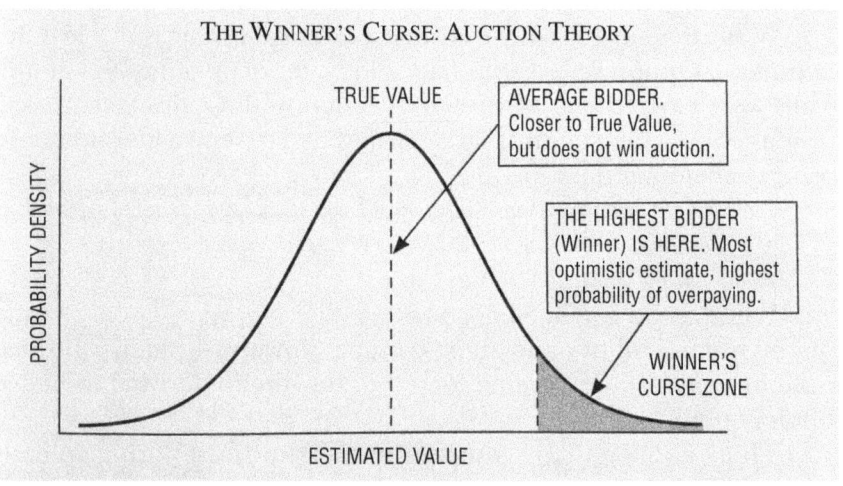

Figure 3.2 The winner's curse in auction theory. The bell curve represents the distribution of estimated values for an asset among different bidders. The vertical line at the center represents the true value. The shaded area on the far right represents the estimates of the highest bidders. The "winner" of the auction is the bidder with the highest estimate, falling in this extreme right tail—and most likely to have overestimated the asset's worth.

of the lease. Some conservative, some close to true value, some overly optimistic.

Who wins the auction? The firm with the highest bid. Who is the highest bidder? By definition, the firm with the most optimistic estimate. They're at the extreme right tail of the distribution. The "winner" has outbid all competitors, but in doing so, has most likely overestimated the asset's value. The victory is a curse. They've probably paid more than the lease is worth.

In trading, every time you "win" a fill, you've won an auction. You were willing to pay the most. You beat Citadel. Beat Virtu. Beat the HFTs. Ask yourself: did you beat them because you're smarter? Or because they saw the trap and stepped aside?

This leads to a state every professional trader knows, but few discuss:

> **The Chronic Dissatisfaction of the Pro.** If you buy and price immediately rises, you're unhappy—you didn't buy enough, your conviction was too low. If you buy and price immediately falls, you're unhappy—you bought at all, your information was bad. There's no outcome that leaves you satisfied. The very fact that you found a counterparty is evidence that someone faster and better capitalized disagreed with you.

The Operator's Protocol

How do you swim in this ocean without getting eaten?

You can't eliminate adverse selection. As long as you're taking risk, you're exposing yourself to information asymmetry. But you can invert the game. Stop acting like prey. Start thinking like the anglerfish.

> **The Null Hypothesis of the Sucker.** The transformation begins when you flip your default assumption. Most traders assume they're right until proven wrong. Invert this. Start from the assumption: "I am the patsy." Before every trade, ask the question the small fish failed to ask: "Why is this liquidity available to me?" If you can't identify the constraint, the panic, or the structural mandate of your counterparty, don't trade.
>
> **Target the Constrained Player.** Once you've stripped away the arrogance, you can begin to hunt appropriately. Alpha is not

created; it is transferred. It moves from those who must trade to those who can trade. Stop looking for value and start looking for distress. Who is being liquidated by a margin call? Who is rebalancing a levered ETF at the close? Who is hedging a regulatory requirement? These are the safe counterparties. They're price insensitive. They're not trying to beat you—they're trying to clear a ticket. When you provide liquidity to them, you're not being adversely selected. You're being paid a premium for service. When you've identified forced flow, an easy fill is exactly what you want. Adverse selection works in your favor when your counterparty is constrained.

Respect the Silence. If you place a limit order and it sits for an hour, with the market trading around it but never touching it, and then suddenly—WHACK—you're filled ... **get out**. Don't celebrate the fill. That fill is a siren. The toxic flow found you. The information has changed, and you're holding the old price. The anglerfish has snapped its jaws.

Take the small loss immediately. Don't wait for the thesis to play out. The fill was the thesis invalidation.

Slippage Is Information. If you try to buy and price runs away from you, don't chase it. That slippage is the market screaming at you. It's telling you that you're late. If you chase, you're eating scraps.

The only good fill is the one that was hard to get. The market is not a store. It's a dark ocean. Every light you see is either food or a trap. Know the difference before you bite.

But if you can't trust the price, and you can't trust the fill, what can you trust? How do you know anything is true? That's where we're going next.

Notes

The Market for Lemons. Akerlof, George A. "The Market for 'Lemons': Quality Uncertainty and the Market Mechanism." *Quarterly Journal of Economics* 84, no. 3 (1970): 488–500. The foundational paper on information asymmetry.

Winner's Curse. Thaler, Richard H. "Anomalies: The Winner's Curse." *Journal of Economic Perspectives* 2, no. 1 (1988): 191–202. Accessible introduction to the concept.

Adverse Selection in Financial Markets. Glosten, Lawrence R., and Paul R. Milgrom. "Bid, Ask and Transaction Prices in a Specialist Market with Heterogeneously Informed Traders." *Journal of Financial Economics* 14, no. 1 (1985): 71–100. The formal model of adverse selection in market microstructure.

Toxic Order Flow. Easley, David, Marcos López de Prado, and Maureen O'Hara. "Flow Toxicity and Liquidity in a High-Frequency World." *Review of Financial Studies* 25, no. 5 (2012): 1457–1493. Academic treatment of how informed flow impacts market makers.

Payment for Order Flow and Internalization. Various SEC reports and industry analyses. For accessible treatment, see Matt Levine's coverage in Bloomberg Opinion.

November 2018 Natural Gas Spike. Contemporary reporting from Reuters, Bloomberg, and industry publications. The OptionSellers.com collapse was widely covered in financial media.

Anglerfish Biology. Pietsch, Theodore W. *Oceanic Anglerfishes: Extraordinary Diversity in the Deep Sea.* University of California Press, 2009.

CHAPTER 4

The Mirage of Certainty

The market is structurally hostile. Your brain is wired to learn the wrong lessons. Even when you find an opportunity, its availability may be evidence of adverse selection. Now the fourth layer, the most disorienting: even when you have a genuine edge, you cannot know that you have it. The certainty you feel about your strategy may be the most dangerous thing about it.

Four Minutes to Impact

At 02:10:05 UTC on June 1, 2009, Pierre-Cédric Bonin did something that makes no sense to a layperson—but terrible, tragic sense to a psychologist. The 32-year-old copilot of Air France Flight 447 pulled back on his sidestick and climbed into the pitch-black darkness over the Atlantic.

There was no reason to climb. The aircraft was flying normally at 35,000 feet, cutting through an equatorial storm between Brazil and Senegal at Mach 0.80. The captain had stepped out for a scheduled nap 15 minutes earlier. Routine. Until it wasn't.

It started with ice. Crystals began accumulating in the pitot tubes—the external sensors that measure airspeed—causing the readings to go haywire. The autopilot, programmed to abdicate responsibility whenever data conflicts, disconnected. An alarm chimed, then a synthetic voice: "Autopilot off."

Any pilot will tell you this is not an emergency. They train for pitot tube icing until they can do it in their sleep. The procedure is boringly simple: maintain angle, maintain altitude, wait. The ice sublimates in less than a minute. The sensors come back online. You go back to drinking your coffee.

Bonin didn't wait. He pulled back. The nose rose. Airspeed decayed. Within seconds, the Airbus A330 entered an aerodynamic stall: the wings were no longer generating enough lift.

The stall warning screamed. A harsh, repetitive synthetic voice: "STALL. STALL. STALL."

For the next three and a half minutes—while the aircraft fell from 38,000 feet at 10,000 feet per minute—Bonin held that stick back. He maintained the exact input that guaranteed they would crash. The warning sounded seventy-five times. His colleague, David Robert, tried to take control. But on the Airbus, the sticks aren't mechanically linked. If one pilot pulls and the other pushes, the computer averages the inputs. Robert was pushing down to save them. Bonin was pulling back to doom them. The plane announced "DUAL INPUT" in a monotone voice while they fought each other all the way down.

At 02:11:43 UTC, Captain Marc Dubois burst back into the cockpit. The transcript captures it: "*Eh ... qu'est-ce que vous foutez?*" (What the hell are you doing?)

Robert: "*On perd le contrôle de l'avion, là!*" (We're losing control of the aircraft!)

Two minutes left.

The cockpit was a cacophony of alarms. The altitude was bleeding away. But here's the detail that transforms this from tragedy to lesson: *the instruments were working.*

The angle-of-attack indicators showed the stall. The warnings screamed the diagnosis. The altimeter was counting down the seconds of their lives. These men had 20,000 hours of combined flight experience. They had the data. They had the training.

What they had was certainty. They were certain the instruments were lying.

Ninety seconds before impact, Robert finally realized what Bonin was doing. "*Alors descends ... Alors, donne-moi les commandes.*" (Descend, then. Give me the controls.) Bonin let go. Robert pushed the nose down. The speed began to recover. For a fleeting moment—maybe three or four seconds—survival was possible.

Then, without a word, Bonin panicked and pulled back again. The ground proximity warning screamed "PULL UP"—the ocean was rushing up to meet them. Hearing "pull up," Bonin did exactly that.

At 02:14:28 UTC, Air France Flight 447 hit the water at 107 knots. Controlled flight. Engines working perfectly. The aircraft fell because a human was commanding it to stall.

This is what happens when a human mistakes confidence for knowledge.

The BEA—France's equivalent of the NTSB—spent three years picking through the wreckage, physical and psychological. Their report reads like a catalog of cognitive failures: attentional tunneling, selective perception, the overconfidence effect. Staring at one number while ignoring the rest. Deciding the sensors were broken because they disagreed with gut instinct. The certainty that comes from training simulations that always have happy endings.

Bonin wasn't incompetent. He had nearly 3,000 flight hours. He was a professional. But under stress, he replaced reality with his internal model of reality. His model said, "If I'm in trouble, I climb." That heuristic had worked thousands of times. His confidence in it drowned out the screaming reality of the cockpit.

You have been here. I know I have.

You have a strategy. It works. Then the stop-loss is blaring. The metrics look wrong. But your brain whispers, "It's just manipulation. It's just a stop run. It'll bounce." You're pulling back on the stick while your equity curve stalls, convinced the market is wrong because you feel certain your strategy is sound.

The only difference: the market won't kill you in four minutes. It'll bleed you out over four months.

The Turkey Problem

The Air France crew had thousands of hours of experience. Their confidence was built on data—years of successful flights. So when does data actually tell you something true about the future? The answer is more disturbing than most traders want to hear.

Bertrand Russell saw this coming in 1912 with his thought experiment about the chicken, later popularized by Nassim Taleb as the turkey.

Imagine a turkey acquired by a farm on September 1st. Each morning, the farmer arrives to feed it. The turkey, being a good empiricist, begins collecting observations. Day one: fed. Day two: fed. Day three: fed. As weeks pass, the turkey accumulates an increasingly robust sample. Fed on sunny days and cloudy days, weekdays and weekends, when the farmer seemed cheerful and when he seemed distracted. The pattern holds regardless of condition.

By late November, the turkey's confidence is at an all-time high. Eighty-four consecutive days of feeding. Substantial sample size. Zero variance. Every data point confirms the hypothesis: the farmer will feed me tomorrow.

On the morning of the 85th day—the day before Thanksgiving—the turkey approaches the feeding trough with maximal certainty. The farmer appears, as expected. But instead of feed, he carries a knife.

The turkey's problem was not insufficient data. Eighty-four observations is a reasonable sample. The turkey's problem was that induction—inferring general laws from particular observations—cannot account for structural breaks in the underlying process. The turkey built a model that captured the surface pattern (farmer appears, food arrives) while remaining blind to the mechanism generating that pattern (farmer is fattening turkey for slaughter). The turkey never asked *why* it was being fed. It only asked *when*.

David Hume identified this in 1739. He called it the problem of induction: there can be no demonstrative argument proving that instances we have not experienced will resemble those we have experienced. The sun has risen every morning of recorded history. This doesn't prove, logically or mathematically, that it will rise tomorrow. We believe it will because we possess theoretical knowledge—astronomy, physics, orbital mechanics—that explains *why* the sun rises. The turkey had no such knowledge. Only pattern recognition operating on an insufficient representation of reality.

Edge validation isn't statistical. It's philosophical.

Your backtest is the turkey. It has observed historical patterns—thousands of trades, perhaps, across multiple years of data. It has documented which configurations worked and which didn't. Sharpe ratio high. Drawdown manageable. Win rate above 50%. By every conventional metric, the strategy has "edge."

But the backtest can't tell you *why* those patterns existed. It can't distinguish between structural phenomena—market microstructure effects that persist because they arise from enduring features of how markets function—and ephemeral coincidences—statistical artifacts that arose from conditions that no longer obtain. The backtest is collecting data on the feeding schedule without understanding the farmer's intentions.

Consider the confidence curve. Day one, confidence is low—a single observation proves little. By day 40, confidence has risen substantially. By day 80, it approaches certainty. Positive slope, roughly linear, asymptoting toward 100%.

Now superimpose actual risk on the same graph. Risk is also rising, but the turkey can't see it. With each passing day, Thanksgiving approaches. The farmer's intent becomes more imminent, not less. Risk rises exponentially while confidence rises linearly—and the two curves are invisible to each other.

On day 84, the curves cross. Confidence at maximum. Risk at maximum. Peak certainty at the exact moment of maximum vulnerability.

This is every trader who sizes up after a winning streak. The wins feel like evidence. They are evidence—of nothing, or everything, or something specific you can't identify with the data you possess. The confidence you derive from those wins has no necessary relationship to the risk you're accumulating. The winning streak might be skill. It might be regime. It might be variance. The pattern itself can't tell you which.

The Impossibility of Certainty

You might object: "Fine, the turkey is a parable. But surely with enough data, with rigorous testing, we can prove our edge the way a scientist proves a hypothesis?" The answer is no. And understanding why requires grasping a distinction most traders never encounter.

The dream of proving edge the way a pharmaceutical trial proves drug efficacy is structurally incompatible with markets.

Pharmaceutical validation works because biology is fixed. A drug either binds to a receptor or it doesn't. The receptor's structure is fixed by biology. The binding mechanism is governed by chemistry and physics. The laws governing these interactions don't change because pharmaceutical companies begin testing compounds. When Pfizer runs a clinical trial for a blood pressure medication, the underlying biology of hypertension remains constant throughout the study. Researchers can isolate their intervention, control for confounding variables, randomize subjects, and measure outcomes against a stable baseline.

Frank Knight, the University of Chicago economist, identified the fundamental distinction in 1921. In *Risk, Uncertainty, and Profit*, he separated randomness into two categories:

Risk exists when you can't know the outcome of a specific event, but you can accurately measure the probability distribution. A casino operates in the domain of risk. The roulette wheel lands on red approximately 47.4% of the time. This probability is fixed by the physical construction of the wheel. A million spins will converge on this distribution. The casino doesn't know whether any particular spin will be red or black, but it knows—with mathematical precision—what its long-run expectation is.

Uncertainty exists when you can't even assign accurate probabilities to outcomes. Knight called this "immeasurable uncertainty"—situations where we can't know all the information we need to set accurate odds in the first place. You can't calculate the probability that China will invade Taiwan in the next decade. You can't assign a reliable percentage to the likelihood that AI will displace hedge fund managers by 2035. These questions involve too many unknown variables, too many interdependent systems, too much reflexive feedback between prediction and outcome.

Markets live in Knight's second category. They generate noise that resembles risk—you can compute historical volatility, measure past drawdowns, calculate observed Sharpe ratios—but these backward-looking statistics don't bind the future. The distribution from which tomorrow's returns will be drawn is not the same distribution from which yesterday's were drawn. The system mutates.

George Soros named this mutation *reflexivity*: participants' actions change the system they're attempting to understand. When you trade size, you move prices. When your edge becomes known, faster traders front-run it, capital floods in, and the opportunity disappears. When volatility shifts, strategies that worked stop working. The system is adversarial and adaptive. It responds to your observations by changing what you're observing.

Andrew Lo formalized this instability in the adaptive markets hypothesis: market efficiency is not a constant state—it cycles as participants learn and adapt. Patterns work until enough capital discovers them. Then they degrade or disappear entirely. McLean and Pontiff estimated that trading anomalies lose approximately 26% out-of-sample and 58% post-publication as arbitrage capital responds.

This creates the fundamental structural problem of professional trading: you need edge to survive. You can't verify you have edge until you've traded long enough to collect meaningful data. By the time you've collected meaningful data, the market has likely changed.

There is no loophole. You're measuring a moving target whose movement is partly caused by your attempt to measure it. (This is the epistemological nightmare that adverse selection thrives in. If you can't know the true state of the system, you're always vulnerable to someone who knows slightly more.)

The Mechanics of Nonstationarity

Many traders comfort themselves with the casino analogy: "I'm like the house. I have an edge. I just need to play enough hands." This analogy will kill you. Here's why.

Destroy the casino analogy.

The casino operates on *stationary processes*—probabilities fixed and unchanging. The roulette wheel's odds are fixed by physics. The house edge doesn't decay because gamblers become more sophisticated. The distribution of outcomes in 2024 is identical to 1984. A hundred years of play doesn't erode the wheel's bias. This is what makes casinos profitable: they face risk, not uncertainty, and risk is manageable through position sizing and diversification.

Markets are *nonstationary*—the underlying distribution of returns shifts over time. Sometimes gradually, sometimes violently, always invisibly at first. Volatility regimes expand and contract. Correlations flip. Liquidity ebbs and flows. Regulatory changes rewrite the rules. Central bank policy reshapes risk-free rates and risk premiums. Participant composition evolves—what worked when retail dominated stops working when institutional algorithms arrive.

You can't see these shifts in real time. By the time nonstationarity manifests in your P&L, the regime has already changed. You're detecting the shift retrospectively, always operating on stale information about the system state.

Clausewitz called this the *fog of war*: the uncertainty, confusion, and incomplete situational awareness that commanders experience in battle. "Three-quarters of the factors on which action in war is based are wrapped in a fog of greater or lesser uncertainty." Successful commanders are not those who pierce the fog—it can't be pierced—but those who develop doctrines robust to operating within it.

Trading presents an identical challenge. You can't know what regime you're in until the regime has ended. You must act confidently despite incomplete information—sizing positions, entering trades, managing risk—while acknowledging that your model of current conditions may be wrong in ways you can't detect.

The tools exist. Hidden Markov models can identify regime states from observable data. Gaussian mixture models can cluster historical returns into distinct volatility regimes. Machine learning can detect structural breaks and flag anomalous behavior. But none of these provides real-time certainty. They provide probabilistic assessments, lagging indicators, and historical pattern recognition applied to a system whose present-to-future relationship may differ from its past-to-past relationship.

You're operating, always, in the fog.

The Wason Selection Task

Given all this uncertainty, you might expect humans to be naturally skeptical. We're not. We are designed to protect our beliefs, not to falsify them.

In 1966, Peter Wason designed an elegantly simple experiment that revealed this flaw.

Subjects were shown four cards. Each had a letter on one side and a number on the other. The visible faces: E, K, 4, 7.

The experimenter stated a rule: "If a card has a vowel on one side, then it has an even number on the other side."

Which cards must you turn over to determine whether the rule is true or false?

The answer is not intuitive.

Most subjects chose E and 4. This seems logical: E is a vowel, so check if it has an even number; 4 is an even number, so check if it has a vowel.

The correct answer is E and 7.

Turning over E is necessary—if E has an odd number on the back, the rule is false. But turning over 4 proves nothing. The rule says, "if vowel, then even." It says nothing about what must be on the back of an even number. K on one side and 4 on the other wouldn't violate the rule.

Turning over 7 is essential. If 7 has a vowel on the back, the rule is false—a vowel paired with an odd number. Most subjects never consider turning over 7 because they're seeking confirmation of the rule, not falsification.

Wason documented what he called *confirmation bias*: the systematic human tendency to seek evidence that supports existing beliefs while ignoring evidence that could disprove them. We are confirmation-seekers, not truth-seekers. Our cognitive architecture evolved to recognize patterns and construct narratives, not to rigorously test hypotheses against disconfirming evidence.

Traders in false certainty live the Wason selection task continuously. They observe winning trades and take them as confirmation of edge. They observe losing trades and explain them away. "Market manipulation." "Slippage." "Bad execution." They never test the hypothesis that their edge doesn't exist because they never turn over the 7. They seek only the E and the 4—evidence that confirms what they already believe.

The problem isn't stupidity. Wason's subjects included trained logicians and scientists. The problem is that human reasoning defaults to confirmation rather than falsification. Testing your hypothesis against disconfirming evidence requires deliberate effort against cognitive gravity.

The Overconfidence Effect

Confirmation bias explains why we don't seek disconfirming evidence. But there's a related phenomenon just as dangerous: our inability to assess how much we actually know.

In 2013, a study at the Houston VA found something that should keep you up at night.

Researchers presented 118 physicians with diagnostic vignettes. Some cases were straightforward: classic presentations with clear symptom patterns. Others were difficult: atypical presentations, overlapping symptoms, unusual conditions.

The results were stark. Physicians correctly diagnosed 55.3% of easier cases and only 5.8% of difficult ones. The nearly 10-fold decline in accuracy was expected. Difficult cases are difficult.

What was not expected: the corresponding decline in confidence was minimal. Physicians rated confidence at 7.2/10 for easy cases and 6.4/10 for difficult cases. Accuracy dropped from 55% to 6%. Confidence dropped from 7.2 to 6.4.

The researchers calculated calibration—the alignment between confidence and accuracy—and found systematic overconfidence. When physicians were most likely to be wrong, their confidence remained nearly as high as when they were most likely to be right. They couldn't feel the difference between knowing and guessing.

More troubling: higher confidence correlated with a decreased likelihood of ordering additional tests or seeking consultation. When physicians felt certain, they stopped gathering information. The cognitive state that should have prompted more investigation—uncertainty about a difficult case—was masked by an unjustified sense of knowing.

For traders, this explains why confidence feels like knowledge when it isn't. Your pattern-recognition system operates automatically, below conscious awareness. It generates outputs—feelings of conviction, intuitions about direction, senses that "this is the setup"—without providing access to its inputs or reasoning. You experience the output as knowledge. It's not. It's a confidence-weighted guess produced by neural machinery evolved for a different environment.

When that machinery faces a difficult case—a market condition outside your experience, a regime shift you haven't seen before, a configuration of variables your training didn't prepare you for—accuracy drops precipitously. But confidence doesn't drop correspondingly. You feel just as certain in the difficult case as the easy case, even though your probability of being right has collapsed.

The traders who blow up aren't usually the uncertain ones. Uncertain traders size small, use stops, monitor constantly. The traders who blow up are the confident ones—who feel certain they understand what's happening, who interpret contradictory evidence as confirmation of manipulation or bad luck, who "know" the position will work because it has worked before, who are pulling back on the sidestick while the aircraft falls because their model of reality has decoupled from reality itself.

The Prediction Paradox: Prophecy vs. Anticipation

There's a contradiction we need to resolve. We've spent this chapter arguing that certainty is a mirage, that the future is unknowable, that anyone who claims to predict the market is a charlatan. Yet later I'll ask you to "grade your conviction" on a five-star scale, to "anticipate" second-order effects.

Are we predicting, or aren't we?

To resolve this, you need to distinguish between two different intellectual acts: prophecy and anticipation.

> **Prophecy** is the attempt to know the outcome. It's deterministic. "The S&P 500 will hit 7,000 by year-end." "Crude oil is going to $60." Prophecy requires a Laplace demon—the hypothetical intellect that knows the position and momentum of every particle in the universe and can therefore calculate all future states. In a reflexive, nonstationary system, prophecy is impossible. When you try to prophesy, you're hallucinating certainty.
>
> **Anticipation** is the attempt to assess the skew. It's probabilistic. "Given current positioning and the volatility regime, a move to the downside has higher velocity potential than a move to the upside." Anticipation doesn't claim to know what will happen. It claims to know what the distribution of possibilities looks like right now.

The casino doesn't prophesy. Ask a pit boss, "Will the next spin be red?" He'll honestly answer, "I don't know." Zero conviction about the outcome. But 100% conviction about the skew. He knows the wheel is structurally tilted in his favor. He anticipates the edge while accepting the uncertainty of the spin.

When we "grade conviction" in this book, we're not measuring our confidence in a specific future event. We're measuring the degree of tilt in the probability distribution. We're asking: "How heavily is the current deck stacked?"

The amateur predicts the card. The professional plays the odds.

The Four Axioms

Everything in this chapter distills to four irreducible truths. Professional trading isn't governed by rules you can engineer around. It's governed by axioms you can only survive.

> **Axiom One: Edge is never a fact; it is a probability.** Physicists deal in constants. Gravity doesn't take a day off. Traders deal in latent variables—quantities like "edge" or "sentiment" that you can't observe directly. You only see the shadows they cast on price and P&L. Because you're dealing with shadows, you never verify an edge absolutely. You estimate it, update it, and learn to live with the residual nausea of never truly knowing. The question is never "Do I have an edge?"—that presumes a binary world that doesn't exist. The question is "Given the shadows I'm seeing, how heavily should I bet?"
>
> **Axiom Two: The ground is moving.** Markets are nonstationary and reflexive. The distribution of returns shifts, often because you and your peers are interacting with it. Alpha creates its own entropy—discovery accelerates decay. But even without publication, strategies rot. Regimes change, technology evolves, the phenomenon you were exploiting evaporates. The trade that minted millionaires in 2019 might bankrupt them in 2024—not because they lost skill, but because the territory erased the map.
>
> **Axiom Three: Randomness contaminates everything.** Short runs of performance prove nothing, yet your brain is wired to treat them as gospel. Tversky and Kahneman documented this half a century ago as the "Belief in the Law of Small Numbers." We expect 10 trades to reveal the truth of a strategy. At that sample size, you're staring at noise. Even a thousand trades can lie to you if your strategy relies on fat tails that haven't appeared yet. You can be right for years and still be wrong about the distribution.
>
> **Axiom Four: Survival is the only metric.** Sharpe ratios and profit factors are vanity metrics for tourists. The professional is obsessed with a single binary: being in the game versus being taken out. Paul Tudor Jones isn't famous because he maximizes upside. He's famous because he assumes he's about to lose money and defends against it viscerally. This seems

paradoxical—why trade if you're focused on loss?—but it's the only way to reach the long run where probabilities actually converge. You don't protect capital to hide it under a mattress. You protect it so you can survive the variance long enough for the math to work.

Normalization of Deviance

There's one more cognitive trap that makes these axioms difficult to follow in practice. It explains how intelligent, experienced professionals drift toward catastrophe while believing they're operating safely.

On January 28, 1986, *Challenger* disintegrated 73 seconds after launch. The cause: an O-ring seal failure triggered by cold weather. Engineers had warned management. Management had overruled them.

Seventeen years later, *Columbia* disintegrated upon reentry. The cause: foam debris striking the wing during launch. Engineers had requested satellite imagery to assess the damage. Management denied them.

Sociologist Diane Vaughan studied the *Challenger* disaster and coined a term every trader should have taped to their monitor: *normalization of deviance.*

It describes how organizations drift into catastrophe. The O-rings had eroded on previous flights, but the shuttle returned safely. The foam had struck on previous flights, but the shuttle landed. Deviation from safety became the new standard of safety. They were turkeys accumulating data points, mistaking luck for structural integrity.

If NASA—with billions in funding, phalanxes of PhDs, and an explicit mandate for safety—couldn't stop itself from normalizing risk, you have no chance of doing it alone unless you're terrifyingly vigilant.

You're a single pilot in a dark cockpit. You don't have a mission control. When you move your stop-loss "just this once," and the trade works out, you haven't won. You've lost. You've taught your brain that the deviation is safe. You've eroded the O-ring. Next time, you'll move the stop further. You'll size up on a hunch. You'll ignore the regime shift because you ignored it last time and got paid. You're normalizing your own destruction, trade by trade, until the morning variance catches up to deviance.

Bayesian Survival

The antidote to this drift isn't more data. It's a different philosophy of knowledge itself.

Thomas Bayes provided the framework. In the Bayesian world, you never "know" anything. You hold a prior—a belief with a specific level of confidence. You encounter new evidence. You update the prior to create a posterior. This posterior becomes your new prior for the next event.

This isn't a math problem. It's a survival mechanism.

The Newtonian trader asks: "Is the market bullish or bearish?" He wants a binary answer so he can be certain. When the market turns against him, he freezes—his reality has been violated. He holds the bag because he needs to be right.

The Bayesian trader asks: "What's the probability the market is bullish, and how much does this price action change that probability?" When the trade goes against the Bayesian, he doesn't experience cognitive dissonance. He experiences an update. The price action is information. It lowers his confidence in the thesis. As confidence drops, position size drops. He isn't fighting the market—he's fluidly adjusting exposure to match his current probability estimate. He flows like water. The Newtonian shatters like glass.

The Protocol

Operate as if you know nothing. Because you don't. You have models, instincts, backtests. None of them are the territory—they're maps, and the terrain keeps shifting.

The protocol is simple, though rarely easy.

Trade small enough that no single surprise can breach the hull.

Seek uncorrelated bets so a failure in one engine doesn't flame out the others.

Cultivate an aggressive willingness to disconnect.

When the feedback loop screams, when instrument readings conflict, when the "impossible" happens—don't be Pierre-Cédric Bonin. Don't pull back on the stick trying to force your model onto the world.

Let go. Flatten the book. Step away from the screens. Choose to be a coward for five minutes so you can be a pilot for twenty years.

Certainty is a luxury for amateurs. The professional lives in uncertainty— as long as they're positioned to survive it.

Notes

Air France Flight 447. Bureau d'Enquêtes et d'Analyses (BEA). *Final Report on the Accident on 1st June 2009 to the Airbus A330-203.* July 2012. Also see Palmer, Brian. The limits of expertise. *Slate*, December 6, 2011.

The Problem of Induction. Hume, David. *A Treatise of Human Nature.* 1739. Book I, Part III. Russell's chicken appears in *The Problems of Philosophy* (1912).

Knightian Uncertainty. Knight, Frank. *Risk, Uncertainty, and Profit.* Houghton Mifflin, 1921.

Reflexivity. Soros, George. *The Alchemy of Finance.* Simon & Schuster, 1987.

Adaptive Markets Hypothesis. Lo, Andrew W. *Adaptive Markets: Financial Evolution at the Speed of Thought.* Princeton University Press, 2017.

Post-publication Decay of Anomalies. McLean, R. David, and Jeffrey Pontiff. "Does Academic Research Destroy Stock Return Predictability?" *Journal of Finance* 71, no. 1 (2016): 5–32.

Wason Selection Task. Wason, Peter C. Reasoning. In *New Horizons in Psychology*, edited by Brian Foss. Penguin, 1966.

Physician Overconfidence Study. Meyer, Ashley N.D. et al. "Physicians' Diagnostic Accuracy, Confidence, and Resource Requests." *JAMA Internal Medicine* 173, no. 21 (2013): 1952–1958.

Normalization of Deviance. Vaughan, Diane. *The* Challenger *Launch Decision: Risky Technology, Culture, and Deviance at NASA.* University of Chicago Press, 1996.

Fog of War. Clausewitz, Carl von. *On War.* 1832. Translated by Michael Howard and Peter Paret. Princeton University Press, 1976.

CHAPTER

Probabilistic Thinking and Expectancy

*W*e've mapped the terrain. It's hostile. Now the question: what do you actually do about it?

If certainty is impossible, how do professionals make decisions? The answer is a different relationship with probability.

The Empty Plane

In the spring of 1971, a young cargo executive named Akira Okazaki sat in the Japan Airlines headquarters in Tokyo with a problem that had no obvious solution.

JAL's 747 freighters flew west from Narita loaded to capacity: Sony transistor radios, Panasonic televisions, Honda motorcycles—the entire exportable output of Japan's postwar industrial miracle. They landed at JFK, unloaded, and then flew home. Empty. The economics were punishing: for every seven tons of goods shipped from Tokyo to New York, only one ton returned. The planes burned the same fuel either way. The crew drew the same salaries. The landing fees were identical. But half the flights generated zero revenue.

Okazaki's job was to fill those planes with something—anything—that Japanese consumers would pay a premium for. The cargo had to be valuable enough to justify air freight rates. It had to be unavailable domestically. And ideally, it had to be something that American sellers didn't realize was valuable at all.

He found it rotting in landfills on Prince Edward Island.

Atlantic bluefin tuna were, in 1971, classified as a nuisance species on Canada's eastern seaboard. Sport fishermen caught them for the fight. A bluefin can exceed a thousand pounds and battle for hours. But the meat was considered worthless. "Horse mackerel," the locals called it. When the charter boats returned to dock, the carcasses were hauled to municipal dumps and buried. Some fishermen paid disposal fees just to get rid of them.

In Tokyo, the same fish sold for more than its weight in silver.

The Japanese had eaten bluefin for centuries, but supplies were limited to what could be caught in nearby waters and consumed within hours. The fish's flesh—deep red, marbled with fat, impossibly delicate—oxidized and spoiled faster than almost any protein on earth. There was no technology to preserve it. There was no logistics chain to move it. The price reflected scarcity created by physics, not economics.

Okazaki saw the gap. He also saw that closing it would require solving problems no one had solved before.

The first challenge was temperature. Bluefin must be kept between 28 and 32 degrees Fahrenheit. Cold enough to halt bacterial growth. Warm enough to prevent ice crystals from destroying the texture. The margin for error was four degrees over a journey of six thousand miles.

The second challenge was time. From the moment a bluefin dies, a biochemical clock starts. Enzymes break down the muscle tissue. Bacteria multiply. Even under perfect refrigeration, the fish remains sushi-grade for perhaps 72 hours. The journey from a boat off Nova Scotia to an auction house in Tokyo—including trucking to an airport, customs clearance, trans-Pacific flight, landing, more customs, more trucking—had to be compressed into that window.

The third challenge was handling. A bruise invisible to the eye would show as a brown spot when the fish was sliced. The auction masters at Tsukiji fish market inspected each specimen with surgical precision. A single flaw could cut the price by half.

Okazaki's team spent more than a year engineering solutions. They designed insulated shipping containers with gel packs calibrated to the exact thermal profile. They developed handling protocols: how to kill the fish instantly to prevent stress hormones from tainting the flesh, how to bleed it properly, how to pack it without pressure points. They negotiated expedited customs clearance.

conditions constant while you test a hypothesis because your test changes the conditions. The system you are measuring mutates in response to your measurement.

This creates a specific cognitive trap for intelligent people. They have succeeded their entire lives by understanding systems. By analyzing inputs and outputs, by identifying causal relationships, by building mental models that predict behavior. They enter markets expecting the same approach to work. They analyze charts, study fundamentals, build models, form predictions.

For a while, it seems to work. They win some trades. The pattern recognition machinery identifies correlations. The narrative machinery constructs explanations. Confidence builds.

Then the market shifts. The pattern stops working. The model fails.

Instead of updating their beliefs—instead of recognizing the system has changed—they defend their model against the evidence.

The Evolutionary Trap

Why do intelligent people defend failing models?

Because the brain is a survival engine, not a statistics processor.

The brain isn't designed to process falsification. When the stall warning sounded in Air France 447, the pilot pulled back. When the market screams that a position is wrong, we add to it.

This isn't a psychological quirk. It's an evolutionary trap. The Wason selection task proves we're hardwired for confirmation—we instinctively turn over the card that confirms our belief instead of the one that could falsify it. In trading, confirmation is death. We must learn to hunt for the falsifying evidence.

We're running cognitive software designed for a different environment.

In the ancestral environment, a Type I error (false positive: running from the wind) cost a few calories. A Type II error (ignoring the predator) cost your life.

Evolution selected for a cognitive architecture that prioritizes the immediate, binary identification of threats. We are hardwired to see patterns where none exist because the ancestors who occasionally ran from the wind lived to reproduce, while the ancestors who waited for statistical significance became lunch.

This architecture served our species well for hundreds of thousands of years. It doesn't serve you in markets.

> **In trading, the cost structure is inverted.** Type I errors—believing you see edge when you're seeing noise—compound into ruin. Every false pattern you trade bleeds capital. Type II errors—failing to see real edge—merely cost opportunity. You can always find another trade. You can't always find more capital.

We are hardwired to see causality where none exists. We construct narratives to explain random sequences because the alternative—admitting that we are navigating a sea of stochastic noise with only partial, decaying information—is psychologically intolerable. We need to feel in control.

And the moment we form a narrative, a far more dangerous mechanism activates: we defend it.

Confirmation bias isn't a character flaw. It's not a quirk you can overcome with discipline. It's an operational failure mode embedded so deeply that fighting it through willpower is like fighting gravity with your legs. You can't think your way out of it.

> *The only defense is structure.* External constraints that force falsification before your intuition can sabotage it. Stop-losses defined before entry. Invalidation criteria written in advance. Risk limits that trigger automatically, removing the decision from your emotional brain.

The Geometry of Expectation

You can't trust your intuition. You need a replacement. That replacement is mathematics—the mathematics of expectancy.

But intelligent people stumble here too. They confuse frequency (being right) with magnitude (making money).

Expectancy is the primary metric of profitability. It answers the question your P&L cares about: for every unit of risk deployed, how much wealth sticks to the account?

The formula is simple:

Expectancy = (Win Rate × Average Win) − (Loss Rate × Average Loss)

There's a dangerous cliché in trading: "Win rate is a vanity metric." Be right 10% of the time and still get rich, as long as your winners are big enough.

Mathematically, this is true. Psychologically, it is a lie.

Win rate is not a vanity metric; it is a *utility* metric. It is the fuel that keeps you emotionally solvent while you wait for the edge to manifest.

Consider a trend-following strategy with a 20% win rate and massive winners. It has positive expectancy. But can you endure 20 consecutive losses? Can you sit there for three months, bleeding capital every single day, and still execute the 21st trade with perfect precision? Most traders cannot. They break. They abandon the system right before the winning streak begins.

Conversely, a strategy with a 60% win rate provides frequent positive reinforcement. It keeps the dopamine flowing. It keeps you engaged.

Professionals face a trade-off.

High win rate strategies are easier to trade—but they often carry left-tail risk. One bad loss wipes out weeks of gains. Low win rate strategies are mathematically superior for compounding—but psychologically brutal to execute.

You're not a robot. You can't optimize solely for mathematical expectancy. You have to optimize for a system you can actually survive. If a strategy has positive expectancy but a win rate so low that it causes you to abandon the discipline, its realized expectancy is zero.

Professional sizing isn't just about maximizing the "R" multiple. It is about balancing the math of profit with the biology of endurance.

The Volatility Tax

There's a darker layer to expectancy mathematics. It explains why two strategies with identical average returns produce wildly different wealth outcomes.

Returns in trading are geometric, not arithmetic. They compound. If you make 50% one year and lose 33% the next, your arithmetic average return is +8.5%. But your actual wealth is unchanged. $100 becomes $150, then $150 becomes $100. You're back where you started. The arithmetic average lies.

The geometric mean—the actual rate at which wealth compounds—is always lower than the arithmetic mean, and the gap grows as volatility increases. Mathematicians call this *volatility drag*, or *variance drain*. The relationship between geometric return (G), arithmetic return (R), and volatility (σ) is approximated by:

$$G \approx R - (\sigma^2/2)$$

This formula looks abstract until you work through the implications. Suppose you have a strategy with 20% arithmetic expected return and 40% volatility. Sounds profitable. But the volatility drag is $(0.40)^2 / 2 = 8\%$. Your geometric return, the rate at which wealth actually compounds, is only 12%.

Now lever that strategy 2× to chase higher returns. Arithmetic expectation doubles to 40%. But volatility doubles to 80%. The drag becomes 32%. Your geometric return is now 8%—*lower* than the unleveraged version despite twice the arithmetic expectation.

Push leverage further and geometric return goes negative. You can have positive expectancy—a genuine edge—and still go broke because variance is too high for your capital base.

Position sizing isn't a secondary consideration. It's not something you optimize after you've found edge. It's as fundamental as the edge itself.

A correct thesis with incorrect sizing is still a losing proposition. The volatility tax eats your returns regardless of how smart your analysis is.

If you're unsure about your edge—if you can't precisely quantify your advantage—size smaller than feels comfortable. The cost of sizing too small is linear: you make less money. The cost of sizing too large is convex: you risk ruin.

The Decision Stack

How does a professional actually operate when the screen is flashing and P&L is moving?

They don't stare at charts searching for confirmation. They don't read news hoping for narrative support. They execute a decision stack—a rapid-fire cognitive loop that prioritizes pricing over prediction.

> **First, Classification.** Before anything else, classify the environment. Is this movement flow or information? Have you seen this pattern before? Who's on the other side?

If the counterparty is a central bank engaging in yield curve control, their capacity to act is functionally infinite. Betting against them is not contrarian. It is suicide. If the counterparty is a retail trader panic-selling at the low, their capacity is exhausted. Providing liquidity is profitable.

This classification happens fast—in seconds, not minutes—because it draws on pattern libraries built over years. You are not analyzing the situation from first principles. You are matching it against templates you have seen before.

> **Second, Pricing.** Before you buy a single share, define the falsification point. What price level kills your thesis? Where's max pain? Calculate the expectancy explicitly, not intuitively. Risk X to make Y with probability Z. Does the math work?

Ask the uncomfortable question: *Why do I get this trade?*

In a competitive market, if a deal looks too good, it's usually a trap. If you're buying, someone is selling. Why are they willing to let you have it at this price? What do they know that you don't?

If you cannot answer that question—if you cannot identify who the weaker party is—you are likely the weaker party.

> **Third, Execution.** Size based on conviction and volatility. Not hope. Not how much you want to make. Size based on how much you can afford to lose if you're wrong.
>
> **Fourth, The Update Loop.** The process doesn't end at entry.

Conditional on being filled, are you happy? If you placed a limit order and got filled instantly, did you misprice the liquidity? Did the market move through you? That's information. Update your probability estimate.

If the price action after entry is sluggish, if the move you expected is not materializing, a 60% probability thesis becomes a 45% probability thesis. Cut exposure. Don't wait for your stop. Don't hope for recovery. Update and act.

This isn't defending the trade. This isn't rationalizing. This is Bayesian updating in real time.

Most people are intuitive frequentists. They think probability requires repeated trials—rolling a die 1,000 times to see that 6 comes up 16.6% of the time. But you can't rerun the present moment 1,000 times. The "now" happens once.

Traders must be Bayesians. We treat probability not as a frequency of future outcomes, but as a degree of belief in a single, unique event. We assign a probability to our thesis, and as new information arrives—price action, news, order flow—we update that degree of belief.

The professional doesn't ask "Am I right?" They ask "Given what I've observed since entry, what's the probability I'm right, and is my size appropriate for that probability?"

The Variance Vaccination

All of this sounds rational on paper. In practice, variance breaks people. At the trading firms where I've spent my time, there's a training step that seems to have nothing to do with markets.

We play poker.

Not for fun. Not to teach the odds of a flush draw. To vaccinate us against variance.

The goal is to experience the specific sickness of getting your money in good. Holding pocket aces against pocket twos—an 82% favorite—and losing. Watching the board run out three twos. Feeling the unfairness. The injustice. The violation of everything that should be right.

And then watching what happens next.

Do you tilt? Do you change your strategy on the following hand, playing tighter or looser because of the bad beat? Do you hesitate the next time you pick up aces because some part of your brain whispers that the cards are cursed?

If you flinch, you become vulnerable.

The market is a liar. It pays you for recklessness just often enough to make you believe recklessness is skill. It rewards bad process with dopamine and conditions you to increase size right before variance turns. By the time you realize it wasn't skill, your account is gone.

Annie Duke calls this *"resulting"*—judging a decision by its outcome rather than its process. A good decision can produce a bad outcome. A bad decision can produce a good outcome. Over small samples, variance dominates.

But over thousands of hands or thousands of trades, process quality converges with outcome quality. The edge expresses itself. The math works.

The job is to survive long enough for the math to work.

Treat profitable trades that violated your rules as toxic. They're not evidence of skill. They're variance that happened to land in your favor, conditioning you to repeat the violation. Penalize the behavior. Size down. Reinforce the process, not the outcome.

Treat trades that followed perfect process but lost money as operational successes. You paid tuition to learn whether the setup works. You gathered information. You updated your model. The fact that this instance lost money is noise. The process was sound.

The Professional Shift

Okazaki's story illustrates everything in this chapter—and points toward the fundamental shift that separates professionals from amateurs.

Okazaki didn't predict that bluefin would become valuable. He didn't forecast that sushi would conquer the world. He identified a structural inefficiency—high value in Tokyo, zero value in Canada, logistical barriers preventing arbitrage—and he built the capacity to act on it.

When he entered the trade, he wasn't betting on his predictions being right. He was betting that his understanding of the logistics, and his capacity to solve the cold-chain problem, exceeded everyone else's.

That's edge. Not prediction. Not pattern recognition. Not chart analysis. The ability to see something others can't see, combined with the ability to act on it in ways others cannot act.

The intelligent people who fail in markets fail because they're playing a game of prediction in a world of probability. They want the comfort of knowing. They want to be right. They want the market to confirm their cleverness.

The market doesn't care about your cleverness.

Professional traders give up the comfort of knowing. They accept that the market won't tell them if they're right—only if they survive. They don't predict; they price uncertainty. They hunt for the falsification point, the evidence that would prove them wrong. They act as the casino, relying on the geometry of edge over many bets rather than the outcome of any single bet.

You don't need to be the smartest person in the room. You need to be the one who understands that being "right" is a vanity metric, and making money is a discipline.

The traders who survive aren't the ones who predict best. They're the ones who update fastest, size smallest, and kill their edge before the market kills them.

They are the ones who found the empty plane.

Notes

JAL Bluefin Trade. Issenberg, Sasha. *The Sushi Economy: Globalization and the Making of a Modern Delicacy.* Gotham Books, 2007. The definitive account of how Atlantic bluefin became a global commodity.

Lebron's Edge Inequality. Lebron, Agustin. *The Laws of Trading: A Trader's Guide to Better Decision-Making for Everyone.* Wiley, 2019. Essential reading on the structure of trading advantage.

First-order vs. Second-order Chaos. Harari, Yuval Noah. *Sapiens: A Brief History of Humankind.* Harper, 2015. The distinction between weather (first-order) and markets (second-order) chaotic systems.

Reflexivity. Soros, George. *The Alchemy of Finance.* Simon & Schuster, 1987.

Volatility Drag. Standard result in portfolio mathematics. The formula $G \approx R - \sigma^2/2$ is an approximation that assumes log-normal returns. For formal derivation, see any graduate text on continuous-time finance.

Bayesian vs. Frequentist Probability. For accessible introduction, see Silver, Nate. *The Signal and the Noise.* Penguin, 2012. For formal treatment, see Jaynes, E.T. *Probability Theory: The Logic of Science.* Cambridge University Press, 2003.

Resulting. Duke, Annie. *Thinking in Bets: Making Smarter Decisions When You Don't Have All the Facts.* Portfolio, 2018.

Type I and Type II Errors in Evolutionary Context. Haselton, Martie G., and Daniel Nettle. "The Paranoid Optimist: An Integrative Evolutionary Model of Cognitive Biases." *Personality and Social Psychology Review* 10, no. 1 (2006): 47–66.

CHAPTER 6

The Operator's Equation

Philosophy doesn't pay the bills. This chapter translates probability into operational mathematics—the equation that governs every professional trading decision. Starting with a story about what happens when intelligent people confuse confirmation with validation.

The Launch

January 28, 1986. NASA faced a binary decision: launch *Challenger* or delay. The forecast called for overnight temperatures dropping to 18°F—far colder than any previous shuttle launch. The coldest prior launch had been 53°F (mission STS-51-C), which itself was an outlier and had shown the most significant O-ring erosion to date.

The engineers at Morton Thiokol had data showing O-ring erosion at lower temperatures. But they also had something else: 24 consecutive successful launches where the O-rings performed adequately. The data was clear. The pattern was established. The shuttle was safe.

Their presentation focused on confirmation: "Look at how well it's worked. Look at the consistent performance."

But one engineer asked a different question: "*At what temperature does it fail?*" He was looking for falsification, not confirmation. He wanted to find the cold-soak test data that would prove the O-rings unsafe. That data didn't exist—they'd never launched below 53°F.

The engineers who approved launch were seeking confirmation. They were turning over the card that couldn't validate their decision. The engineer who objected was trying to turn over the 7 card—hunting for the condition that would prove them wrong.

The next morning, *Challenger* launched at 36°F. Seventy-three seconds later, the O-rings failed. Seven astronauts died.

The most expensive cognitive error in expert decision-making isn't lacking information—it's confusing repeated success with validated edge. The engineers had 24 confirming instances. They had zero falsifying instances—not because the system was safe but because they'd never tested the relevant conditions.

Every day you trade, you run the same decision process.

When you discover a pattern that has "worked" 17 times in a row, you're NASA in the conference room. When you backtest a strategy and see a beautiful equity curve, you're looking at 24 successful launches. The only question that matters—the falsifying condition—is the one most traders never ask: "*Under what conditions does this fail?*"

What follows is the equation for asking that question correctly, not as philosophy, but as daily arbitration between three competing voices.

Edge, Expected Value, and Expectancy

But first, let's clean up some vocabulary.

It took me years to get precise about three terms traders use interchangeably: edge, expected value, and expectancy.

An **edge** is the underlying market phenomenon that creates systematic advantage. It's the *why*—the causal mechanism. When a stock gets added to the S&P 500, passive index funds must buy billions of dollars regardless of price. That's an edge. The pattern you might observe—"price rises into inclusion date"—is merely the signal. If enough traders front-run that flow and the opportunity evaporates, your pattern persists but your edge dies.

Expected value (EV) is the theoretical expression of that advantage for a single bet. "What should this trade be worth if I could repeat it thousands of times under identical conditions?" Math, not reality. What the trade *deserves* to produce in a perfect simulation.

Expectancy is what you've actually realized over many real trades. Your historical track record—the unit economics of your actual trading business. While EV is theoretical, expectancy is empirical fact.

Most traders confuse these catastrophically. You can have theoretical EV of +0.35R per trade and realized expectancy of −0.08R. Nothing theoretical went wrong. Everything practical did. Terrible fills. Hesitation on entries. Moving stops. Edge on paper, donation to the market in practice.

If you can't express your edge as positive expectancy—if you can't measure it—you're operating on faith. Faith in markets leads to poverty.

Get them wrong and the market extracts tuition.

The Three Voices and the Operator's Equation

Every trading decision involves three competing claims inside your head. Most traders experience these as vague emotions—confidence, fear, hesitation. Professionals recognize them as distinct voices.

> **The Optimist:** Your edge model says "This setup has +0.40R expectancy. The conditions align. Execute."
> **The Pessimist:** Your risk model says "You're already down 2.3% this week. Three consecutive losses. Another loss and you enter psychological spiral territory. Sit this one out."
> **The Accountant:** Your friction model calculates "Round-trip costs are 2.3 ticks slippage, 1 tick commission. You're starting this trade 3 basis points underwater. Is your edge really that big?"

The arbitration between these voices—the decision process that determines performance—most traders don't recognize as formal. They just feel something and act. Or freeze.

The system is an equation:

$$\text{Performance} = (\text{Expected Value} \times \text{Optimal Exposure}) - \text{Friction}$$

Three variables. Three knobs to turn.

EV: Your edge. The average profit per trade if you could execute thousands of times. Without positive EV, nothing else matters—you're subsidizing other participants.

Optimal Exposure: Your position size relative to capital and conviction. Too small and your edge doesn't compound. Too large and variance destroys you before the edge manifests. Not about maximizing size—about *optimizing* it. Massive difference.

Friction: Every cost that eats your edge. Spreads. Commissions. Slippage. Market impact. Opportunity costs. The hidden tax that kills most "profitable" strategies before they ever reach your account.

You're not a predictor. You're an operator of a probability engine. When traders fail, it's because they optimized one variable while ignoring the others.

The Edge-Chaser finds setups with massive theoretical EV but never calculates true costs. A 50-basis-point edge that costs 75 basis points to execute is a loss disguised as discovery.

The **Size Junkie** reads about Kelly Criterion, calculates what "optimal" sizing should be, and risks 25% of capital per trade. He ignores that his EV estimate carries massive uncertainty (Kelly assumes you know the probabilities—you don't) and that one bad regime shift destroys the entire account. Three consecutive losses at 25% risk: down 58%, game over.

The **Penny-Pincher** minimizes friction obsessively—limit orders only, tightest spreads, negotiated commissions to nothing. But he passes on his best ideas because they might cost one extra tick. Saves pennies while forgoing dollars.

The equation works when all three variables align. The market doesn't care about your edge if you size yourself into oblivion. It doesn't care about your friction minimization if you never take any trades.

The Sample Size Trap

The *Challenger* engineers had 24 successful launches. The trap they fell into has a mathematical dimension.

You find a pattern. Backtest it. It works 17 times in a row. Your brain screams: "This is real!" You've found confirmation every time. You never ask about the evidence you haven't seen.

Here's the problem: you need roughly 380 trades to achieve 95% confidence that a 55% win rate isn't random luck. That's two years if you take five trades per day. 17 years if you take one trade per month.

Yet traders commit serious capital after 30–50 trades. They're not validating an edge. They're gambling on noise and calling it evidence.

The standard sample size formula (for the statistically inclined) lands you at roughly 380 trades for 95% confidence with 5% margin of error:

$$n = \frac{z^2 \times p \times (1 - p)}{e^2}$$

where z is the confidence level, p is the expected proportion, and e is the margin of error.

But this assumes each trade is independent—like a coin flip. In markets, trades cluster. You win during trends. You lose during chop. Autocorrelation means your effective sample size is smaller than your trade count. Your confidence intervals are dishonestly narrow.

I've been this trader. I discovered a gap fade that "worked" 17 times in a row. Scaled to 3% risk per trade. Trade 18 came during a Fed announcement. Volatility exploded. I lost 6% in one morning. My "edge" had been variance wearing the costume of skill.

The law of large numbers doesn't rescue you from small samples—it punishes you for misunderstanding it. As sample size approaches infinity, observed results converge to true results. It says nothing useful about what happens at $n = 50$. At $n = 50$, you're at maximum confidence and maximum fragility.

The Volatility Tax

We covered volatility tax in Chapter 5. Here's how it operates when you compare two real strategies.

Two traders with identical "average profit per trade" can produce wildly different wealth outcomes.

Strategy A (The Grinder): 65% win rate. Average win 1.2R. Average loss 1.0R.

Strategy B (The Sniper): 35% win rate. Average win 3.0R. Average loss 1.0R.

Strategy A:
$$(0.65 \times 1.2) - (0.35 \times 1.0) = 0.43R$$

Strategy B:
$$(0.35 \times 3.0) - (0.65 \times 1.0) = 0.40R$$

They look roughly equivalent. Strategy A actually looks slightly better. But now let's look at the volatility tax.

Wealth grows geometrically, not arithmetically. It compounds. The enemy of compounding is variance:

$$G \approx \text{Arithmetic Return} - \left(\frac{\text{Variance}}{2}\right)$$

Strategy B has massive variance. Long losing streaks followed by huge jumps. That variance creates "drag" on the portfolio. If you lose 50%, you need 100% just to break even. Strategy B spends most of its time digging out of holes.

Strategy A (The Grinder) has a smooth equity curve. Its variance is low. It pays very little volatility tax. Therefore, more of its "gross expectancy" converts into "net wealth."

The path matters. A strategy that makes 50% one year and loses 35% the next has an average return of +7.5%. But you actually lost 2.5%. $100 → $150 → $97.50.

Professionals obsess over win rate and smoothness because smoothness creates geometric efficiency. A lower-return, lower-volatility strategy can be leveraged to produce more wealth than a high-return, high-volatility strategy that constantly interrupts its own compounding.

Sharpe Ratio as Turbulence

If you mention Sharpe ratio to day traders, half will roll their eyes. Fair enough. The textbook version has real issues—Two Sigma published a paper on them. It assumes returns are independent (they're not), treats upside and downside volatility identically, and is blind to skew.

Most discretionary traders discard Sharpe as "quant bullshit for hedge fund PMs." I did too, until I realized I was missing the point.

Sharpe is a proxy for turbulence. How violently does your equity curve wiggle relative to the returns it generates? How much pain do you endure between profits? How likely are you to be forced to liquidate at the worst moment?

This is the difference between an edge you can hold and an edge that holds you hostage.

The volatility tax is real. If you make 50% one year and lose 50% the next, your arithmetic average is zero but your capital is down 25%. The more jagged your path, the more compounding works against you. You can be right in expectation and still lose in practice because the path was too wild.

Here's what most traders miss: controlling turbulence lets you apply strategic leverage.

If your strategy runs at a 2.0 Sharpe (very few do), you can prudently lever it to target far higher absolute returns while maintaining the same risk-adjusted profile. The smoothness gives you capacity to size. A 0.5 Sharpe strategy, even with higher raw expectancy, cannot be levered safely. The turbulence will eventually land you in a drawdown that exceeds your risk tolerance or margin limits.

This is why professional desks obsess over Sharpe—it tells them whether they can press. For a day trader: can I size up when conditions are good, or will the volatility of the path blow me up?

You don't need to calculate Sharpe precisely. But look at your equity curve and be honest: is it a smooth compounding line, or a sawblade? If it's a sawblade, you won't be able to press size when the edge is real. The volatility tax will eat you.

Bayesian Thinking

You need roughly 380 trades to validate an edge statistically. But what if your strategy generates 30 trades per year? Are you supposed to wait 16 years?

No. Bayesian thinking saves you.

Kahneman and Tversky posed a famous problem. You're given a description of Steve: "Very shy and withdrawn, invariably helpful but with little interest in people or reality. A meek and tidy soul with a need for order and structure and a passion for detail."

Librarian or farmer?

Most people say "librarian." The description matches the stereotype. But this is irrational. It ignores the *base rate*: there are roughly 20 farmers for every librarian. Even if 40% of librarians fit the description and only 10% of farmers do, there are so many more farmers that Steve is more likely to be on a tractor than in the stacks.

Rationality isn't about knowing facts. It's about knowing which facts are relevant.

In trading, Steve is your chart pattern.

You see a setup that looks "meek and tidy"—a perfect bull flag, a textbook breakout. It matches your mental stereotype perfectly. You ignore the base rate: in this volatility regime, 80% of breakouts fail. You're betting on the description while ignoring the prior.

Bayesian thinking corrects this. Visualize probability not as a number, but as a *geometry of belief*.

Imagine all possibilities as a 1 × 1 square. Your prior belief is a slice of that square. When you see new evidence—a breakout, a news event, an order flow imbalance—you aren't just adding points to a score. You are restricting the space. You are slicing away the parts of the square that are no longer possible.

If your prior is strong—"breakouts fail in bear markets"—it takes enormous evidence to justify a long trade. A simple chart pattern isn't enough. You need flow, volume, cross-asset confirmation.

Bayes' Theorem looks intimidating, but in plain English: *Your updated belief equals your prior times the strength of the new evidence.*

The power comes from rewarding causal reasoning. If your edge is structural—built on mechanics that won't disappear—you can start with a high prior. Maybe 70%. Index funds must buy stocks added to the S&P 500. Passive rebalancing happens on schedules. Tax-loss selling follows calendar patterns. These mechanisms are mandated.

If your edge is purely *statistical*—a pattern you data-mined with no economic logic—your prior should be low, maybe 20%. Most statistical patterns are mirages. Correlations that break the moment you trade them.

Watch what Bayesian updating means practically.

> **High-prior structural edge:** After 10 confirming trades, confidence rises to 85%. After 30 trades, 92%. You can start scaling.

Low-prior statistical pattern: After 10 confirming trades, confidence only rises to 35%. After 30 trades, maybe 55%. You need far more evidence because you started skeptical.
Same data. Different conclusions. Structural edges require less validation because the mechanism is robust. Statistical edges require enormous validation because they're prone to break.

This lets you think clearly when you don't have enough data. Instead of "I don't know," you say, "given what I know about *why* this should work, here's my rational confidence level, and here's how much new evidence I need to increase it."

The Negative-sum Game

Most traders never calculate what the game costs them.

In poker, for every dollar one player wins, another loses exactly one dollar. Zero-sum.

Trading is worse. For every dollar winners gain, losers lose more than a dollar. The difference goes to transaction costs—commissions, spreads, market impact, slippage, exchange fees, data costs, the entire infrastructure of modern markets. The market extracts a tax on every interaction.

In ES futures, this becomes explicit. You're long when it rallies 10 points. Your gain: 10 points. The short's loss: 10 points. Zero-sum so far.

But factor in round-trip costs. Your 10-point gain becomes 9.7 points (commissions and slippage). The short's 10-point loss becomes 10.3 points. The system extracted 0.6 points total.

The *inefficiency budget*—the total edge available to extract—is tiny. Markets maintain just enough inefficiency to compensate information gatherers and liquidity providers. But that budget must first pay all transaction costs. What remains—actual extractable edge—is measured in basis points, not percentage points.

At our desk, we run strategies with gross expectancy of 30 basis points per trade. After execution costs? Maybe 8–10 basis points net. That's professional trading: fighting over scraps.

You have limited interactions with the market. Each costs capital, time, mental energy, and opportunity. The question isn't just "are you profitable?" It's "are you generating returns at minimum cost, risk, and effort?"

The Friction Tax

Friction is a tax you pay before you keep any profits.

Think of your strategy as a thermodynamic engine. No engine is 100% efficient—energy is always lost to friction. Your strategy converts gross expectancy into net expectancy. The difference is *implementation shortfall*.

> **Explicit Costs:** Commissions, exchange fees, platform fees—the visible taxes. Easy to calculate, relatively small.
>
> **Implicit Costs:** Bid-ask spread, slippage, market impact, adverse selection—the hidden taxes that kill most strategies. I've seen traders with 40 basis point edges that cost 42 basis points in execution. They're running charities for their brokers.

The professional countermove is *biasing*. If your model predicts a price rise, you don't just sit on the best bid and hope. You bias your order—moving it toward the ask to ensure participation. You pay a fraction of the spread because your alpha says the move is imminent. You use your prediction to fight the friction.

> **Psychological Costs:** Hesitation on entries, premature exits, revenge trading, moving stops. The self-imposed taxes. I've seen +0.50R gross strategies deliver –0.10R net because the trader couldn't execute as designed.

A strategy with +0.40R gross expectancy might net +0.10R after all friction. Your edge just shrank 75%.

Institutional traders understand what retail doesn't: in a negative-sum game, friction determines winners and losers more than edge quality. The firm with 0.30R gross edge and 0.05R friction crushes the retail trader with 0.50R gross edge and 0.40R friction. Not about being smarter—about structural advantages in the friction component.

The Hurdle Rate

Even positive net expectancy isn't enough. You must clear your hurdle rate—the minimum return that justifies risk.

Example: +0.20R expectancy, 200 trades/year, 1% risk on $100,000 account.

Annual return: $200 \times 0.20R \times \$1{,}000 = \$40{,}000$ (40%)

Sounds great. But your opportunity costs: Risk-free rate at 5% is $5,000. Equity index at 10% is $10,000. Your time: 1,000 hours/year managing this.

$$\text{Your true alpha: } \$40,000 - \$10,000 = \$30,000$$
$$\text{Hourly rate: } \$30,000 / 1,000 \text{ hours} = \$30/\text{hour}$$

This barely compensates for the cognitive load and capital risk.

Most traders never do the cold math. They see 40% returns and get excited. They don't subtract opportunity costs, don't value their time, and don't price the stress and cognitive load.

At our desk, we require strategies to clear 25% risk-adjusted returns above the hurdle rate before committing proprietary capital. Below that, it's a hobby, not a business. Below 15%, it's not worth the headspace.

The Five Decisions

What does a realistic decision pipeline look like for a discretionary day trader?

It's not a checklist. It's a sequence of questions you run through, usually in under a minute, because the market doesn't wait.

First: Where might I have edge today? A specific product (ES over NQ because of macro). A specific time window (the open, the London close, the lunch lull). A specific flow event (earnings, a Fed speaker, a rebalance). What kind of trade makes sense right now and why?

This is the shift from time-based trading (the market is open) to predicate-based trading (a specific condition is met). You're a predator waiting for a vibration in the web. No vibration, no trade.

Second: Once a setup appears, run a friction check. What's the spread? How jumpy is the tape? How often does this product slip your stop? If you can't argue that the edge exceeds the costs, let it go. Don't put yourself in a position where, even if you're right, you're breakeven after friction.

Third: If you have multiple ideas but limited capital or attention, which one gets your focus? "Given my playbook, do I want to be fading this move in crude or playing continuation in ES around the fix?" Choose the one with the best combination of edge, clarity, and tradability for you right now.

Fourth: Pick size. Not vibes, but rules. Baseline risk per trade (0.5–1% of capital), plus a bump or cut based on conviction and recent performance. If you're tilted, size down automatically. If the setup is clean, in your wheelhouse, supported by narrative and cross-market confirmation, size modestly higher—but stay in a band that keeps ruin probability low.

Fifth: After the trade, does this kind of trade deserve a place in your future? Log it, tag it, periodically look at your stats: which setups survive the hurdle of friction and psychology, and which ones are just noise you like pressing?

Underneath, that is still the same equation: Performance = EV × Exposure – Friction. You've translated it from white paper to how you actually click buttons between 9:30 and 16:00.

One final nuance: speed of resolution. If two trades have similar net edge but one resolves in an hour and the other drags across five days, the faster one is usually better. It frees your capital. It frees your headspace. You're not waking up three mornings in a row checking your swing before you've had coffee.

The Objective Function

The five previous decisions assume you know what you're optimizing for. Most traders don't.

Most will tell you their goal is "to make money," which is wonderfully unfalsifiable. Under the surface, everyone has a real objective function.

Some traders maximize Sharpe-like smoothness. They hate drawdowns more than they love big wins. They'd rather clip consistent 0.5–1.0R days than shoot for 5R weeks that come with –4R drawdowns. These traders do best with high-frequency, modest-edge, low-variance plays.

Others are clearly maximizing raw expectancy. They don't mind taking real pain for real gain. They will happily sit through an intraday puke to stay in a multi-day swing that can print 10R. For them, the challenge is not math; it is building the psychological and financial buffers to withstand the volatility tax.

Some, especially those with other obligations, are really trying to maximize return per hour of attention. They want the highest dollar outcome for the least amount of intense, screen-bound concentration. For them, certain very active scalp styles are a terrible fit no matter how good the Sharpe is; the "cost" in life energy is too high.

And a smaller subset, usually with substantial capital and high risk tolerance, are trying to maximize compounding in a more literal sense. They think in Kelly-like terms, accept that their P&L path will be wild, and are optimizing for long-term wealth rather than annual comfort.

The point isn't that one is "correct." The point is that mixing them unconsciously is lethal.

If you size like a compounding-maximizer, demand the comfort of a Sharpe-maximizer, and expect the free time of a return-per-hour trader, you're going to be in a permanent state of dissatisfaction and confusion.

Be explicit. "This year, my goal is X. I'll favor these trades, these holding times, these sizing rules." Now your daily decisions have a spine.

The Pipeline

One more thing: every edge decays.

The intraday nuance you find today—that little lag between ETF arbitrage legs, that time-of-day pattern in crude, that reliable reaction to a particular econ release—has a half-life. As more capital discovers it, the raw Sharpe compresses. Your friction doesn't go down, so net edge shrinks.

Traders who survive a decade or more don't find some eternal golden setup and defend it to the grave. They manage a pipeline of edges.

Structural edges rest on rules or institutions slow to change. Regulation-driven flows, calendar effects tied to tax law, predictable behavior around a central bank fixing window. These decay slowly.

Behavioral edges exploit recurring human tendencies—panic at certain levels, mean-reversion in quiet regimes, predictable overreaction to headlines. Durable but not permanent.

Informational edges are fleeting. Mispricings when a product is new, venue structure creating an exploitable lag. These vanish quickly.

Your job is to treat your playbook like a portfolio of edges, each with its own decay rate. Watch their expectancies over time. When a setup that used to average +0.5R is now printing +0.2R, scale it down. When it drifts toward zero after costs, retire it and look for the next one.

This isn't glamorous work. It's also where the real money is made.

From Probability to Survival

At this point, the pattern should be clear.

You're not in the business of prediction in the way people casually use that word. You're running a messy, human-in-the-loop probability machine.

The three voices—optimist (edge), pessimist (risk), accountant (friction)—aren't annoyances to be silenced. They're the three terms in the equation that determines whether your trading life trends up or flatlines.

EV tells you what your trades "deserve" to make. Expectancy tells you what they actually make.

A common trap: Confusing the average trade (arithmetic) with wealth growth (geometric). A strategy with a positive expectancy can still bankrupt you if the position sizing is too aggressive. Expectancy measures the quality of the trade. Geometric growth measures the quality of the trader.

Sample size and Bayes tell you how seriously to take your own results. Sharpe reminds you that the shape of your equity curve matters as much as its slope. Friction tallies the tax you pay for each trade. The hurdle rate asks whether the enterprise beats the alternatives. The pipeline forces you to accept that nothing works forever.

The final step is connecting all of this to survival.

Here's the brutal twist: you can do everything "right" in expectation and still go broke.

Not because your edge was fake, but because your sizing was too aggressive for the variance—or because your particular sequence of wins and losses hit an absorbing barrier before the math had time to bail you out.

The ensemble of all possible paths for a given strategy can be beautifully profitable. The one path you live through can still end at zero.

That's the real operator's equation: not just how to make good bets, but how to structure them so your path stays in the subset of trajectories that survive.

That's the work of Part II.

Notes

Challenger Disaster. Presidential Commission on the Space Shuttle Challenger Accident (Rogers Commission). *Report to the President.* June 6, 1986. Also see Vaughan, Diane. *The Challenger Launch Decision.* University of Chicago Press, 1996.

Lord Kelvin on Measurement. Thomson, William (Lord Kelvin). *Popular Lectures and Addresses*, Vol. 1. 1889. "When you can measure what you're speaking about, and express it in numbers, you know something about it."

Sample Size Calculation. Standard statistical result. See any introductory statistics text. The formula assumes simple random sampling and independent observations.

Sharpe Ratio Limitations. Two Sigma. "A Sharpe Ratio Is Not Enough." 2016. Available at twosigma.com.

Sortino Ratio. Sortino, Frank A., and Lee N. Price. "Performance Measurement in a Downside Risk Framework." *Journal of Investing* 3, no. 3 (1994): 59–64.

Steve the Librarian/Farmer. Kahneman, Daniel, and Amos Tversky. "On the Psychology of Prediction." *Psychological Review* 80, no. 4 (1973): 237–251. The original base rate neglect study.

Bayes' Theorem. For accessible introduction, see McGrayne, Sharon Bertsch. *The Theory That Would Not Die.* Yale University Press, 2011.

Implementation Shortfall. Perold, André F. "The Implementation Shortfall: Paper versus Reality." *Journal of Portfolio Management* 14, no. 3 (1988): 4–9.

Kelly Criterion. Kelly, J.L. "A New Interpretation of Information Rate." *Bell System Technical Journal* 35, no. 4 (1956): 917–926. For practical application and limitations, see Thorp, Edward O. "The Kelly Criterion in Blackjack, Sports Betting, and the Stock Market." In *Handbook of Asset and Liability Management*, 2006.

PART II
Mental Models

CHAPTER

Where Edge Comes From

"The only way to beat roulette is to steal the money when the dealer isn't looking."

—Attributed to Albert Einstein

Part I was the diagnosis. Part II is the prescription. If the game is rigged against you, where isn't it?

The Man Who Beat the Wheel

In 1961, Edward Thorp walked into a casino in Reno. He wasn't there to gamble. He was running a physics experiment.

For 200 years, the roulette wheel had been the symbol of pure, unbeatable randomness. The house edge was mathematical and absolute. In American roulette, with its 0 and 00 pockets, the casino held a 5.26% advantage on every spin. Over time, the law of large numbers guaranteed that the player would be ground to dust. Einstein himself is widely attributed as saying that the only way to beat roulette is to steal the money when the dealer isn't looking. Whether Einstein actually said this is disputed, but the sentiment captures two centuries of conventional wisdom.

Thorp disagreed. He didn't see a game of chance. He saw a system of differential equations.

A roulette wheel is a mechanical device. A ball is spun in one direction; a rotor spins in the other. Friction, gravity, and angular momentum determine the outcome. Thorp realized something.

If you could measure the velocity of the rotor and the ball at release, you couldn't predict the exact number—but you could predict which octant the ball would land in. Not certainty. A probability distribution heavily skewed in your favor.

To prove this, Thorp teamed up with Claude Shannon, the father of information theory, in a basement lab at MIT. Together, they built the world's first wearable computer. It was the size of a pack of cigarettes, hand-soldered, and wired into a shoe. Thorp would tap his toe when the ball passed a reference point to time the revolutions. The computer would calculate the orbital decay and transmit a musical tone to a tiny earpiece, telling him which section of the wheel to bet on.

He wasn't guessing. He wasn't "feeling lucky." He'd converted a game of chance into a game of physics.

He started winning. He won so consistently that casinos became suspicious. They didn't know how he was doing it—the computer was invisible—but they knew that he was doing it. They banned him. They changed the wheels. Eventually, Thorp realized that physical edges scale poorly; the "pit boss risk" was too high. So, he moved to a more scalable inefficiency: the financial markets.

Thorp founded Princeton Newport Partners, the first true quantitative hedge fund. There, he applied the same rigor to warrant pricing (working with economist Sheen Kassouf) and risk management. In a 20-year run (1969–1988), the fund compounded at 19.1% net of fees with zero down years.

Thorp is the patron saint of professional trading because he understood the fundamental truth that separates the professional from the amateur:

The lesson: you don't play the game. You play the inefficiency in the game.

Most people walk into a casino—or a market—and accept the rules as given. They try to be "lucky" or "smart" within the constraints of the game. Thorp looked at the game and asked: where's the flaw in the mechanism?

In roulette, the flaw was physics. The wheel wasn't random; it was just complex.

In blackjack, the flaw was memory. The deck didn't reset after every hand; the odds shifted based on what had been played. Thorp's book *Beat the Dealer* pioneered card counting and remains a classic of applied probability.

In markets, the flaws are subtler, but they are just as real. They are the structural, behavioral, and informational inefficiencies that allow a trader to extract value from a zero-sum system.

If you're trying to make money by "predicting the future," you're playing the game the casino wants you to play. You are guessing red or black. You might win for a while, but the transaction costs and the bid-ask spread will eventually eat you alive.

To survive, you must stop trying to predict and start trying to locate the flaw. You must find the place where the odds are broken. You must find your edge.

The Poker Principle

Thorp's story illustrates how to find edge. But there's a prior question most traders never ask: *against whom?*

Edge doesn't exist in a vacuum. It exists relative to a counterparty.

Trading is a zero-sum game. (Net of commissions, it's negative-sum.) For you to generate alpha, someone else must generate negative alpha. You can't win unless someone loses.

Imagine you're the ninth-best poker player in the world. You are a genius. You have mastered game theory, psychology, and probability. You have "positive expectancy" in a vacuum. Now, imagine you sit down at a table with the eight players ranked one through eight.

What happens?

You lose. You lose everything

It doesn't matter that you're the ninth-best player on the earth. It doesn't matter that you're better than 99.9999% of the human population. At that specific table, in that specific game, you're the "fish." You are the source of alpha for the other eight players.

Edge is not absolute. Edge is relative. This is the single most important concept for a retail trader to internalize. You are not competing against "the market." You are competing against specific counterparties in specific timeframes.

When you buy a stock, someone sold it to you. Who?
When you sell a future, someone bought it from you. Who?
So who are you actually trading against?
The answer depends on where you trade.

You might think you're competing against Citadel or Jane Street. It's more nuanced. If you're a retail trader sending a market order to buy equities, your order gets intercepted by a wholesaler like Citadel Securities or Virtu. They pay for the right to take the other side because they've categorized you as "uninformed flow"—industry jargon for dumb money. They know you have no edge, so they capture the spread with a statistical certainty so powerful it's effectively printing money. You're not fighting them. You're the product they're processing.

But step into the futures market or dark pools and you're sitting at the table with sharks: macro hedge funds, HFT firms, multi-strategy giants like Millennium or Point72. They have faster data, lower fees, better models, deeper pockets.

Do you have an edge against them? If the answer is, "I don't know," then you don't.

But there's hope. That same retail trader might have a massive edge in micro-cap distressed debt, a specific crypto altcoin, or small-cap biotech earnings reactions. Why? Because the multi-billion-dollar funds can't play at that table. Their size prevents them from entering markets that can't absorb their liquidity. The competition is softer. The fish are plentiful.

The question isn't, "Am I good?"

It's "Am I better than the person on the other side of this trade right now?"

If you can't identify your edge—specifically, what type of edge you have—you're providing liquidity to those who can. There are only four sources of edge in financial markets.

Informational Edge

The first of the four sources is the most obvious—and for retail traders, the hardest to pursue.

This is the edge of "knowing something they don't."

In the 1980s, this was how money was made. A guy on the floor. A contact inside the company. Getting the newspaper before the guy in Iowa. You knew the earnings were good before price reflected it.

Today, for retail traders, informational edge is mostly a myth.

Two things killed it: regulation and technology.

> **Regulation FD**, enacted by the Securities and Exchange Commission (SEC) in 2000, mandated that public companies release material information to everyone simultaneously. No more whispering in analysts' ears.

The Arms Race: High-frequency trading algorithms now parse news headlines, earnings releases, and economic data feeds in microseconds. They use Natural Language Processing to read the sentiment of a Federal Reserve statement before the pixels have even loaded on your monitor.

By the time you see the headline on Bloomberg or Twitter, price has already moved. The "news" you're reading is history. If you try to trade on it, you're trading stale data against machines that reacted 50 milliseconds ago.

Grossman and Stiglitz argued that markets can't be perfectly efficient—if they were, no one would bother gathering information, and they'd become inefficient. There's always some reward for information. But today that reward goes to those buying satellite imagery to count cars in Walmart parking lots or scraping credit card data to predict revenue. Unless you're spending millions on alternative data, you're informationally disadvantaged.

The Janitor Story

Imagine you're a janitor at a Major League Baseball stadium. You overhear the team doctor telling the star pitcher—whose endorsement deal drives a public shoe company's stock—that his elbow is blown and he's out for the season.

You know this before ESPN. You know this before the high-frequency algorithms. You could buy puts on the shoe company and make a fortune.

This is a pure Informational Edge. It is also *illegal*.

This is called **Material Non-Public Information**—MNPI. If you trade on it, you're not a "smart trader." You're a criminal. The SEC can fine you up to three times the profit you made.

The problem: by the time information is legal to trade—published in a press release—the machines have already repriced the stock. You're either a criminal (first) or the liquidity provider (last). There's no third option.

The Exception

Can a retail trader ever have informational edge? Yes, but almost never in the liquid indices or mega-cap tech stocks where the world's eye is fixed.

The opportunity for information arbitrage exists in inverse proportion to liquidity and attention.

If you're trading small-cap crypto tokens where the real updates happen in a developer's Discord channel or GitHub repository, you might have an informational edge. If you're trading local real estate, you know the neighborhood better than the Blackstone algorithm does. If you're trading distressed debt in a micro-cap company where you have read the court filings that the quants ignored, you have an edge.

But in the arena of liquid, public markets? You are not going to beat the machine on information. You are the last to know.

Analytical Edge

If everyone has the same information, how do you win? You process it better.

This is analytical edge.

This is the domain of **variant perception**. You see the same data as everyone else—the same earnings, the same chart, the same macro print—but you draw a different conclusion. And that conclusion turns out to be right. Steinhardt defined it as holding a view that's "materially different from the consensus."

The problem: distinguishing skill from luck. Analytical edge is incredibly hard to sustain because the consensus is usually pretty smart. And you have to distinguish being right from being lucky. As Mauboussin notes, in activities where luck plays a role, short-term results are poor indicators of skill. You might make 10 winning trades in a row simply because you're aggressive in a bull market. That's not analytical edge. That's survivorship bias.

In the modern era, analytical edge has largely moved to the quants. Renaissance Technologies doesn't "read" the news like you do. They ingest it as data points, measure sentiment velocity across petabytes of historical data, find correlations invisible to the human eye. They process massive datasets to find a 51% probability that Asset A will move with Asset B, then scale that 1% advantage across millions of trades.

Specialization

For a discretionary trader, analytical edge usually comes from extreme specialization. You can't analyze everything. You won't be smarter than the market on the S&P 500, oil, gold, Apple, and Bitcoin simultaneously.

But you *might* be able to be smarter than the market on a specific sector of mid-cap software stocks. If you spend 10 hours a day studying that one sector, reading every transcript, understanding the product cycles, tracking the customer sentiment—you might develop an intuition that the generalist algorithm misses.

You might see that a company's "missed earnings" were actually a strategic pivot that will pay off in two quarters. The algo sells the miss. You buy the pivot. That is analytical edge.

But this requires work. Real work. Not looking at a chart for five seconds and seeing a "head and shoulders." That's not analysis. That's *pareidolia*—seeing meaningful patterns in random noise, like faces in clouds.

Structural Edge

The third source doesn't require knowing more or thinking better. It requires understanding the *mechanics* of the market itself.

If informational edge is "I know more," and analytical edge is "I think better," then structural edge is *"I am paid to help you."*

Structural edge arises from the mechanics of the market itself. Certain participants are forced to trade regardless of price.

In Chapter 3, we covered Adverse Selection, the problem of avoiding informed traders who know more than you. Structural edge is the opposite: it is about finding **forced players**.

A forced player is a participant who is not trading for profit. They are trading to satisfy a mandate, a regulation, a margin call, or a hedging requirement. They are price insensitive. They need liquidity now, and they are willing to pay for it.

The Gamma Squeeze

A powerful modern example is the gamma squeeze, famously demonstrated during GameStop in 2021.

> **The mechanics:** When retail traders buy out-of-the-money call options en masse, the market makers who sell those options are legally and mathematically required to hedge. They are short the option, so they are short "gamma" (the acceleration of directional exposure—essentially, how fast their risk changes as price moves). As the stock price rises, the market maker's delta becomes more negative. To stay neutral, they must buy the underlying stock.

The higher the stock goes, the more they must buy.

Traders who understood this mechanism weren't betting on GameStop's fundamentals (which were poor). They were exploiting a structural loop: retail buys calls → market maker buys stock → price rises → market maker buys more stock.

Volmageddon

February 2018. Volmageddon.

A popular product called XIV—inverse VIX—had a structural mandate to rebalance daily. As volatility spiked, the fund's prospectus required it to buy VIX futures to cover its short exposure. This created a death spiral: fund buys VIX → VIX rises → fund value drops → fund must buy more VIX.

Traders who read the prospectus and understood the rebalance mechanic knew that XIV was a forced buyer. They front-ran the flow. XIV lost 96% of its value in a single session and was liquidated.

Structural Edges You Can Trade

Institutional structural edges—like HFT arbitrage between ETF baskets and their components—are inaccessible to retail. But macro structural edges are visible on the calendar and in the data. You can trade them.

Index Inclusion

When a stock gets added to the S&P 500, passive index funds are mandated to buy it at the close on the inclusion date. They can't wait for a dip. They're price-insensitive forced buyers. Their buying interest isn't a guess—it's a certainty, a function of the $13 trillion tracking the S&P 500 and the stock's weight in the index.

Traders who buy ahead of the inclusion date are front-running a guaranteed wall of money. The historical data is clear: stocks added to the S&P 500 experience an average price appreciation of 3–5% on inclusion, driven almost entirely by forced passive buying. You are not guessing; you're reading the institutional mandate on the calendar.

Month-end Rebalancing

Pension funds have strict allocation mandates—60/40, for example. If equities rip 10% in a month, they must sell equities and buy bonds at month-end to reset. This isn't preference. It's regulatory requirement. The flow is price insensitive.

Retail traders can predict the direction of the flow based on the month's performance and trade ahead of the "fix." If the market rallies hard in November, pension funds must rebalance at month-end (selling equities, buying bonds). This creates predictable pressure on equity prices in the final trading day of the month—a structural edge you can see on the calendar.

MOC Imbalance

Every day at 3:50 p.m. ET, the NYSE publishes Market on Close imbalances. This tells you how many shares institutions are required to buy or sell at the close.

If there is a "$2 Billion Buy Imbalance," it means institutions—pension funds, mutual funds, index rebalancers—are structurally forced to buy $2B of stock in the final 10 minutes of the day. Intraday traders can use this data to ride the wave.

The mechanics are not mysterious. The MOC imbalance creates temporary price pressure in the final minutes. An aggressive trader can buy at 3:50 p.m. when the imbalance is revealed, ride the buying pressure up for nine minutes, and *sell into the closing liquidity at 3:59 p.m.* You are not speculating; you're front-running a known forced flow and passing the bag to the institutions who are forced to execute at 4:00 p.m.

Tax-loss Selling

In December, mutual funds and individuals sell their biggest losers to realize losses for tax purposes. This isn't preference—it's a mandate to minimize tax liability. The flow is price insensitive and seasonal.

This artificial selling pressure depresses the prices of "hated" stocks below fair value in late December. Retail traders can buy these beaten-down names in December and hold through the seasonal rebound in January (the "January effect"). You are exploiting a structural calendar edge created by tax incentives.

If you're trading against a hedge fund manager, you're in a fair fight—or a losing one. If you're trading against a corporate treasurer executing a mandated currency conversion, or an index fund forced to buy an S&P 500 addition, you have structural edge. They're price insensitive. You're not. You win.

Behavioral Edge

The final source of edge is the most durable—because it depends on something that never changes: human nature.

This is the edge of being a stoic in a room full of maniacs.

Markets are composed of human beings (and algorithms programmed by human beings). Humans are subject to fear, greed, panic, and euphoria. These emotions cause prices to deviate from value.

The Science of Irrationality

Kahneman and Tversky's prospect theory proved that humans feel the pain of a loss twice as intensely as the pleasure of an equivalent gain. This leads to the **disposition effect**: traders sell their winners too early (to lock in the good feeling) and hold their losers too long (to avoid the pain of realizing the loss).

George Soros took this further with his theory of **reflexivity**. He argued that these biases don't just affect prices; they affect reality. If investors believe a tech company is the future, they bid up the stock. The high stock price allows the company to raise cheap capital, hire the best engineers, and acquire competitors, effectively making them the future. The bias creates the fundamental.

Why Behavioral Edge Lasts

Informational edges disappear (internet). Structural edges decay (algos adapt). But behavioral edge never disappears. Why? Because human nature doesn't change. We are running the same hardware we had 100,000 years ago on the savannah.

The reason you can make money from behavioral edge is that other market participants are trapped in a cognitive architecture of failure. They are making systematic errors that you can exploit. But to do so, you must first ensure you're not making them yourself.

Three mechanisms create the opportunity (and the trap):

Attribution Bias. The left hemisphere of the human brain functions as an "interpreter," constantly inventing narratives to explain sensory input in ways that preserve the ego. In trading, this manifests as attribution asymmetry. When the amateur wins, the internal monologue is clear: "I read the flow perfectly. My thesis was spot-on. I am a skilled operator." They assign the outcome to internal competence. When they lose? "The algorithms hunted my stop. The Fed surprised everyone. I got unlucky." They assign the outcome to external malevolence. This creates a market full of participants who never learn from their mistakes. They repeat the same errors because they have rationalized them away. Your edge comes from being the person who accepts the error, learns, and doesn't repeat it.

Hindsight Bias. After a market crash, the narrative crystallizes instantly. "Of course the market crashed. The yield curve was inverted. Valuations were high." It looks obvious now. But in the moment of decision, it was not obvious. Hindsight bias erases the uncertainty from the past, making the market appear deterministic and solvable. This causes amateurs to be overconfident. They believe they "knew it all along," so they take excessive risk on the next trade, believing they have a crystal ball. They don't. You can profit from their overconfidence.

The Intelligence Trap. You might think smart people are immune to these biases. The opposite is true. High-IQ individuals are often more susceptible to motivated reasoning than average populations—and their intelligence makes their rationalizations more sophisticated and harder to detect. Why? Because if you are intelligent, you are exceptionally good at rationalizing. A novice panic-sells and admits, "I got scared." A genius panic-sells and writes a 10-page memo about "structural regime shifts" to justify the emotional collapse.

Execution Patience

This is the most accessible behavioral edge for the independent trader.

Most institutional traders operate under strict constraints—career risk. Monthly or quarterly performance targets. They're forced to be impatient. A pension fund manager with $5 billion in exposure doesn't care if the chart looks terrible. They need to buy $500 million of stock by 4:00 p.m. because their mandate requires it. If the stock drops during the day, they must buy more. They're price insensitive because they have no choice.

You have an option they don't: *you can sit in cash.*

No boss. No quarterly report. No investors who'll redeem if you have a bad month. You can sit in cash for five hours if the chart looks terrible. Wait for the forced liquidation to finish before you step in.

This is **intraday time horizon arbitrage**. When an institution is forced to execute a block trade at market price, prices become temporarily dislocated. You buy at the dislocated price, hold for 10 minutes while the institutional wave passes, exit at the normal price. Your edge isn't holding for years. It's the ability to not trade until the odds are perfect.

The edge comes from understanding why they're trading (mandate, not discretion) and when they must trade (calendar, data feeds). While they're forced to execute, you're free to execute only when you have an edge.

This is structural in origin—the forced buyer creates the opportunity—but it requires behavioral discipline to exploit: the discipline to not trade, the patience to wait, and the wisdom to know the difference.

The Alpha Check

How do you apply this in real time?

Before you click "Buy" or "Sell," stop and answer three questions.

The framework: "I am taking the other side of [specific participant] who is forced to transact because [specific constraint]."

A stock crashes 30% in two days on high volume. You want to buy. The alpha check: "I'm taking the other side of leveraged retail traders and risk-managed funds who are forced to transact because they're receiving margin calls and hitting stop-loss limits. The selling is mechanical, not fundamental." Verdict: valid structural edge.

A parabolic tech stock up 200% in a month. You want to short. The alpha check: "I'm taking the other side of FOMO-driven retail buyers and momentum algos who are transacting because they're chasing performance and fear missing out. Price has detached from reality." Verdict: valid behavioral edge.

Now you want to buy EUR/USD because it "looks low." The alpha check: "I'm taking the other side of … um … the market? Because … I think it's going up?" Verdict: no edge. Delete the order.

If you can't identify the sucker at the table, you're the sucker.

Edge Decay

Even when you find genuine edge, there's a melancholy truth: *it dies.*

Edges are organic. They're born, they mature, and they decay.

Andrew Lo's **adaptive markets hypothesis** is more useful than Fama's efficient markets. Markets aren't static machines—they're evolutionary ecosystems. When a strategy makes money, it attracts predators.

The cycle of decay follows a predictable pattern. First, discovery: a few pioneers find an inefficiency (the "January effect" in small caps, or the index rebalance) and make massive returns. Then, imitation: other traders notice the returns or read the academic papers. They reverse-engineer the strategy. Capital floods in. Then, crowding: as Cliff Asness of AQR has noted, factor crowding compresses premiums. Everyone tries to front-run the front-runners. The entry price gets bid up earlier and earlier. Finally, inversion: the trade becomes so crowded that it becomes a trap. The slightest deviation causes a massive unwind as everyone tries to exit the same door at once. The edge becomes a liability.

The professional trader knows this. They don't marry their edge. They date it. They monitor performance, watch for signs of decay—smaller wins, larger drawdowns, more slippage. And when the edge is gone, they move on. Back to the casino floor, looking for the next wobbly wheel.

The BAIT Framework

There's a useful framework called **BAIT**:

Behavioral: Exploiting predictable irrational decisions by other traders

Analytical: Processing the same information better than the consensus

Informational: Knowing something material that the market doesn't

Technical (Structural): Exploiting the mechanics and forced flows embedded in the market itself

For the independent trader, the formula is simple:

Forget Informational Edge. It requires illegality or speed you don't have.

Specialize in Analytical Edge. Pick a niche (one sector, one asset class) and become genuinely smarter than the competition in that space.

Hunt for Structural Edges. Learn to read the calendar (month-end rebalancing, tax-loss selling, index additions). Learn to read the data (MOC imbalances, options expiration pinning). The forced flows are printed on the exchange data feed.

Exploit Behavioral Edge Through Patience. Your superpower is that you don't have to trade. Sit in cash until the institutional churn creates a dislocated price, then execute.

The best trades stack multiple edges: a structural setup (MOC imbalance) combined with a behavioral opportunity (panic selling into the close) combined with an analytical insight (this micro-cap always pops into earnings). But a single, clearly identified edge is enough.

Biasing and Predicate-based Timing

Finding edge is half the battle. Executing on it is the other half. Two concepts from the professional world:

When you sit at a professional trading desk, you notice something immediately. They don't just "take the trade." They bias into it.

This is the countermove to friction we discussed in Chapter 6. If your model predicts a price rise, you don't wait for a perfect fill on the passive side. You bias your order aggressively toward the ask. You are willing to pay a fraction of the spread because your edge says the move is imminent. Your prediction justifies the friction cost.

Retail traders fight every tick. Professionals pay what the edge is worth.

Then there's timing. Time-based timing is the mark of the amateur. They trade because the market is open. Because they're bored. Because they "have a feeling."

Professionals use **predicate-based timing**. They're predators waiting for a vibration in the web. No vibration, no trade.

The vibration might be a specific order imbalance pattern in the Level 2. It might be a dealer gamma hedge level approaching.

It might be a cross-market signal that pulls three assets into misalignment for a few seconds.

The point is: you don't trade because you can. You trade because a specific predicate has been satisfied. You are not a day trader. You are a conditional operator.

Back to the Wheel

Thorp's story doesn't end with roulette. Or even with the market.

After he beat the casinos and the market with Princeton Newport Partners, he focused on money management. He used the Kelly criterion—a formula from information theory that tells you exactly how much to bet on a given edge to maximize wealth without going broke. We'll build on this in Chapter 9.

The formula is ruthless. If your edge is zero, the optimal bet size is zero.

Thorp didn't beat roulette because he was a better gambler. He beat it because he refused to gamble. He identified a structural edge (physics) and an analytical edge (the computer). He ignored the noise and played the flaw.

When you sit down at your trading desk tomorrow, look at your screen.

Don't look for "money." Money is the byproduct.

Look for the flaw.

Look for the forced player.

Look for the panic.

Look for the structural constraint that forces someone to do something stupid.

If you can find that, you have an edge. If you can't, turn off the computer.

Because if you sit down at the table and you don't know where the edge comes from, you aren't the player. You're the chips.

Notes

Edward Thorp. Thorp, Edward O. *A Man for All Markets: From Las Vegas to Wall Street, How I Beat the Dealer and the Market.* Random House, 2017. Also see Thorp, Edward O., and Sheen T. Kassouf. *Beat the Market: A Scientific Stock Market System.* Random House, 1967.

Beat the Dealer. Thorp, Edward O. *Beat the Dealer: A Winning Strategy for the Game of Twenty-One.* Blaisdell, 1962. The book that launched card counting.

Claude Shannon and the Wearable Computer. Thorp describes the collaboration in *A Man for All Markets.* The computer predated publicly known wearable computing by decades.

Regulation FD. Securities and Exchange Commission. "Final Rule: Selective Disclosure and Insider Trading." August 2000.

Material Non-Public Information (MNPI). For SEC enforcement authority, see Securities Exchange Act of 1934, Section 10(b) and Rule 10b-5. Penalties under Securities Enforcement Remedies and Penny Stock Reform Act of 1990.

Grossman-Stiglitz Paradox. Grossman, Sanford J., and Joseph E. Stiglitz. "On the Impossibility of Informationally Efficient Markets." *American Economic Review* 70, no. 3 (1980).

Variant Perception. Steinhardt, Michael. *No Bull: My Life In and Out of Markets.* Wiley, 2001.

The Success Equation. Mauboussin, Michael J. *The Success Equation: Untangling Skill and Luck in Business, Sports, and Investing.* Harvard Business Review Press, 2012.

Index Inclusion Effect. Chen, Honghui, Gregory Noronha, and Vijay Singal. "The Price Response to S&P 500 Index Additions and Deletions: Evidence of Asymmetry and a New Explanation." *Journal of Finance* 59, no. 4 (2004): 1901–1929.

MOC Imbalance Data. NYSE Market on Close Order Imbalance Information. Published daily at 3:50 p.m. ET. Available via NYSE data feeds.

Prospect Theory. Kahneman, Daniel, and Amos Tversky. "Prospect Theory: An Analysis of Decision Under Risk." *Econometrica* 47, no. 2 (1979).

Disposition Effect. Shefrin, Hersh, and Meir Statman. The disposition to sell winners too early and ride losers too long: Theory and evidence. *Journal of Finance* 40, no. 3 (1985).

Reflexivity. Soros, George. *The Alchemy of Finance.* Simon & Schuster, 1987.

Adaptive Markets Hypothesis. Lo, Andrew W. *Adaptive Markets: Financial Evolution at the Speed of Thought.* Princeton University Press, 2017.

Factor Crowding. Asness, Cliff. *How Can a Strategy Still Work If Everyone Knows About It?* AQR Capital Management, 2015.

Kelly Criterion. Kelly, J.L. "A New Interpretation of Information Rate." *Bell System Technical Journal* 35, no. 4 (1956). For practical application, see Thorp's writings on optimal bet sizing.

GameStop and Gamma Squeezes. Various contemporary reporting from Bloomberg, Reuters, and academic analysis. See also Barber, Brad M. et al. "Attention-induced Trading and Returns: Evidence from Robinhood Users." *Journal of Finance* 77, no. 6 (2022).

Attribution Bias. Kunda, Ziva. "The Case for Motivated Reasoning." *Psychological Bulletin* 108, no. 3 (1990).

Hindsight Bias. Fischhoff, Baruch. "Hindsight ≠ Foresight: The Effect of Outcome Knowledge on Judgment Under Uncertainty." *Journal of Experimental Psychology* 1, no. 3 (1975).

Motivated Reasoning in High IQ. Stanovich, Keith E., and Richard F. West. "On the Relative Independence of Thinking Biases and Cognitive Ability." *Journal of Personality and Social Psychology* 94, no. 4 (2008).

CHAPTER 8

Structural Discipline

You know where edge lives. Now the problem is executing on it without sabotaging yourself. This is the gap where most traders lose their money.

The Interference Effect

It's 2:00 p.m. on a Wednesday. You're stalking a trade in crude oil.

You've done the work. You identified a structural support level at $75.50. You mapped the liquidity. Inventory data was bearish, but price refused to break down. Classic absorption signal. You are waiting for the retest of the low to enter long. Your plan is precise: Entry at $75.55, Stop at $75.30, Target at $76.80.

You are calm. You are prepared. You are a sniper waiting for the target to cross the crosshairs.

Then you start thinking about your thinking.

"Am I being patient or just passive? Is this discipline or fear? What if this is the setup I've been waiting for and I freeze? What if it's a trap and I'm about to get run over?"

The price ticks down. $75.65. $75.60. Your entry is approaching.

But now you're monitoring yourself. You're checking your pulse. You're asking: "Am I calm because I'm prepared, or am I calm because I've already decided not to take the trade?"

$75.55. Your level.

You hesitate. Not because the setup is wrong. Because you're too busy analyzing your own psychology to execute the plan.

$75.60. $75.75. $76.00.
The trade works perfectly. Without you.

Sports psychologists call this **reinvestment**. It's what happens when an athlete tries to consciously control a movement that should be automatic. A professional golfer who thinks about his wrist angle during the downswing will shank the ball. He forced a process that belongs in the fast, automatic brain into the slow, analytical one. The interference destroys the performance.

I call this the **interference effect**.

When you try to "monitor your psychology" in real-time—watching yourself for signs of fear, greed, FOMO, or tilt—you create a feedback loop of noise. You become the quarterback and the color commentator at the same time.

Your brain cannot run both processes at peak efficiency. The analytical load of "watching yourself" steals the cognitive fuel needed to read the tape. The result is paralysis, hesitation, and late execution.

And here's the worst part: you knew it was happening. You could feel yourself hesitating. The quiet voice said, "Just take the trade." But the louder voice asked, "What if I'm wrong about myself?" That louder voice was the interference. It usually is.

Later that night, you're doing the autopsy. "I need to be more disciplined. I need to work on my psychology."

You buy a meditation app. You journal more. You re-read *Trading in the Zone*.

Stop.

You don't have a psychology problem. You have a *hygiene* problem.

The Concept of Decision Hygiene

Decision hygiene isn't a metaphor.

The industry tells you the solution is more mindfulness. "Be aware of your emotions." They're wrong. The solution isn't more self-observation. It's externalization.

You can't think your way out of interference. You move the decision out of your head and onto the desk.

If you're asking "Is this FOMO?" in the moment of execution, you've already lost. A professional doesn't introspect. They look at their checklist. Does the trade meet the criteria? Yes or no.

If the boxes are checked, the trade is valid. How you feel about it is irrelevant.

Shift authority from your internal state to an external system and the interference disappears. You stop being a psychologist. You start being an operator.

This is what I call structural discipline.

The Lie That Sells Books

The trading education industry survives on a profitable lie: *You're broken, and you need to be fixed.*

"Master your emotions." "Eliminate bias." Work hard enough on your mindset and you can become an emotionless, perfectly disciplined machine.

This is nonsense.

You can't eliminate emotions. You're a biological organism. Your brain evolved on the African savannah. Immediate threat detection meant survival. You're wired at the hardware level to feel fear when you perceive a threat and dopamine when you perceive a reward. Your brain was built for a different environment. The market exploits that mismatch ruthlessly.

You can't mindset your way past three million years of evolution.

Most traders do exactly what the industry tells them. They meditate. They journal obsessively. They recite affirmations. They read *Trading in the Zone* until they've highlighted the entire book. They attend seminars on "trading psychology."

And yet.

When the VIX spikes to 40 and their P&L is flashing red, they still panic. When they're up $10,000 on the day, they still get greedy and risk it all for round numbers.

Why? Nothing changed. The hardware is the same. The emotional triggers still fire. They just added guilt: "I know I shouldn't feel this way, and I'm trying not to, but I still am."

Now they're not just afraid—they're afraid of being afraid. Anxious about their anxiety. Policing their own nervous system in real-time.

The professional understands something different. They accept the hardware. They stop trying to fix the human.

Instead, they fix the system.

NASA doesn't train astronauts to "not make mistakes." They assume mistakes will happen, especially under pressure. So they design cockpits, checklists, and protocols that function despite human error. The system catches the human.

This is **structural discipline**.

Decision hygiene starts with recognizing that you're the weakest link in your own trading system. The goal isn't to become perfect. It's to build guardrails that prevent the imperfect you from driving off the cliff.

The Overthinking Trap

The mechanism is neurological. More insidious than most traders realize.

Here's what I've noticed. The traders who try hardest to "manage their psychology" tend to be the ones who blow up.

Why? They're running two processes at once. A secondary system that competes with the primary. Both are exhausting.

When you're analyzing whether your impulse to buy is "intuition" or "FOMO," you're activating System 2—the slow, deliberate, analytical brain. But trading execution requires System 1—the fast, automatic, pattern-recognition brain. Here it becomes operationally critical. These two systems compete for resources. Your brain literally cannot run both simultaneously at full efficiency.

Kahneman proved System 2 is lazy. Every time you waste it on introspection, you drain the battery you need to trade. You're not multitasking. You're doing two things badly at once.

You miss the entry analyzing whether it's FOMO. You screw up the exit wondering if it's fear. You're so busy managing your thoughts that you can't execute.

The more you try to control your psychology, the less control you have.

A trader I work with sent me a message about six months into his career. He said, "I know I overtrade when I'm bored. I revenge trade after losses. I struggle with FOMO. I've been working on these problems for years. But I'm still doing them."

Years of introspection. Years of self-work. Still the same patterns.

His solution wasn't another psychology book. It was a simple rule: once he closed his laptop for the day, he couldn't open it again until the next morning. Full stop. Not unless there's a market emergency (there isn't). Not unless I think of a "must-see" setup (I won't).

He used software to lock himself out of the platform after hours. That's how serious he was. He couldn't trust his own willpower. His P&L improved dramatically. Not because he became a better person. Because he removed the option to be a bad trader.

Did that fix his psychology? No. He's still bored, still impulsive, still prone to FOMO.

But the system now makes those traits irrelevant to his P&L.

Building a System That Works When You Don't

The best traders I know have internalized this: *the system must function independently of your psychological state.*

We have a trader on our desk. Manages significant capital. One of the most consistently profitable traders I've met. By his own admission, an anxious wreck.

Overthinks everything. Sees danger everywhere. Crippling imposter syndrome. If you met him at a dinner party, you'd think, "This guy has the worst personality for trading imaginable."

But he prints money.

How?

He told me once: "My psychology is terrible for trading. So over the years I've built systems that trade despite me."

He didn't try to become someone else. He accepted he's neurotic. Then he engineered around it.

Chronic anxiety meant he hesitated at entries. Solution: once he approves a setup, an algorithm executes it. Hands off the keyboard. No second-guessing.

Analysis paralysis meant he could spend three hours analyzing a trade before clicking. Solution: a 60-second timer. If he hasn't clicked, the trade is void. The clock decides, not his brain.

Loss aversion meant he wanted to override position sizing rules. Solution: position size is locked by a volatility formula. He can't adjust it.

He didn't fix himself. He made himself irrelevant to the execution.

Old thinking: "I need to become less emotional." New thinking: **"I need a system that works regardless of my emotions."**

The old thinking says: "I need to stop revenge trading." The new thinking says: *"I need a circuit breaker that physically prevents me from trading after three consecutive losses."*

Where the Fighter Pilots Got It Right

Those traders figured this out through trial and error. There's an entire profession that has systematized it: military aviation. Fighter pilots face the same problem we do: high-stakes decisions under extreme time pressure when the human brain is demonstrably terrible at it. They've spent billions solving it.

Hasard Lee—F-22 and Thunderbird pilot—wrote *The Art of Clear Thinking*. He had to solve exactly this: how do you make decisions under extreme pressure when the human brain is demonstrably terrible at it?

The Air Force's answer is the **ACE Helix**: Assess, Choose, Execute. Not a thinking process. *A protocol.*

They engineered the thinking out of the critical moment. That's exactly what you need to do with your trading.

The **Assess** phase happens before you need it. Gather information, you think through scenarios, run through possible failures. On the ground, when you're calm, when your prefrontal cortex is online.

The **Choose** phase is fast. You've already identified the options. Pick one.

The **Execute** phase is automatic. You've rehearsed so many times your hands know what to do without your conscious mind interfering.

This is why pilots "chair fly" missions. Before every flight, they sit in a chair, close their eyes, and mentally walk through every step. Not success scenarios—failure scenarios. Engine flameout at 40,000 feet. Hydraulic failure. Radio outage.

When the real emergency happens, they're not inventing solutions. They're executing pre-loaded code.

Your **pre-flight ritual** is your chair flying.

Here's what most traders miss: you're not visualizing success. You're rehearsing failure.

What if crude breaks my stop and I feel panic? I check the VIX. If VIX is below 20, I trust the stop and move on.

What will I do if I'm up $10,000 and feel invincible? I will reduce size by 50%. I will move my stop to break even on the next trade. I will close the laptop at noon.

This isn't positive visualization. This is **pre-commitment**. You're locking your future self into a protocol before that self is compromised.

The Dopamine Trap

So far: fear. Paralysis, hesitation, interference. But there's an equally dangerous state that gets far less attention. Winning.

We talk about tilt as a response to losing. There's a more dangerous form nobody warns you about: winner's tilt.

You just nailed a massive trade. You're up big. Brain flooded with dopamine. You feel invincible. Like you can "see the matrix."

At this exact moment, your judgment is worse than when you're down.

Here's why. There's a cognitive bias called the **house money effect**. When you're up, you start thinking about profits as "the market's money," not yours. "I'm up $5,000 today. I can risk $1,000 on this flyer. Even if I lose, I'm still up $4,000."

This is seductive because it's partially true. It's also a trap.

The moment that $5,000 closes out, it's your money. In your equity. Real. Risking it is no different than writing a check from your savings account. Your dopamine-soaked brain doesn't believe that.

Your risk perception is impaired. You're drunk.

Dan, one of our risk managers, tells this story. Late afternoon at a prop firm. The trader was up £990,000 on Eurostoxx futures. Day of his life. One tick away from a round million.

He wanted that number. Wanted the screenshot.

So, he loaded up 1,000 lots. He needed one tick. £10 per tick. One tiny tick.

The market ticked against him. He didn't cut it. "Just a pullback," his brain said. "I'm up a million. I can handle this."

The risk alarms started screaming. In 10 minutes, the trader went from +£990,000 to flat. Zero.

The trader was physically shaking. Not from fear—from the dopamine crash. The visceral withdrawal from a neurochemical high. Winner's tilt makes you an addict. The market is your dealer.

He didn't lose money on the day. He obliterated a career-defining win because he was trading under the influence of his own neurochemistry.

Give-back Protocols

This is why professional firms don't trust traders who are up big. They've seen it too many times. A trader up 5% on the day is just as dangerous as a trader down 5%. So they build hard rules that activate when you're profitable.

> **The 50% Rule:** You're never allowed to give back more than 50% of your day's high-water mark. If you're up $10,000, your stop for the rest of the day is +$5,000. Hit +$5,000 and you're flattened. Liquidated. Done.
>
> **Position Sizing Decay:** As your P&L extends into outlier territory—2+ standard deviations from your average daily win—your max position size *decreases*. Not increases. *Decreases*.

Why? You're compromised. You're high. You shouldn't be operating heavy machinery.

The goal: capture the fat tail of returns without giving them back.

The Flaw Audit

You need a system. But before you can build guardrails, you need to know what kind of car you're driving.

Brent Donnelly calls this Nosce Te Ipsum—know thyself. Not as a Zen principle. As a practical prerequisite for building a system that works.

Different flaws, different guardrails.

Some traders are **anxious overthinkers**. See danger everywhere. Analyze endlessly. Hesitate at the trigger. Miss entries, then chase the move. Paralyzed by the fear of making a mistake.

For this type, the fix isn't "be more confident." It's removing the decision from the moment. Use a rigid "If/Then" checklist. Criteria met? You click. No analysis. Give yourself a 30-second timer. If you don't click by 0:00, the trade is void. The clock decides, not you.

Some traders are **impulsive action-takers**. See opportunity everywhere. Trade first, think later. Overtrade because they're bored. "Invent" setups. Incapable of sitting still.

For this type, the fix is friction. Slow down the loop between "see" and "click." Before every trade, write it down on paper: setup, stop, target, thesis. Can't write it? Can't trade it. Usually, by the time you pick up the pen, the impulse fades.

Some traders are **emotional empaths**. They viscerally feel the market. When it crashes, their stomach drops. When it rips, they feel euphoria. They get swept up in crowd sentiment. Panic when everyone else panics.

For this type, outsource your feelings to data. When you feel panic, don't trust the feeling. Check the VIX. Check the put/call ratio. Check the structure. If those aren't screaming panic, your feeling is a signal about your state, not the market's. Use your emotions as a contrarian indicator. "I feel sick, so the bottom is probably close."

You're not trying to fix the flaw. You're building around it.

"But what if I'm a mix of all three?" You probably are. Most traders are. Identify which flaw costs you the most money and build the guardrail for that one first. You don't need to solve everything. Just stop the biggest leak.

The Circuit Breaker

The ultimate tool in your hygiene kit: the circuit breaker.

Exchanges have circuit breakers. S&P 500 drops 7%, trading halts for 15 minutes. Why? Stop the panic. Give cooler heads time to think. Break the feedback loop before it becomes catastrophic.

You need a personal circuit breaker.

Not a stop loss on a trade. A stop loss on the trader. A hard rule that stops you from trading.

> **The Rule of Three:** Three losses in a row, you walk away for 60 minutes. Full stop. No exceptions. No "one more try."

I know the voice in your head. "But what if the next one is the winner? What if this is the setup I've been waiting for?"

That's your amygdala. That's exactly what the circuit breaker is designed to silence. The voice is wrong. It's always wrong in that moment.

Leave the room. Go for a walk. Reset your physiology.

> **The Daily Stop:** Lose X% of your account in a day, you're done. Platform closes. Change your password if you have to—so you can't access it until tomorrow.

Why?

Revenge Trading.

Revenge trading isn't a strategy. It's a biological fight response. When you lose money, your amygdala perceives it as a physical attack. Floods your body with adrenaline. Shuts down your prefrontal cortex.

You become stupider. Not metaphorically—neurologically.

You can't willpower your way out of an adrenaline dump. Remove the stimulus. Stop trading.

The circuit breaker doesn't make you less emotional. It removes your ability to act on the emotion until the neurochemistry resets.

The Ritual

Rules are useless if you don't follow them. So how do you ensure you follow them?

Anchor them in a ritual.

You can't go from scrolling Twitter or arguing with your spouse directly into trading high-frequency futures. You need a buffer. A shift from civilian mode to professional mode.

Pilots have pre-flight checklists. Surgeons have scrub-in procedures. Traders need a pre-flight ritual.

Doesn't have to be long. Fifteen minutes is enough.

The first week you do this, it will feel ridiculous. You'll feel like you're play-acting. That's normal. The pros feel that way too. They do it anyway. By week three, it stops feeling like acting and starts feeling like switching on.

Five components:

> **One:** Review the overnight. What happened in Asia? London? Where's the inventory? What levels broke or held?
> **Two:** Check the calendar. Fed noise today? Earnings that matter? Economic data that could spike volatility?
> **Three:** Hygiene check. Am I tired? Hungover? Angry? (If yes to any, reduce size or don't trade.)
> **Four:** Write the plan. Two or three scenarios you're willing to trade today: "If ES holds 4450, I look for longs into the FOMC." "If crude breaks 75 and holds, I look for shorts on the retest." Anything else is noise. You will not trade it.
> **Five:** Activate your professional identity. This tells your brain: "Play time is over. Work time has begun."

Brent Donnelly put it well: one of the biggest blind spots traders have is not understanding their own personality. Not in a deep psychological sense—in a practical sense. What does the data say about you? What time of day do you trade best? What setups does your journal show you nail? Which do you consistently screw up?

He discovered his trading fell apart after 11 a.m. Morning trades: clean and profitable. Afternoon trades: chaotic. So he built a rule: squares up most of his risk by 11 a.m. After that, if he's trading, it's smaller, thesis-based, and not noise.

That's not self-improvement. That's self-knowledge applied to system design.

The Cargo Cult Danger

I've given you a lot of rules. Checklists, protocols, rituals. Before you build them, a warning about the biggest failure mode of this approach.

Feynman's "Cargo Cult Science" speech: After WWII, some Pacific Islanders built bamboo airplanes and coconut headphones, mimicking what they'd seen American soldiers do. They had the form. Not the function. The planes never came.

In trading, this becomes **process rigidity**.

You can follow a checklist perfectly and still blow up if the checklist is designed for a market that no longer exists. You can fill out your trade ticket dutifully and still lose money if your thesis is wrong. You can follow circuit breaker rules and never take a real trade because the rules are too tight.

A "buy the dip" algorithm that worked beautifully from 2010 to 2021 became a suicide machine in 2022. If your discipline is so rigid, it prevents you from adapting to regime change, it's just a slow death wearing the costume of process.

The difference: a **protocol** is a tool you use to execute. It serves you. A **ritual** is a habit you perform for comfort. It serves itself.

If you're filling out your trade ticket mindlessly, just to "get it done" so you can take the trade you already decided to take, you're wearing the coconut headphones.

Here's what a real system review looks like. Every Friday at 4 p.m., ask yourself three questions:

Which rules prevented me from taking a trade that would have been profitable? *(False negative.)*

126   The Art & Business of Professional Trading

Which rules allowed me to take a trade that lost money? *(False positive.)*

Which rules saved me from a catastrophic loss? *(True positive.)*

If a rule generates more false positives than true positives, tighten it or scrap it. If a rule generates false negatives, loosen it. If a rule saved you once, keep it—even if it feels annoying.

This is System 2 reviewing System 1. This is how you avoid becoming a cargo cult.

The Liberation

Checklists, rules, circuit breakers, rituals. Sounds like a straitjacket.
It's the opposite.
The more you constrain your actions, the freer your mind becomes.

When you don't have to decide whether to trade, or how much to risk, or when to stop, you free up enormous cognitive bandwidth.
The internal war ends.
You stop fighting yourself. Stop wondering if you're "disciplined enough." Stop doing psychological introspection while the market is moving. Just run the system.

That energy you wasted on "managing your psychology"—anxious thoughts about your thoughts, self-monitoring, second-guessing—is now available for managing the trade. You can read the tape clearly because you're not reading it through the fog of your own internal conflict.

You become a trader. Not an amateur psychologist pretending to trade.

Back to 2:00 p.m. Wednesday

Same trader. Same market. Same temptation. Different system.

2:00 p.m. Wednesday. You're stalking the crude oil trade at $75.50.

> **8:00 a.m. Pre-flight ritual:** You ran your checklist. Identified "Crude Long at $75.50" as one of your three A+ setups. Wrote it down. Also wrote: "I get distracted by NQ volatility. Today I close the NQ chart at 10:00 a.m. if I'm stalking a crude setup."
> **2:00 p.m. The setup:** Price hits $75.55. You're ready.
> **2:01 p.m. The distraction:** A Twitter notification. "Shorting NQ here. Tech looks heavy."

Your brain feels the pull. Dopamine spikes. You want to look.

But your protocol is already live. You have a rule: "No new ideas after noon unless they're on the morning watchlist."

Is NQ on the watchlist? No.

Therefore: no.

You don't have to use willpower. Don't have to analyze the NQ chart or debate with yourself. The decision was made four hours ago by a calmer version of you.

You swipe the notification away. Don't even open the NQ chart.

2:02 p.m. The execution: Focus entirely on crude. See the absorption. Click "Buy" at $75.55.

The trade works. Hit your target at $76.80.

Later, you check NQ. It chopped around and ripped higher. The Twitter guru got stopped out.

You smile. Not because you predicted NQ—because you survived yourself.

There's a strange satisfaction in that. A quiet pride that feels different from the dopamine hit of a big win. The pride of having outsmarted your own worst instincts. That's what a working system feels like.

Same human. Same market. Same temptation.

Different outcome.

The system worked.

Notes

Reinvestment (Sports Psychology). Masters, R.S.W. "Knowledge, Knerves and Know-How: The Role of Explicit versus Implicit Knowledge in the Breakdown of a Complex Motor Skill Under Pressure." *British Journal of Psychology* 83, no. 3 (1992): 343–358. The foundational research on how conscious attention to automatic processes degrades performance.

System 1 and System 2. Kahneman, Daniel. *Thinking, Fast and Slow.* Farrar, Straus and Giroux, 2011. The foundational work on dual-process theory in decision-making.

Trading in the Zone. Douglas, Mark. *Trading in the Zone.* Prentice Hall, 2000. A widely read book on trading psychology that emphasizes mindset.

The Art of Clear Thinking. Lee, Hasard. *The Art of Clear Thinking: A Stealth Fighter Pilot's Timeless Rules for Making Tough Decisions.* St. Martin's Press, 2023. The ACE Helix framework for decision-making under pressure.

House Money Effect. Thaler, Richard H., and Eric J. Johnson. "Gambling with the House Money and Trying to Break Even: The Effects of Prior Outcomes on Risky Choice." *Management Science* 36, no. 6 (1990): 643–660.

Nosce Te Ipsum. Donnelly, Brent. *Alpha Trader.* Harriman House, 2021. Also, his trading notes on self-knowledge and system design.

Cargo Cult Science. Feynman, Richard. *Cargo Cult Science.* Caltech Commencement Address, 1974. Reprinted in *Surely You're Joking, Mr. Feynman!* W.W. Norton, 1985.

NASA Human Factors. For background on cockpit design and error management, see Reason, James. *Human Error.* Cambridge University Press, 1990.

Pre-commitment and Self-Control. Ariely, Dan, and Klaus Wertenbroch. "Procrastination, Deadlines, and Performance: Self-Control by Precommitment." *Psychological Science* 13, no. 3 (2002): 219–224.

Amygdala and Financial Decision-Making. Kuhnen, Camelia M., and Brian Knutson. "The Neural Basis of Financial Risk Taking." *Neuron* 47, no. 5 (2005): 763–770.

CHAPTER

Position Sizing

"The first thing I heard when I got in the business was bulls make money, bears make money, and pigs get slaughtered. I'm here to tell you I was a pig. And I strongly believe the only way to make long-term returns that are superior is by being a pig."

—Stanley Druckenmiller

Druckenmiller can be a pig because he's earned it. Decades of calibrated risk-taking. An ability to size up that was built, not given. You haven't earned it. Yet. This chapter is about how you get there.

How much should you risk on any given trade? Get it wrong and edge won't save you. Get it right and even mediocre edge compounds into wealth. Position sizing is where theory meets your account balance.

The Setup on Your Screen

It's 9:47 a.m. on a Tuesday in late February. You're short WTI crude at $75.82.

You have your reasons. The narrative is clean: OPEC+ is jawboning about extending cuts, but the Saudis are quietly selling into the rally. Fundamentals are murky—inventory data mixed, but the print came in higher than whisper expectations. Technicals are aligned: crude is testing a major resistance cluster. Sentiment is euphoric: retail piling in long, speculators near record net long per the Commitment of Traders.

Every pillar is aligning. High conviction.

But here's the question that actually matters: *how many contracts do you short?*

Not the thesis. Not the entry price. The size.

Crude is trading at $75.82. The last swing high—the one that matters structurally—is at $76.15. That's the invalidation point. If crude trades through $76.15, you're wrong. Stop goes above that. You add a buffer for stop-hunting algorithms (paying the vig to market makers) and pick $76.21.

Thirty-nine cents of heat.

You're trading a $500,000 account, but you don't size based on that. You size based on **risk capital**—the maximum drawdown you'll tolerate this year. Yours is $100,000. You're up $12,000 YTD, so adjusted risk capital is $112,000. Baseline risk per trade: 1% of that. $1,120.

The math:

$$\text{Barrels} = \$ \text{ Risk} \div |\text{Entry} - \text{Stop}|$$

$1,120 ÷ $0.39 = 2,872 barrels

Crude trades in 1,000-barrel contracts. That's 2.87 contracts—round to two or three?

Most amateurs round up because they're greedy. You choose two. $780 risk, 0.7% of adjusted risk capital. Discipline over maximizing a single instance.

You short two contracts at $75.82. Stop is in the market, hard, at $76.21. If you're wrong, you lose $780. If you're right, target is $74.50—a 3.4R trade. (R is your unit of risk. 3.4R means you make 3.4 times what you risked.)

You think about the risk, not the profit. Hands off the keyboard.

Crude ticks up to $75.85. Then $75.90. Down $160. Then $76.00, down $360. You don't touch the mouse. The stop is your governor. At $76.21, you're out. Not a debate. Not a second thought. The decision was made before you clicked.

At 10:13 a.m., crude taps $76.18. You feel the adrenaline spike—biology screaming at you to do something. But you don't flinch. The stop holds. Offer lifts. Crude rolls over. By noon, $75.60. By 2:30 p.m., $75.10. By 3:45 p.m., $74.50. Target fills.

Net profit: $2,640. You compounded your risk capital by 2.4% in one day.

You close the laptop. Don't high-five. Don't tweet. You executed a system. The system worked because the sizing was right.

The Learning Problem

The previous trade worked. But here's the uncomfortable truth: you couldn't know in advance that it would work. Conviction isn't certainty.

Most traders think position sizing is about risk management. How much can I afford to lose?

The real question: *how do I stay alive long enough to learn whether my edge is real?*

Trading is a learning problem disguised as a financial one. You're always operating in the fog. You have a theory about the market—a belief that certain conditions predict certain outcomes. This theory might be true. It might be an artifact of overfitting, survivorship bias, regime luck, or narrative fallacy. You don't know which.

The only way to find out is to run experiments. You trade, observe outcomes, update beliefs. But statistical significance requires sample size. A 55% win rate isn't distinguishable from 50% until you've run hundreds of trials. Maybe thousands.

If you blow up at trade #47 because you bet too big on a "sure thing," you never reach the sample size required to know if your edge was real. You destroyed the lab before the experiment concluded.

Position sizing is sample size protection. The discipline that keeps you in the game long enough to convert belief into knowledge.

But here's what took me years to understand: position sizing isn't just about survival. It's about optimization. Specifically, optimizing the geometric growth of your wealth over time. That's the goal. Not the outcome of any single trade, but the trajectory of your account across hundreds or thousands of trades.

The objective: maximize long-term geometric growth while staying alive long enough to get there.

The Kelly Gift—and Its Trap

If the goal is geometric growth, there's a mathematical framework that addresses it directly: the Kelly criterion. We touched on it in Chapter 7. Now you need to understand it more deeply, both its power and its limitations.

In 1956, John Kelly at Bell Labs published a paper called "A New Interpretation of Information Rate." He wasn't thinking about stocks or gambling. He was building on Claude Shannon's information theory, trying to figure out how to transmit data over noisy telephone lines without corruption.

Kelly realized Shannon's equations for information capacity could be repurposed. If a noisy channel could transmit information, maybe a gambler with an edge could transmit that edge into capital growth over time.

In solving that problem, Kelly gave traders a powerful framework for optimal capital growth under uncertainty. His work answers the core question of position sizing: given a repeatable edge, what fraction of capital should you risk on each bet to maximize wealth over the long run?

The intuition: a sweet spot must exist. Bet too little and you leave money on the table—your account grows too slowly to matter. Bet too much and inevitable drawdowns become so severe that volatility drag destroys your compounding even when the average outcome is positive. Your long-term growth rate gets driven toward zero, then negative, eventually to ruin.

For a simple bet with two outcomes, the optimal fraction of capital to risk—the Kelly fraction—is:

$$f^* = \frac{bp - q}{b}$$

where b is the net odds (payoff to 1), p is the probability of winning, and q is the probability of losing $q = 1 - p$.

In trading contexts where wins and losses are measured in R-multiples with asymmetric payoffs, this generalizes to

$$f^* = \frac{pW - qL}{WL}$$

where W is the average win size in R-multiples and L is the average loss size in R-multiples.

A strategy with a 60% win rate ($p = 0.60$) and even-money payoffs ($b = 1$):

$$f^* = (1 \times 0.60 - 0.40)/1 = 0.20$$

Kelly says risk 20% of your account on every trade. If you plot expected long-run growth as a function of f, the Kelly curve peaks at full Kelly and drops off sharply. The penalty for overbetting is catastrophic; the penalty for underbetting is merely slower growth. In simulations and empirical studies, half Kelly emerges as a robust compromise—roughly three-quarters of maximum growth with substantially less volatility and drawdown risk.

Why Kelly Fails in Practice

Kelly's formula works cleanly when probabilities and payoffs are fixed, known, and stable. Kelly's context was data transmission through a noisy but fully specified channel. Thorp's applications were in blackjack and other games with fixed rules and well-defined state spaces. In those environments, the road conditions are controlled, the engine's redline is clearly marked, and the map is complete.

Financial markets are not that world.

Markets are complex, adaptive systems—structural uncertainty, regime shifts, feedback loops. Not stationary, quantifiable risk. Probabilities are never truly known. They're estimated from incomplete, path-dependent data, and they evolve as other participants adapt.

Applying full Kelly sizing amounts to making very strong claims about how accurately you know your edge and payoff distribution. Any estimation error or model misspecification is effectively leveraged. Overconfidence in p, b, W, or L can turn a theoretically optimal strategy into one that's fragile, overexposed, and prone to catastrophic drawdowns.

The most critical failure: parameter uncertainty. You're claiming perfect knowledge of your win rate based on a backtest that's almost certainly optimistic due to overfitting. To use full Kelly is to treat your backtest as gospel truth, not biased estimate. It's an act of fatal intellectual arrogance.

This is why I apply what I call the backtest tax before I even think about position sizing.

Your backtest tells you a 58% win rate and 1.3:1 payoff ratio. These numbers feel precise. They came from data. But they're not truth—they're estimates derived from a process that's structurally biased toward optimism. You tested hundreds of parameter combinations and kept the ones that worked. You stopped the backtest at a point that looked good. You excluded the data that didn't fit.

The backtest tax is simple: assume your real-world parameters will be worse than your backtest suggests. Discount your estimated win rate by 10–20%. Discount your payoff ratio similarly. Then calculate Kelly on the discounted numbers.

Graham called this the margin of safety. Buy assets at a discount to intrinsic value—not because you know the value is wrong, but because you know your estimate is uncertain. The discount protects against your own analytical error.

The backtest tax serves the same function. You're not protecting against the market. You're protecting against yourself.

A Word on Kelly in Practice

Kelly sounds great in theory, and the math is elegant, but when you talk to discretionary traders who've been doing this for any length of time, many will tell you they don't actually use Kelly day to day. Not explicitly.

During my years of active trading, I wasn't sitting there calculating Kelly fractions before every entry. I'd start with my risk limits—daily stops, maximum position sizes, drawdown thresholds—and back into the sizing from there. The question wasn't "What does Kelly say?" It was "What can I afford to lose on this trade without compromising my ability to trade tomorrow?"

That said, Kelly gives you something valuable: a framework for thinking about the relationship between edge and sizing. It makes explicit what many traders feel intuitively—bigger edge justifies bigger bets, but only up to a point. And it quantifies the severe cost of overbetting.

The practical reality: if you're going to use Kelly at all in a discretionary context, you need to size down substantially. Not half Kelly. Quarter Kelly or below. Some traders I respect use tenth Kelly as their ceiling. *The formula assumes perfect knowledge. You have imperfect knowledge. Therefore, you discount the output dramatically.*

The good news: calculating Kelly has never been easier. With modern AI tools, you can get instant Kelly calculations, sensitivity analyses, Monte Carlo simulations. All the things that used to require custom spreadsheets or programming. The computational barrier is gone.

But computation isn't the hard part. Getting the inputs right is. And for discretionary traders, the inputs are always uncertain.

There are other approaches worth knowing. Lance Breitstein—partner at the firm, Market Wizard trader—advocates exponential bet sizing. Scale position size exponentially with conviction rather than linearly. A five-star setup isn't just marginally better than a four-star; it's categorically different, and your sizing should reflect that nonlinearity. It's aggressive, requires genuine calibration (which we'll discuss shortly), but it's intellectually coherent.

The point isn't that Kelly is the only way, or even the best way. The point is that you need some systematic approach to translating conviction into position size, and that approach should optimize for what Kelly optimizes for: geometric growth over time. Whether you use Kelly, exponential sizing, fixed fractional, or some hybrid—find what works for your psychology and trading style. Just make sure you understand what you're optimizing for.

The Volatility Tax

You've seen the volatility tax before. Here's why it matters for sizing specifically. Now let's see how it applies to position sizing, because this is where the abstract concept becomes operationally critical.

Why does overbetting destroy wealth even when expected value is positive?

Because of asymmetry in percentage math.

You've seen the volatility tax before. Here's why it matters for sizing specifically.

If you lose 10%, you need 11% to recover. Lose 20%, you need 25%. Lose 30%, you need 43%. Lose 50%, you need 100%—a double—just to get back to even.

The deeper you fall, the harder gravity pulls. A 50% drawdown isn't twice as bad as 25%. It's categorically worse—the recovery math becomes nearly impossible. Think about how it felt the last time you were down 30%. How large the mountain suddenly looked. That feeling is the volatility tax made visceral.

High variance creates deep drawdowns. Deep drawdowns require exponentially larger recoveries. Even with positive expected value, the tax on volatility can exceed the profits from edge.

Two traders with identical edges—same win rate, same payoff ratio—can have opposite outcomes based purely on sizing. Trader A risks 2% per trade and compounds steadily. Trader B risks 10% and occasionally makes spectacular gains. But B's drawdowns trigger the volatility tax, eating returns faster than edge generates them. Over time, A builds wealth while B becomes a cautionary tale.

This is why geometric growth—not arithmetic expectation—is the right optimization target. A strategy with lower expected value but lower variance can outperform a higher-EV, higher-variance strategy over time. The volatility tax is real. It compounds against you.

The Rationality of Restraint

If full Kelly is a fast path to ruin, what do we do?

What professionals always do: respect the theory but adapt it to the environment. Treat Kelly as a benchmark, a theoretical speed limit. Operate at a conservative fraction of that limit—fractional Kelly. Usually half or quarter, though I'd argue for even less in discretionary trading.

This is often framed as a practical compromise—trading optimality for safety. But it's more than that. Choosing a fractional approach isn't just safer. It's a philosophically superior and more rational way to behave when you acknowledge the limits of your own knowledge.

The **precautionary principle** encapsulates this perfectly.

The precautionary principle is a framework for decision-making under deep uncertainty when the stakes involve existential risk. It states that if an action has a suspected risk of causing severe, irreversible harm, the burden of proof that it's not harmful falls on those taking the action.

Apply this to your trading operation. Your capital base faces the threat of irreversible harm—ruin, the absorbing barrier from which there's no return. Full Kelly sizing maximizes theoretical growth but simultaneously maximizes volatility and the speed at which you approach ruin if your assumptions are even slightly wrong.

Therefore: don't use full Kelly sizing if your primary goal is survival. Applying the full formula—knowing the fragility of the inputs and the catastrophic consequences of being wrong—is not aggressive. It's reckless. A fractional bet is the only rational choice for an operator who admits they don't have perfect knowledge of the future.

The Variance Problem

Before we build the sizing architecture, you need to understand variance—because it will test every rule you create. Most traders underestimate how dramatically it affects performance.

In statistics, variance means that in a series of numbers with a given average, individual data points will be spread away from that average. So even if your average daily P&L over the last few years is +$2,000, you might still lose $5,000 five days in a row. This may not mean you did anything wrong. It's just variance.

A thought experiment: a trader with a 50% win rate and 1.67:1 payoff ratio (average winner $2,000, average loser $1,200). This is a profitable strategy—expected value of $400 per trade. Over 250 trading days, you'd expect roughly $100,000.

But that's the expected outcome. Run a thousand simulations of this exact strategy and you'll see annual returns ranging from $50,000 to $150,000, purely from variance. Same edge. Same process. Wildly different outcomes. Some years you look like a genius; other years you question everything. Neither perception is accurate. It's just the distribution doing what distributions do.

> **Variance looks like this:** I was wrong a lot. Being wrong is part of trading. I got unlucky—I was long and unexpected news came out. When I'm wrong and lose money but stuck to my risk management system, I shrug and move on. That's trading.
>
> **Not variance looks like this:** I've been right and reading the market well, but I'm still losing money. (Red flag—something is wrong with my process.) I traded with no plan. I'm overtrading, making a series of small bets on random ideas and leaking money every day. I left a stale order in overnight and it triggered a loss. My discipline is poor—I broke my rules, positions were too big, I kept moving my stop instead of cutting.

If losses stem from the second category, that's not variance. That's bad trading, bad process, or bad mindset. Cut all your risk and figure out how to get things back on track.

Path Dependence

Variance matters trade by trade. But there's a larger pattern that governs your entire year.

In most trading operations, one year is the most important unit of performance. To survive long-term, you want your yearly performance to look like a call option: flat or small losses in bad years, medium to huge gains in good years.

To achieve this distribution, you must understand **path dependence**: future steps of a process depend on its history. A series of coin flips isn't path dependent—if you flip 10 tails, the coin has no memory, and the 11th flip is still 50/50. But each month in a trading year is path dependent. Your performance in January determines your risk capital and state of mind for February.

The most important principle: never take actions in one period that could be overly detrimental to future periods.

Start slow and increase risk as year-to-date P&L builds. You can't have the same risk appetite on January 1 with zero P&L as you can on August 15 when you're up significantly. There's something special and scary about the zero bound. Going from +$50,000 to +$25,000 feels significantly less bad than going from +$10,000 to –$15,000, even though both are $25,000 declines.

Any red number next to your name feels bad.

This isn't just psychological. As your P&L falls below zero, your ability to take risk decreases. There's a nonlinear real-world impact. When you're below zero, you wear a straitjacket. If you're trading at a firm, that straitjacket might be literal—your risk manager cuts your limits. If you're trading your own capital, the straitjacket is psychological, but no less real.

Start the year slow and build up. How you start has a big influence on where you end up. If you lose 20% of your risk capital in January, the odds of hitting your annual goal are nearly zero. If you make 4% in January and 6% in February, you're behind budget but still in position.

The idea is to get safely away from the zero bound and then, when a mega-opportunity arrives and you have a cushion, go for it.

Defining Risk Capital

Before I can establish my sizing framework, I need to know my risk capital: the amount of money I can afford to lose.

Risk capital isn't your total account equity. It's the maximum drawdown you're willing to tolerate for the year. If your account is $500,000 and you decide that losing $100,000 (20%) means you stop trading for the year to preserve the core, your risk capital is $100,000.

All sizing should be calculated as a percentage of risk capital, not account equity. A 1% risk in this framework is $1,000. Relative to total equity, that's 0.2% position risk.

Why does this matter? If you risk 1% of total equity ($5,000 per trade), a string of 20 losses wipes out your entire risk capital buffer. You're out of business. If you risk 1% of risk capital ($1,000 per trade), you can sustain 100 consecutive losses without breaching your shutdown threshold. The math is the same. The survivability is radically different.

This buffer is your longevity.

Your risk capital is path dependent. **Adjusted risk capital** = initial risk capital + year-to-date P&L. If you started with $100,000 and you're up $30,000, adjusted risk capital is $130,000. If you're down $20,000, it's $80,000. The number moves with your performance.

This creates a natural throttle on your risk-taking. When you're winning, you can afford to be more aggressive—playing with "house money" (though I dislike that phrase; the profits are real). When you're losing, the system automatically constrains you, forcing smaller positions when you can least afford large losses.

The Governor on the Engine

We've established how to determine the percentage of capital you're willing to risk. Now: translate that abstract percentage into a concrete position size for a specific instrument in a live, moving market.

If you have a 1R budget for a trade in a sleepy utility stock and a trade in a volatile cryptocurrency, the implementation must be vastly different. To use the same notional dollar amount for each is to let the market's volatility dictate your risk rather than the other way around.

The discipline of keeping your risk constant when the environment is not: **volatility-normalized sizing**.

This isn't a modern financial invention. It's the application of a 200-year-old engineering principle: the governor.

James Watt faced a critical problem with his steam engines: their speed fluctuated wildly, sometimes racing so fast they'd explode. His solution was the centrifugal governor—a feedback control system that automatically regulated speed by adjusting steam flow based on rotational velocity. When the engine sped up, the governor's spinning weights flew outward, reducing steam flow and slowing the engine. When it slowed down, the weights dropped, increasing steam flow. Self-correcting.

Your volatility-normalized position size is your governor. It automatically adjusts your exposure to maintain constant risk, regardless of the market's speed.

$$\text{Position Size} = \$ \text{Risk} \div |\text{Entry} - \text{Stop}|$$

But the stop must be set based on market structure and volatility, not arbitrary percentages. A professional stop is placed where the trade is invalidated, plus a buffer for market noise—the vig to market makers, the cost of ensuring your stop isn't triggered by random noise before the trade has a chance to work.

A $100,000 account with a 1% risk budget ($1,000 per trade): in a low-volatility utility stock with a $1.00 stop distance, you take 1,000 shares. In crude oil with a $0.50 stop distance, two contracts. In Bitcoin with a $2,000 stop distance, 0.5 BTC.

Position sizes vary dramatically, but dollar risk remains constant. The governor throttles you automatically. The market's volatility governs your size, not your emotions.

Earn the Right

Now the most contentious part of position sizing: betting bigger when you feel confident.

The intuition is strong. If you see a fat pitch, you want to swing harder. But this intuition rests on a massive assumption: that your feeling of confidence is reliably correlated with your actual accuracy.

If this correlation doesn't exist—and for most humans, it doesn't—then varying your bet size based on conviction is worse than useless. It introduces noise and increases variance.

So here's the mandate: *You must measure it.*

Until you have a dataset of at least 100 trades showing a statistical correlation between your conviction rating (three stars vs. five stars) and your realized Sharpe ratio, you're forbidden from using conviction sizing. The number 100 isn't arbitrary—it's roughly the minimum sample size needed to distinguish signal from noise given typical win rates and payoff distributions.

Most traders find their "high conviction" trades actually perform worse than their standard setups. Confirmation bias. They feel certain because they've ignored contradictory evidence, not because the evidence is stronger.

Until you have the data to prove your feelings correlate with reality, you're a Tier 1 operator. You flat size everything. Trade 1R on every setup. *You don't get to use conviction sizing until your data proves your conviction has value.*

This might feel limiting. Good. The limitation protects you from your own overconfidence. If your conviction truly has predictive value, the data will show it—and you'll earn the right to size up. If it doesn't, you'll have avoided blowing yourself up on trades that felt great and were actually mediocre.

The Three Types of Trades

Once you've earned the right—once the data proves you're calibrated—you can graduate to a tiered system. This framework is adapted from Brent Donnelly's path-dependent sizing model in *Alpha Trader*. Other methodologies exist—fixed fractional, volatility targeting, exponential conviction scaling—but this architecture strikes the right balance between aggression and survival.

Not all trades deserve equal capital. The industry-standard advice—risk 1% on every trade—is designed for survival, and for beginners, it's the right approach. But for the calibrated trader, flat betting becomes a drag on performance. You're treating a routine technical setup with the same capital weight as a historic macroeconomic dislocation. Under-betting your highest EV opportunities and over-betting your marginal ones.

This tiered system is built on the **anti-Martingale principle**: increase bet size only after winning, never after losing. The math is favorable. During a winning streak, capital grows geometrically. During a losing streak, the variable component of your risk budget shrinks or vanishes, automatically reverting you to conservative sizing. The system forces you to trade smallest when you're performing worst.

Type I: The Standard Trade

Your bread-and-butter setup. The run-of-the-mill opportunity you'd take on any given day. Technical alignment, fundamental non-contradiction, acceptable sentiment. It meets your criteria, but it's not screaming at you. Part of your regular process.

Risk 1% of adjusted risk capital. No more, regardless of how profitable you've been. The goal of Type I trades isn't to make you rich—it's to keep you in the game and generate the inventory of profits

142   The Art & Business of Professional Trading

required to fund Type II and Type III trades. If you're new to this framework, stay here until your calibration data justifies graduation.

Type II: The High-conviction Trade

These trades are characterized by a narrative shift. The market isn't just moving—the reason it's moving is changing. A central bank pivoting from hawkish to dovish. A commodity breaking out of multi-year consolidation due to a supply shock. A mispricing in your area of expertise that the broader market hasn't recognized yet.

> **The formula:** Risk 3% of your initial risk capital (your starting capital, fixed at the beginning of the year) plus 10% of your year-to-date profits, subject to a cap of 5% of adjusted risk capital. The cap is the safety governor; it prevents a hot streak from becoming a blow-up.

The math differs with P&L levels, assuming $100,000 initial risk capital:

> **If you're flat on the year (YTD = $0):** Base risk is $3,000 (3% of $100,000), variable is $0 (10% of nothing), total risk is $3,000. Adjusted risk capital is $100,000 (you haven't made or lost anything), so the 5% cap is $5,000. Cap doesn't bind (your total is below the cap). Your Type II risk is $3,000.
> **If you're up $20,000:** Base is $3,000, variable is $2,000 (10% of your $20,000 profit), total is $5,000. Adjusted risk capital is $120,000 (your starting capital plus your profits), cap is $6,000 (5% of $120,000). Cap doesn't bind. Your Type II risk is $5,000.
> **If you're up $50,000:** Base is $3,000, variable is $5,000 (10% of $50,000), total is $8,000. Adjusted risk capital is $150,000, cap is $7,500. Cap binds (your $8,000 total exceeds the $7,500 cap). Your Type II risk is $7,500.
> **If you're up $100,000:** Base is $3,000, variable is $10,000, total is $13,000. Adjusted risk capital is $200,000, cap is $10,000. Cap binds. Your Type II risk is $10,000.

The asymmetry is built in. When you're in a drawdown, the variable component vanishes (10% of zero or negative is zero or negative, so the formula naturally forces you into defense). When you're profitable, you press the accelerator, but the governor prevents recklessness. You cannot size up to "make it back." You can only size up to press the winner.

There's a psychological dimension. Trading large size is emotionally taxing. Fear of loss causes traders to exit winners early or hesitate on high-conviction setups. By framing the variable component as "accumulated profits" rather than "my money," you grant yourself psychological permission to be aggressive. You're not risking your rent—you're risking the market's previous contribution to your account. This reframing reduces the emotional load.

Type III: The Fat Pitch

Rare, idiosyncratic events, historic dislocations where the market has fundamentally mispriced a binary outcome or regime change: Soros breaking the Bank of England in 1992. The Abenomics short-yen trade in 2012. The blow-off top when Bitcoin futures launched in 2017. You might see one or two genuine Type III setups per year. Maybe none.

Risk the maximum allowable within your survival constraints, typically 5–8% of adjusted risk capital, depending on your volatility tolerance.

But only if you're in a strong position. If you're down on the year, you keep it small (even on perfect setups). This is not punishment; this is architecture. A Type III opportunity perceived from deep drawdown is a trap. The psychological pressure to "make it back in one trade" will lead to execution errors: tight stops, early exits, hesitation. The framework demands that even the perfect trade must be sized defensively if your account is not in surplus. The professional never lets a great opportunity become a career-ending mistake because they took maximum risk from a position of weakness.

The Correlation Trap

A naive application of this framework can blow you up if you ignore correlation risk. Say you identify a "risk-off" narrative and take three Type II trades: short S&P, short AUD/USD, long gold. You think you have three independent positions. You don't. You have three expressions of the same bet (long volatility, short risk appetite). If you're wrong, you're wrong on all three simultaneously.

The risk budget applies to the portfolio theme, not just the ticker. If you have multiple correlated positions expressing the same view, the combined risk must not exceed your safety governor. Failing to aggregate correlation turns a Type II allocation into a 15% bet on a single market outcome (three "independent" 5% positions that move together). That's not a Type II trade. That's ruin waiting to happen.

The Five Steps

How do you size your positions in real time? The process is straightforward.

> **Step 1: The Idea.** You decide to buy TBT (ultrashort bond ETF) because you think bonds are going to sell off into nonfarm payrolls.
> **Step 2: The Conviction.** You check your calibration data. You are a calibrated trader, and this setup matches your Type II criteria—multiple pillars aligning, narrative shift underway.
> **Step 3: The Risk Budget.** You are up $30,000 on the year. Your Type II allocation is 3% of initial risk capital ($3,000) plus 10% of YTD profits ($3,000) = $6,000. Your adjusted risk capital is $130,000, so the 5% cap is $6,500. The cap doesn't bind; your risk is $6,000.
> **Step 4: The Stop.** You analyze the chart. TBT is at $100.00. The structure breaks at $98.00—that's where the thesis is invalidated. That's $2.00 per share of risk.
> **Step 5: The Output.** Position Size = $6,000 ÷ $2.00 = 3,000 shares.

Bad traders work in the opposite direction. They say: "I want to buy 10,000 shares because I want to make a lot of money, so I'll put my stop at $99.50 to make the math work."

That is how you blow up. The market doesn't care about your wallet. It cares about the level. Always start with dollars at risk, then determine your stop by analyzing the market. The position size is the output, not the input.

The Stop-loss Fallacy

Everything we've discussed assumes your stop will execute at the price you specified. This assumption is often false.

In 2015, I was trading natural gas futures. Three months of steady profits. A strategy that passed every backtest. By close, 40% of my account sat in a single thesis.

The next morning, natural gas gapped down 4%.

Not *through* my stop. *Past* it. A discontinuity—a hole in the price chart where my risk management was supposed to exist.

My stop was sitting at a level that implied –8% if hit. The market opened at –35%. Not on a trade. On the day.

Three weeks later, gas rallied 12%. My thesis played out exactly as anticipated. I watched from the sidelines, knowing I'd been right about everything except the one thing that mattered.

The lesson isn't about natural gas. It's about the stop-loss fallacy.

A stop-loss is a request, not a command. It says: "When price reaches this level, please execute a market order." Two hidden assumptions: that price will reach your level rather than jumping past it, and that liquidity will be there when you need it.

In a crisis, neither holds. Ask anyone who was long EUR/CHF when the Swiss National Bank unpegged the franc in January 2015. Stops at 1.19 filled at 0.85—or worse. Traders leveraged 50:1 went negative—they owed their brokers money. The stop-loss was a market order, not a promise.

Your actual risk on any position isn't your stop distance. It's Stop Distance + Gap Risk. If you're risking "2% to my stop" holding overnight, you're actually risking 2% plus the probability-weighted magnitude of an overnight catastrophe. For overnight holds in volatile markets, gap risk can dwarf your intended risk.

Position sizing isn't just about calculating the formula correctly. It's about understanding what the formula leaves out.

Circuit Breakers

Circuit breakers serve a specific position-sizing function: the final layer of defense protecting your entire operation from systemic risk, correlated errors, and your own human fallibility.

> **Drawdown Locks.** A daily stop at –2R means you stop trading for the day, no exceptions. A weekly hibernate at –6R means you stop trading for the week. When I hit a weekly hibernate, I don't just stop trading—I conduct a deep review. Am I missing something in the market? Is my process broken? Or is this just variance? The answer determines what happens next.

Streak Governor. This automatically reduces your next trade's size by 50% after three consecutive losses. It is a mechanical defense against the tilt spiral—that psychological state where losses beget frustration, frustration begets impulsive trading, and impulsive trading begets more losses.

Correlation Caps. If you're long EUR/USD and long GBP/USD, you don't have two independent positions; you have two ways of being short the dollar. Your total risk across correlated positions should be capped at a maximum of 10% of risk capital. (This is harder to implement than it sounds because correlations shift. What looks like a diversified portfolio can become a concentrated bet overnight if correlations spike during a crisis.)

The Sleep Point. The maximum P&L swing that lets you think clearly. Beyond it, every trade has negative expected value regardless of setup quality—you become incapable of executing rationally. Your effective maximum bet size is the lesser of the mathematical optimum and the sleep point. If the math says bet 5% but you can't sleep with a position that size, the sleep point governs.

The sleep point is personal. It depends on your net worth, your financial obligations, your psychological makeup. There is no formula. You discover it through experience—usually by exceeding it once and learning what that does to your judgment.

The Glass Box

After the natural gas blowup, I built rules. Not from theory. From scar tissue—specific failures, specific costs, specific lessons about which mistakes I kept repeating under pressure.

The architecture laid out here—Kelly as a theoretical ceiling, fractional Kelly as a robust operating range, the backtest tax as a margin of safety, volatility-normalized sizing, calibration-gated conviction, path-dependent tiers, circuit breakers—is the synthesis of those lessons.

It's not a black box. It's a glass box. You can see every component. You understand why each piece exists. You can modify it to fit your style, your psychology, your risk tolerance.

But here's what you can't modify: the underlying goal. Everything in this chapter serves one objective—maximizing the geometric growth of your wealth over time while staying in the game long enough to achieve it. That's the optimization target. That's what Kelly was really solving for. That's what every sizing decision should trace back to.

The system doesn't promise perfection. It promises to keep you in the game long enough to discover whether your edge is real.

That's the only thing that matters.

Notes

R-multiples. Tharp, Van K. *Trade Your Way to Financial Freedom.* McGraw-Hill, 1998. The foundational work on thinking in terms of risk units.

Kelly Criterion. Kelly, J.L. "A New Interpretation of Information Rate." *Bell System Technical Journal* 35, no. 4 (1956). For practical application and limitations, see Thorp, Edward O. "The Kelly Criterion in Blackjack, Sports Betting, and the Stock Market." In *Handbook of Asset and Liability Management*, 2006.

Fractional Kelly. MacLean, Leonard C., Edward O. Thorp, and William T. Ziemba. *The Kelly Capital Growth Investment Criterion.* World Scientific, 2011.

Margin of Safety. Graham, Benjamin. *The Intelligent Investor.* Harper & Brothers, 1949. Chapter 20: Margin of Safety as the Central Concept of Investment.

Precautionary Principle. Taleb, Nassim Nicholas. *Skin in the Game.* Random House, 2018.

Anti-Martingale Strategy. Standard betting theory. The opposite of the Martingale (doubling down after losses), the anti-Martingale increases bet size only after wins, producing geometric compounding during winning streaks and automatic risk reduction during drawdowns.

House Money Effect. Thaler, Richard H., and Eric J. Johnson. "Gambling with the House Money and Trying to Break Even." *Management Science* 36, no. 6 (1990).

Path-dependent Sizing. Donnelly, Brent. *Alpha Trader.* Harriman House, 2021. The tiered sizing architecture, conviction-based allocation, and safety governor concepts are adapted from Donnelly's institutional macro methodology.

Exponential Bet Sizing. Breitstein, Lance. Discussed in his 50in50 series and trading education materials.

Sleep Point. Carver, Robert. *Systematic Trading.* Harriman House, 2015. Also *Leveraged Trading* (2019) for detailed discussion of leverage and risk.

SNB Flash Crash. January 15, 2015. Contemporary reporting from Reuters, Bloomberg, and the *Financial Times*. Multiple retail brokerages faced insolvency due to client negative balances.

James Watt's Governor. Standard engineering history. The centrifugal governor became the foundational example of feedback control systems.

Druckenmiller Quote. From the Lost Tree Club speech, widely circulated.

CHAPTER 10

Risk Definition

*P**osition sizing assumes you understand what you're risking. Most traders don't. They think they're taking one bet when they're actually taking a bundle of bets—and the bets they didn't analyze are the ones that destroy them. This chapter is about seeing the full picture.*

The Summit and the Storm

On May 10, 1996, at 11:30 a.m. Nepal time, 33 climbers from three separate expeditions were strung out along the final ridge of Mount Everest, waiting in a slow-moving queue at the Hillary Step—a 40-foot vertical rock face just 300 meters below the summit.

The weather was perfect. The thesis was right.

Rob Hall, the most respected high-altitude guide in the world, had done everything correctly. His Adventure Consultants team had acclimatized for weeks. They had stocked camps with oxygen, fixed ropes along the route, chosen an ideal weather window. His client success rate was legendary: by 1996, he had guided 39 clients to the summit without losing a single one. His competitors joked that Hall had "built a yellow brick road to the top of the world."

His turnaround rule was absolute: if you haven't summitted by 2:00 p.m., you turn back. No exceptions. After 2:00 p.m., the math changes. Not enough daylight. Not enough oxygen. The margin for error collapses.

At 1:00 p.m., the queue was still backed up at the Hillary Step. Fixed ropes that should have been placed hours earlier weren't there. Climbers stood motionless in the death zone—above 8,000 meters, where the human body is slowly dying from oxygen deprivation—burning through their supplemental oxygen while they waited.

At 2:00 p.m., the turnaround time, several climbers were still an hour from the summit. Hall's rule said turn back.

They didn't turn back.

Hall's client Doug Hansen had attempted Everest the year before and failed just 100 meters from the top. He had scraped together the money to return—the $65,000 fee was enormous for a postal worker. Hall felt responsible. The expedition's business model depended on summit success rates. The narrative was too compelling: help Doug finish what he started.

By 4:00 p.m., climbers were still summiting. Scott Fischer, leader of the rival Mountain Madness expedition, reached the top at 3:45 p.m.—nearly two hours past the deadline. The weather was still holding.

Then it wasn't.

At 5:00 p.m., a storm materialized with almost no warning. Winds exceeded 100 miles per hour. Visibility dropped to zero. Temperature plunged. Climbers who had been celebrating on the summit were now scattered across the upper mountain, stumbling blind through a whiteout, their oxygen running out.

Rob Hall never made it down. He was found frozen near the South Summit, his arm around Doug Hansen's body. Scott Fischer collapsed 1,200 feet below the summit and died where he fell. Eight people perished that day—the deadliest day in Everest history at the time.

The thesis was right. The weather window was real. The route was correct. Hall's system was sound—"nobody's were better," Jon Krakauer wrote in *Into Thin Air.* And it didn't matter.

What killed them wasn't the storm. Storms happen on Everest; that's a known risk.

What killed them was a bundle of risks they never analyzed as a bundle.

Crowding risk: three expeditions attempting the summit on the same day created bottlenecks that burned oxygen and time. Correlation risk: when one team fell behind schedule, all teams fell behind—their fates were coupled. Competitive pressure: Hall and Fischer were business rivals; neither wanted to be the first to turn clients around.

The professional trader's job is to convert as much uncertainty as possible into risk—to move exposures from Urn B into Urn A. But here's the catch: you can never fully empty Urn B. There's always a residue of irreducible uncertainty. The market is not a casino with fixed rules. It's a complex adaptive system that changes its behavior in response to the behavior of its participants.

Your backtest measures risk. The market delivers uncertainty.
Your model assumes stationarity. The market isn't.
Your stop loss defines risk. Gap risk ignores it.

This is why the Knightian distinction matters: if you treat uncertainty as risk, you'll consistently underestimate your exposure. The most confident traders—the ones who've "modeled everything"—are usually the most exposed. Their confidence blinds them to what the model doesn't capture.

You'll size positions as if you know the odds when you don't. You'll feel confident because your model is elegant, when elegance has nothing to do with accuracy in a nonstationary environment.

Rob Hall had a system. The system was based on decades of Everest data. That data told him the risks: altitude, weather windows, oxygen consumption rates, client fitness levels. What the data couldn't tell him was the uncertainty: what happens when three expeditions crowd the same route on the same day, when competitive pressure overrides safety protocols, when a storm materializes in a 15-minute window that the forecasts missed.

He treated uncertainty as risk. He died.

Defining the Problem

The Knightian framework gives us a way to think about what we're up against. But to operationalize it, we need a working definition of risk that goes beyond the abstract.

If you ask most traders to define risk, they say: "Losing money."

This isn't a definition. It's a symptom. It describes the pain, not the pathology. If risk is just "losing money," then a stop loss should solve it. Set a price, get out, problem solved.

But a stop loss doesn't protect you from a gap open. It doesn't protect you from an exchange outage. It doesn't protect you from a correlation failure where your entire portfolio moves against you at once.

Risk is the distribution of all possible negative outcomes and their probabilities.

Risk is a set—not a single number like "volatility" or "value at risk," but a collection of specific scenarios that can go wrong, each with different mechanics, different probabilities, different magnitudes. And each scenario has a probability. A negative outcome without a probability is just anxiety. A negative outcome with a probability is a variable you can price, hedge, and manage.

When you buy a stock, you're accepting a specific bundle of outcomes.

There is **thesis risk** (Urn A)—the stock moves against your thesis. This is the risk you analyzed. But then there is the rest of the bundle (Urn B).

> **Market risk:** The entire market crashes, dragging your stock with it regardless of its individual merit.
> **Sector risk:** The industry falls out of favor (your stock is fine; the category is not).
> **Liquidity risk:** You can't exit the position when you need to because the bid disappears.

Then there is **execution risk** (you get filled at a worse price than expected), **correlation risk** (your "diversified" positions all move together because they share hidden exposures), and **counterparty risk** (your broker fails).

And don't forget **gap risk** (price discontinuity where markets close and reopen somewhere else entirely) and **operational risk** (your internet fails, your platform crashes, or you fat-finger a trade). The pre-flight ritual from Chapter 8 is a risk management control, not just a habit.

The professional doesn't just list these risks. They weight them. They ask: *Which of these am I being paid to take?*

The Core Principle

We've catalogued the risks in the bundle. Now the principle: *take only the risks you're paid to take. Hedge, eliminate, or minimize everything else.*

In practice:

Suppose your thesis is that Apple will beat earnings expectations. You've done the work. You've analyzed the supply chain, spoken to channel checks, modeled the revenue. You have an informational edge—or at least you believe you do.

> **Your edge:** Apple's specific performance relative to consensus
> **Not your edge:** The direction of the S&P 500

Risk Definition

If you simply buy Apple stock, you're betting on your earnings thesis plus the direction of the overall market. If the S&P crashes 5% tomorrow, Apple will likely drop 3% even if your earnings call is perfect. You'll lose money despite being right about the thing you actually analyzed.

This is a failure of isolation. You allowed Urn B (market risk) to pollute Urn A (thesis risk).

The professional isolates the edge.

They might buy Apple stock and simultaneously short an equivalent beta-weighted amount of SPY or QQQ. If the market crashes, the short offsets the long. The only thing driving P&L is the relative performance of Apple versus the market—which is precisely what their thesis predicts.

You've stripped away the noise. You're exposed only to the specific risk you have an edge on.

This is what Agustin Lebron means in *The Laws of Trading*: "take only the risks you're paid to take." If you're being paid to predict Apple's earnings, don't take implicit bets on market direction, sector rotation, or risk-on/risk-off sentiment. Hedge those. Neutralize them. Isolate the edge.

Hedging has costs: transaction costs, tracking error, capital drag. The decision isn't always simple. But the principle is clear: every unhedged exposure should be a conscious choice, not a passive default.

The Bundle That Kills

Most trading careers don't end because the trader was bad at picking stocks. They end because the trader was exposed to a structural risk they didn't understand.

Three mechanisms.

Path Dependence

In Chapter 9, we discussed how leverage interacts with the volatility tax. Here's the deeper problem: leverage doesn't just amplify returns. It creates path dependence.

If you buy an asset with cash, you only need to be right about where the price ends up. A 10% drawdown followed by a 15% rally still leaves you ahead.

If you buy the same asset with 10× leverage, you need to be right about the path it takes to get there. That 10% drawdown wipes you out before the 15% rally arrives.

The destination might vindicate your thesis. But leverage forced you to bet on the journey—every tick, every swing, every overnight gap. Unless your edge specifically includes path prediction (and it almost never does), leverage adds a risk you're not compensated for.

This is what happened to the traders who shorted inverse volatility products before February 2018. (We examined the XIV collapse in Chapter 7.) Their thesis was correct: volatility tends to mean-revert. But the products' rebalancing mechanisms created path dependence they didn't model. The feedback loop destroyed the products before the thesis could play out.

Liquidity Risk

You buy a small-cap stock. It looks cheap. You size it big—maybe 10% of your portfolio.

Then bad news hits. You want to sell. But nobody's buying. The "bid" on your screen shows 100 shares at $8.25, and you're holding 50,000 shares. To exit, you must crash the price yourself.

This is the dark matter of financial risk: the risk that doesn't appear until you try to move.

Liquidity risk is asymmetric. It's invisible on entry and catastrophic on exit. It's fine when everyone else wants what you have. It's lethal when everyone wants out at the same time.

As Brent Donnelly says: "Never enter a trade unless you know you can get out." If you're a directional trader (not a market maker), you're a liquidity taker, not a liquidity provider. You pay the spread; you don't collect it. Trading illiquid instruments means accepting the risk of being trapped without collecting the premium for providing liquidity.

If you aren't a market maker, don't take liquidity risk. Stick to instruments where you can enter and exit freely. (And even in liquid markets, remember that liquidity is conditional—it evaporates precisely when you need it most.)

Correlation: The False Diversification

The most dangerous risks are the ones you can't see because you thought you'd already handled them.

Consider what I call the "Tech Worker Portfolio":

Income: Software engineer at a major tech firm
Real Estate: Condo in San Francisco

Investments: Long a basket of high-growth tech stocks
Options: Vested equity in employer's stock

This person believes they're diversified. They have a job, a home, and an investment portfolio—three different buckets. In reality, they're 100% long a single factor: "tech boom."

If the sector turns, they lose their job, their home equity drops, and their portfolio crashes simultaneously. The correlation was hidden because the exposures looked different. They were categorically different (employment, real estate, securities). But they were all expressions of the same underlying bet.

The professional checks the correlation matrix. Not just among their trades, but across their entire financial life. If assets move together under stress, they count as one position. If you want to take five independent risks, they must be five genuinely independent risks—which is much harder than it sounds.

Correlation is unstable. Assets that appear uncorrelated in normal markets become highly correlated in crisis. This is when diversification fails—precisely when you need it most. The correlations you measured in your backtest are not the correlations you'll experience in the drawdown.

The Risk Audit

We've identified the mechanisms of destruction. Now we need a systematic way to apply this knowledge before every trade.

The risk audit: before every trade, list the risks in the bundle. Label each one: **Yes** (I have an edge and accept this risk), **No** (I have no edge and should eliminate this risk), or **Neutral** (I accept this risk as the cost of doing business, but I'm not paid for it).

For every No, you need an action: hedge it, reduce size, change instruments, or don't take the trade.

Example: long crude oil (CL) based on a supply/demand thesis.

> **Thesis Risk** (supply/demand imbalance): **Yes**—this is my edge, the whole point of the trade.
> **Market Risk** (broad risk-off event): **Neutral**—I'm not hedging this, but I'm sizing accordingly.
> **Sector Risk** (energy sentiment shift): **Neutral**—comes with the territory, managed through position size.

Liquidity Risk: Yes—crude futures are highly liquid, this is acceptable.

Gap Risk (overnight/weekend): **No**—I will not hold over weekends; if I must hold overnight, I reduce size by 50%.

Correlation Risk: Checking—is this adding to existing energy exposure? If my portfolio is already long natural gas, this trade increases concentration.

Operational Risk: Managed—stops are in the market, not mental.

This audit takes five minutes. It forces you to confront the bundle before you click Buy. Most importantly, it separates the risks you're choosing from the risks you're inheriting.

The amateur thinks: "I'm long crude because I think supply is tight."

The professional thinks: "I'm long crude, short weekend gap risk, neutral on energy sentiment, and I've confirmed this isn't adding to existing correlation exposure."

Same trade. Completely different understanding of what's actually being risked.

The Risk You're Being Paid For

Zoom out.

Trading is fundamentally a business of getting paid to warehouse risk. You take a position that someone else doesn't want to hold. The "fee" you receive is the edge—the expected profit from the trade. Risk is not something to be avoided; it's the monetization mechanism for edge. Without risk, there's no return.

The question is not "how do I minimize risk?" The question is *"which risks am I being paid to take?"*

If you're a fundamental analyst, you're being paid to take thesis risk. You've done work that others haven't. Your edge is informational.

If you're a momentum trader, you're being paid to take trend risk. Your edge is behavioral—you're betting that other traders will continue to do what they've been doing.

If you're a market maker, you're being paid to take liquidity risk. Your edge is operational—you can quote tighter than competitors and manage inventory better.

Each edge (Chapter 7) comes bundled with risks the trader isn't being paid for.

The fundamental analyst isn't being paid to predict market direction. The momentum trader isn't being paid to predict company fundamentals. The market maker isn't being paid to predict which way the stock will move.

Professional risk management is the discipline of unbundling. You isolate the risk you're paid for. You hedge, eliminate, or minimize the rest. What remains is your edge in its purest form—undiluted by exposures you didn't choose and can't predict.

Next chapter: decomposition—the mathematical conclusion of unbundling.

Why Models Fail

Why do sophisticated funds blow up?

They treat uncertainty as risk. They build models that assume the world is Urn A when it's actually Urn B.

Every model embeds assumptions. Most of these assumptions are invisible to the model's users—they're baked into the data, the functional forms, the parameters. The model works beautifully within its assumptions. Then reality violates the assumptions, and the model doesn't just underperform—it catastrophically fails.

Consider value at risk (VaR), the standard risk metric used by banks and hedge funds worldwide. VaR answers the question: "What's the maximum I could lose, at a 99% confidence level, over a given time horizon?"

The problem is that traditional VaR models assume returns are normally distributed. They're not. Financial returns exhibit "fat tails"—extreme events occur far more frequently than simple models predict. The 2008 financial crisis was a "25σ event" under normal distribution assumptions—meaning it should occur once every 10^{135} years. Obviously, the model was wrong. The tails weren't thin; they were fat. And banks that relied on VaR were unprepared.

Nassim Taleb calls this the "ludic fallacy"—treating uncertainty like a game with known rules. In a casino, the odds are fixed. In markets, the odds themselves are uncertain. When you forget this distinction, your "risk management" becomes a false sense of security. You think you've measured your exposure. You've actually just measured a model's fantasy about your exposure.

The map is not the territory. The backtest is not the future. The VaR is not the risk.

Living with Urn B

So, if uncertainty can't be measured, what do you do?

You don't eliminate it. You can't. But you can structure your operation to survive it.

- **Acknowledge its existence.** The most dangerous traders believe they've converted all uncertainty into risk. They've modeled everything; they're confident in their parameters; they've backtested across regimes. And they're one tail event away from ruin. Epistemic humility isn't weakness—it's survival. As Robert Carver puts it: "The uncertainty of the past is largest for risk-adjusted returns." Even your historical data is uncertain.
- **Build buffers.** Chapter 9 introduced fractional Kelly and the margin of safety. These aren't just position-sizing tools—they're uncertainty buffers. You size smaller than "optimal" because you know the parameters feeding "optimal" are uncertain. You tax your backtest results because you know they're biased. The buffer exists precisely because you can't measure what it's buffering against.
- **Maintain optionality.** In an uncertain world, the ability to adapt is more valuable than the ability to predict. Don't lock up capital in illiquid positions. Don't commit to strategies that require specific outcomes. Don't take positions that can't be unwound. Keep dry powder. Stay nimble. The trader who survives uncertainty is the one who can respond to it, not the one who predicted it.
- **Respect gap risk.** Gaps are where uncertainty materializes. Markets close; the world keeps moving; markets reopen somewhere else. Your stop loss exists only in continuous price space. Reality operates in discontinuous jumps. If you can't survive the gap, you can't survive the uncertainty.
- **Diversify genuinely.** Not across names—across sources of risk. Genuine diversification means your positions are driven by different factors, respond to different regimes, fail in different scenarios. If everything works in the same environment and fails in the same crisis, you're not diversified—you're concentrated with extra paperwork.

The Three Questions

Before you enter your next position, ask:

> **What is the full bundle of risks I'm taking?** List them. All of them. Thesis risk, market risk, sector risk, liquidity risk, correlation risk, gap risk, operational risk. Be specific. If you can't list them, you don't understand the trade.
>
> **Which of these do I actually have an edge on?** Be honest. Your edge is narrow—probably narrower than you think. Most risks in the bundle are not risks you're being compensated to take.
>
> **Can I eliminate or hedge the others?** If yes, do it. If no, size smaller. If the bundle can't be cleaned up, the trade might not be worth taking.

This is the unbundling discipline. It converts the vague anxiety of "risk" into specific, actionable categories. It forces you to confront the difference between the trade you think you're making (Urn A) and the trade you actually are making (Urn B).

If you can't answer these three questions, you're not trading. You're gambling. And the casino—the bundle of risks you didn't analyze—always wins in the end.

The Lesson from the Mountain

Back to the mountain.

Rob Hall was one of the greatest mountaineers who ever lived. His systems were rigorous. His track record was unmatched.

He didn't understand the bundle.

The storm was a known risk—weather on Everest is capricious, and any experienced climber accounts for it. What Hall didn't account for was the complex of interdependencies that turned a manageable risk into a catastrophe: the bottleneck created by multiple expeditions, the competitive pressure that eroded safety margins, the emotional commitment that overrode the turnaround rule, the correlation of all climbers' fates when everyone needed to descend at once.

He had the thesis right. The bundle killed him.

"With enough determination, any bloody idiot can get up this hill," Hall once said. "The trick is to get back down alive."

The trick, for traders, is the same. Getting into a position is easy. The thesis is seductive. The entry feels like progress.

But the exit is where you live or die. And the exit depends not on the thesis, but on the bundle—the liquidity, the correlations, the gaps, the path dependencies, all the things that determine whether you can get out when you need to.

The professional trader is not the one with the best thesis. It's the one who understands the full bundle of risks they're accepting—and who refuses to accept risks they're not being paid to take.

The thesis gets you in. The bundle determines whether you get out.

Notes

1996 Everest Disaster. Krakauer, Jon. *Into Thin Air: A Personal Account of the Mt. Everest Disaster.* Villard, 1997. Also, Boukreev, Anatoli, and G. Weston DeWalt. *The Climb.* St. Martin's Press, 1997.

Ellsberg Paradox. Ellsberg, Daniel. "Risk, Ambiguity, and the Savage Axioms." *The Quarterly Journal of Economics* 75, no. 4 (1961): 643–669. The foundational paper on ambiguity aversion.

Knightian Uncertainty. Knight, Frank H. *Risk, Uncertainty and Profit.* Houghton Mifflin, 1921. The classic distinction between measurable risk and unmeasurable uncertainty.

Taking Only Paid Risks. Lebron, Agustin. *The Laws of Trading.* Wiley, 2019. See especially Law 2: "Know the Edge."

Liquidity Risk. Donnelly, Brent. *Alpha Trader.* Harriman House, 2021. On liquidity as a directional trader.

Value at Risk Critique. Taleb, Nassim Nicholas. *The Black Swan.* Random House, 2007. Also "The Fourth Quadrant" and various technical papers on fat tails and VaR limitations.

Ludic Fallacy. Taleb, Nassim Nicholas. *The Black Swan.* Chapter 9: "The Ludic Fallacy, or the Uncertainty of the Nerd."

Correlation Instability. Longin, François, and Bruno Solnik. "Extreme Correlation of International Equity Markets." *The Journal of Finance* 56, no. 2 (2001): 649–676.

Uncertainty of Historical Data. Carver, Robert. *Systematic Trading.* Harriman House, 2015. On the uncertainty embedded in back-tested parameters.

February 2018 Volatility Event. See Chapter 7 notes. The XIV collapse is the canonical example of path dependence destroying a thesis-correct trade.

CHAPTER 11

Decomposition

Most traders see their P&L and tell themselves a story about skill. The real story is usually about tides and currents they never understood. This chapter is about separating signal from noise in your own track record—answering the most uncomfortable question a trader can ask: Am I actually any good at this?

The Hot Hand That Wasn't

In 1985, three psychologists published a paper that upended how we think about skill.

Thomas Gilovich, Robert Vallone, and Amos Tversky (the latter a founding father of behavioral economics) studied basketball players to answer a simple question: Does the "hot hand" exist? When a player makes several shots in a row, are they more likely to make the next one?

Everyone believed the answer was yes. Players believed it. Coaches believed it. The Philadelphia 76ers organization, which provided the data, believed it. The hot hand was so obvious, so viscerally felt, that questioning it seemed absurd.

The researchers analyzed thousands of shots from 76ers home games. They tracked sequences: what happened after a make, what happened after a miss. They ran the statistics.

Their conclusion: the hot hand was a myth.

The probability of making a shot after a string of makes was statistically indistinguishable from the probability after a string of misses. The "streaks" that players and fans perceived were nothing more than the normal clustering that occurs in any random sequence. Flip a coin 100 times, and you'll see runs of five or six heads in a row. That's not the coin getting hot. That's just probability.

The paper became one of the most cited in behavioral economics. Daniel Kahneman, who would later win the Nobel Prize, called the hot hand "a massive and widespread cognitive illusion." For 30 years, it stood as a canonical example of how humans see patterns in randomness, how we confuse luck for skill.

Then, in 2015, two economists found a flaw.

Joshua Miller and Adam Sanjurjo, working independently, discovered that the original study had made a subtle but devastating statistical error. When you condition on a streak of successes and then measure the next outcome, you introduce a selection bias that makes true hot-hand effects invisible. The math is counterintuitive (it involves the difference between unconditional and conditional probabilities), but the implication was stark. When they corrected for the bias, the hot hand emerged as real.

The "hot hand fallacy" was itself a fallacy.

But here's what matters for traders: even after the correction, the hot hand effect was small. Much smaller than players and coaches believed. The perception of streakiness vastly exceeded the reality.

When a basketball player makes five shots in a row, three things are happening. First, there is the base rate: they're a good shooter (say, 45% from three-point range) regardless of recent history. Second, there is variance: random sequences produce streaks, and five makes in a row happens regularly by chance alone.

And finally, there is the hot hand (alpha): a small, real effect where their probability bumps to maybe 48% after a string of makes.

The player feels like a genius. The crowd roars. The coach calls plays to get them the ball. But most of what they're experiencing is base rate and variance. The actual skill component, the alpha, is a thin residue on top of factors they don't control.

They think they're great swimmers. They're floating.

The Trader's Delusion

We overestimate our contribution to our own success. For traders, this is lethal.

In the previous chapter, we defined risk as the specific set of ways your edge can fail. But that definition assumes something dangerous: that you actually have an edge.

Most traders don't.
Most traders are riding a tide they cannot see, confusing a rising ocean with their own ability to swim. When they make money, they tell themselves a story about their skill. When they lose money, they tell themselves a story about bad luck. The attribution is backward in both cases.

Privatize gains, socialize losses.

A professional reverses this. When they make money, they ask: How much of this was just the market going up? When they lose money, they ask: Did I pay for a risk I didn't intend to take?

This process is called **decomposition**. It is the mental model that turns trading from a gambling addiction into a scientific pursuit. It is the discipline of separating what you actually did from what happened to you.

Chapter 9: How much should I bet?
Chapter 10: What am I actually betting on?
This chapter: *Am I betting on anything at all?*

The Formula

Decomposition isn't a metaphor. It's a mathematical framework with a specific formula. Understanding this formula is essential to understanding your own returns.

The return of any trade or portfolio decomposes into three components:

Return = Market Beta + Factor Exposures + Alpha

The regression version:

$$R_i = \alpha + \Sigma \beta_k F_k + \varepsilon_i$$

where R_i is the return, α (alpha) is your idiosyncratic skill, β_k represents your exposures to factors F_k, and ε_i is the residual noise.

The mental model: **Beta** is the tide—the broad current that lifts all boats. **Factors** are the currents—predictable forces that reward specific positioning. **Alpha** is your swimming speed—what you generate after the ocean has done its work.

Let's examine each component.

Beta: The Tide

Beta is the return you earn simply by taking baseline exposure to an asset class. It is the gravitational pull of the market. When the tide rises, all boats rise with it, and your boat rising has nothing to do with your skill.

If you buy a stock and the S&P 500 rises 10%, and your stock rises 10%, you have generated zero skill. You rented your capital to the market. You could have achieved identical results with a cheap index fund and no work at all.

A common confusion: traders mistake timing beta for alpha. If you successfully time the market (buying the S&P 500 before it rises, selling before it falls), that timing constitutes alpha. You made a discretionary decision based on a predictive edge. But if you're simply "long crypto" because you're a believer, and crypto appreciates, that is not genius. That is beta. You did not predict the move; you stood in its path and benefited from the tide. One is skill. The other is exposure.

Factors: The Currents

Factors are returns you capture by exposing yourself to known, systematic risks. Predictable forces that reward specific positioning.

Academic research has documented dozens of factors. The ones most relevant to discretionary traders:

> **Momentum:** buying assets that have appreciated recently, riding their continued strength
> **Value:** buying assets cheap relative to fundamentals, harvesting the premium when the market reprices them
> **Carry:** buying high-yielding assets and shorting low-yielding ones, collecting the yield differential
> **Volatility Risk Premium:** selling insurance (puts, call spreads, short vol) to anxious hedgers, paid for bearing tail risk
> **Size:** buying smaller-cap names, which have historically outperformed larger peers

Each of these has generated positive returns over extended periods. Each can also destroy you when the regime rotates.

Suppose you generate 20% returns while the market is flat, but you achieved this by selling naked puts through a calm year. You are not a genius. You are a risk premium harvester, paid to provide insurance to nervous traders. This is a valid business, but it is not alpha. It is factor exposure. And it carries embedded risks (the left-tail crash) that will eventually settle.

You may possess skill in execution: better strike selection, superior risk management, smarter timing of when to harvest the premium. But the core return stream is a documented, knowable premium. It is not a unique discovery. It is not alpha.

Alpha: The Residual

Alpha is what remains.

It is the return you generated after neutralizing market beta and accounting for your factor exposures. It is the measure of your specific, idiosyncratic skill: the value you added that cannot be replicated by passive positioning or documented academic factors.

Alpha is rare. Alpha is difficult. Alpha is what most traders claim to possess and almost none actually do. It is the only return stream that originates from you, not from the market.

When you strip away beta and factors from the returns of most traders, the residual approaches zero. Often it is negative. The "skill" they believed they possessed was really just exposure to forces they did not fully understand and did not correctly price for risk.

The Archegos Anatomy

Let me show you what happens when someone confuses leveraged beta for alpha.

Bill Hwang was a protégé of Julian Robertson, founder of Tiger Management, one of the most successful hedge funds in history. Hwang ran his own fund, Tiger Asia, until 2012, when he pleaded guilty to wire fraud related to insider trading in Chinese bank stocks and paid $44 million in fines. Banned from managing outside money, he converted Tiger Asia into a family office called Archegos Capital Management.

Between 2013 and early 2021, Hwang turned roughly $200 million into more than $35 billion.

The returns were extraordinary. If you looked at the performance chart, you would have concluded that Bill Hwang was one of the greatest traders who ever lived.

He wasn't.

Hwang had discovered something, but it wasn't a trading edge. He had discovered a loophole in the disclosure system.

By using total return swaps (derivatives where one party receives the total return of an asset in exchange for a financing cost rather than owning the underlying shares directly) instead of buying stocks outright, Archegos could accumulate massive positions without triggering the SEC's 5% ownership disclosure requirements. The swaps were held by banks (Goldman Sachs, Morgan Stanley, Credit Suisse, Nomura) who owned the underlying shares as hedges. Archegos appeared on no filings, even as it controlled more than 50% of the freely traded shares in companies like ViacomCBS and Discovery.

Hwang replicated similar positions across multiple prime brokers—each bank saw only their piece of the puzzle, none understanding the full scale of Archegos's exposure, which at its peak reached approximately $160 billion in gross positions on $35 billion in capital: leverage of roughly 5:1 across the whole book, but reportedly as high as 8:1 on individual positions.

Let's decompose what Hwang was actually doing:

Beta: Long the US equity market. When stocks went up, Archegos went up faster.

Factor exposures: Long momentum (buying stocks that were already rising), long tech/media sector (concentrated in a single industry), long small-cap/mid-cap (many of his positions were in less liquid names), and implicitly short volatility (leverage creates path dependence that punishes volatility, as we explored in Chapter 9).

Alpha: What unique insight did Hwang have about ViacomCBS or Discovery that justified owning more than half the company? None that has ever been articulated. His "thesis" appeared to be that his own buying would push prices higher, letting him borrow more, enabling him to buy more. This is a feedback loop, not alpha.

Hwang had constructed a machine that printed money in calm, rising markets. His returns were beta and factors, amplified by leverage, disguised as genius.

On March 22, 2021, ViacomCBS announced a secondary stock offering to raise capital. The stock dropped 9%.

For Archegos, this was the first crack. The concentrated position in ViacomCBS, held on margin, suddenly required more collateral. But Archegos was already fully deployed. There was no cushion.

On March 24, ViacomCBS fell another 23%. Archegos's banks began making margin calls.

Crucially, because of the opacity of the swaps, the banks did not know they were all calling the same client on the same collateral. When Archegos couldn't meet the calls, a "prisoner's dilemma" ensued. Goldman Sachs and Morgan Stanley moved first, liquidating billions of dollars of block trades to cover their exposure. Credit Suisse and Nomura hesitated, hoping for a coordinated workout. By the time they decided to sell, the price had collapsed. They were left holding the bag for billions in losses.

Hwang was later convicted on 10 of 11 criminal charges, including fraud and racketeering. While the legal verdict was fraud, the mechanical cause of the blowup was a classic leverage spiral exacerbated by opaque derivatives that hid the true accumulation of risk.

But set aside the fraud charges. Even if Hwang had done nothing illegal, the decomposition tells the story: *He thought he was generating alpha. He was harvesting leveraged beta and factor exposure in a rising market. When the tide went out, there was no swimming speed underneath.*

Every Trade is an Experiment

Archegos is an extreme example. But the same decomposition logic applies to every trader, including you. If you don't know where your money comes from, you can't know when it will stop coming. You are running experiments. Each trade is a hypothesis. The P&L is data. But data is only useful if you can interpret it correctly.

If you make $50,000 this year and attribute it to your brilliant stock-picking, but the real source was beta (the market went up 25%) plus momentum factor (you chased winners) plus luck (variance), then your belief about your own skill is miscalibrated. You'll size future trades as if you have an edge you don't. You'll hold through drawdowns expecting mean reversion that won't come. You'll blow up.

The professional views each trade as a controlled experiment. They ask: What am I actually testing here?

If your thesis is "Apple will outperform Microsoft," you don't just buy Apple. If you buy Apple alone, you're betting on Apple (the thesis), plus the tech sector (noise), plus US equities (noise), plus global risk sentiment (noise).

If the market crashes, you lose money on your "Apple vs. Microsoft" thesis even if you were right. The noise drowned out the signal. You can't learn anything from the outcome because the experiment was contaminated.

To trade this thesis professionally, you decompose the bet. You isolate the variable you want to test: Long Apple, Short Microsoft (or short QQQ to hedge sector exposure).

Now if the market crashes, your short protects you. If tech rallies, your short drags you down, but your long pulls you up. You've neutralized the beta and the sector factor. What remains is the pure residual: Apple minus Microsoft.

This is what professional hedging actually means. Retail traders think hedging is "buying insurance so I don't feel pain." Professionals know hedging is isolating the edge. It is stripping away the risks you're not paid to take (as we established in Chapter 10), so you can concentrate on, and size up, the risk you *are* paid to take.

The Leverage Trap

Common objection:

"If I buy a 3× leveraged S&P 500 ETF and the market goes up 10%, I make 30%. I beat the benchmark by 20%. Isn't that alpha?"

No.

That is leveraged beta. You took three times the risk to get three times the return (minus the cost of leverage and decay). You did not outsmart the market. You just made the same bet with a megaphone.

This distinction is critical because leverage amplifies the consequences of your positioning without changing the nature of your bet.

If you have alpha (true skill), leverage makes you rich.

If you have beta (market exposure), leverage just makes you volatile.

If you have negative alpha (you're bad at this), leverage makes you bankrupt faster.

Hwang's Archegos looked like genius because his leveraged beta produced returns that dwarfed the index. But his Sharpe ratio (return per unit of risk) was probably no better than, and possibly worse than, simply owning SPY. He wasn't generating risk-adjusted outperformance. He was generating levered market exposure disguised as outperformance.

Many "star" traders in bull markets are just people running 2× or 3× beta who haven't blown up yet. They look like geniuses on the way up. On the way down, they discover what they actually are.

The Strategy Factor Trap

Even "unique" strategies are often just disguised factors.

In the early days of quantitative trading, pairs trading (buying Pepsi, selling Coke) was alpha. It was novel. Few people did it. The returns were genuine outperformance.

Today, pairs trading is a commodity. Thousands of algorithms run mean-reversion strategies on correlated securities. The "easy edge" has been arbitraged away. What remains is a strategy factor: the mean reversion risk premium, which is harder to capture and more prone to crowding.

If you run a basic pairs trading strategy in 2025, you're not generating alpha. You are harvesting a known premium that's available to anyone with a Python script and a brokerage account.

This matters because strategy factors, like market factors, get crowded. When a strategy becomes a factor, returns compress (everyone is chasing the same premium), correlations increase (everyone holds similar positions), and crash risk rises (everyone exits at the same time).

Consider momentum. If you buy a stock because "it's going up," you might feel like you made a specific, skillful decision. But if you're just buying the top decile of winners over the last 12 months, you're not a stock picker. You're a factor investor. You're harvesting the momentum risk premium.

That's fine. Momentum has generated positive returns over long periods. But it's not alpha. And when the "momentum crash" happens (as it did in 2009, when the momentum factor lost 40% in a single quarter), you'll discover that your "unique" portfolio is correlated with every other trend-follower on earth.

- **Alpha:** You found a unique data source that predicts earnings surprises. Hard to replicate. Sustainable until the signal decays.
- **Strategy factor:** You're running a standard trend-following model. Easy to replicate. Prone to crowding. Returns compress over time.

If you confuse the two, you will size your "unique" strategy as if it's special, only to find that in a crisis, you're correlated with every hedge fund running the same strategy.

The Decomposition In Practice

You made 35% this year. Congratulations. Let's find out what you actually did.

> **Subtract the beta contribution.** The S&P 500 returned 20%. Your portfolio has a beta of approximately 1.2 to the market (you hold riskier stocks). Beta is the sensitivity of your returns to market returns; a beta of 1.2 means you move 1.2% for every 1% the market moves. Your beta contribution:
>
> $$1.2 \times 20\% = 24\%$$
>
> **Subtract the factor contributions.** Tech outperformed the broad market by 8%. Your portfolio is overweight tech by about 30%. Factor contribution: approximately 2.5%. The momentum factor returned 6% this year. Your strategy tends to chase recent winners. Estimated momentum exposure: approximately 0.5. Factor contribution: approximately 3%. You have a slight tilt toward smaller companies. The size factor returned 2%. Contribution: approximately 1%. Total factor contributions: approximately 6.5%.
>
> **Calculate the residual.**
> Raw return: 35%
> Beta contribution: 24%
> Factor contributions: 6.5%
> **Residual (alpha): 4.5%**

You didn't make 35%. You made 4.5%. Everything else was tide and currents.

Now ask: Is 4.5% statistically significant given your sample size? If you've been trading for one year, the answer is almost certainly no. That 4.5% could easily be noise. You need multiple years of positive residual returns before you can conclude with any confidence that you actually have skill.

A rough heuristic: to distinguish a 55% win rate from a 50% win rate with statistical significance, you need several hundred trades. To distinguish genuine alpha from factor exposure, you need multiple years of data across different market regimes. Most traders never accumulate enough sample size to know whether their edge is real. This is the sample size problem we discussed in Chapter 9, now applied to your entire career.

The Acid Test

Decomposition is the acid test of your ego.

Strip the beta. Did you beat the index, or did you just leverage it?

Strip the factors. Did you beat the style (value, momentum, tech, small-cap)?

Inspect the residue. What's left is your alpha.

If the residue is zero, or negative, you don't have an edge. You have an expensive hobby. And if you have an expensive hobby that involves leverage, you're not a trader. You're the liquidity.

Here's the brutal math most traders never confront: the average actively managed mutual fund underperforms its benchmark by approximately 1% per year after fees. These are professionals with research teams, Bloomberg terminals, and decades of experience. If they can't generate alpha, what makes you think you can?

The answer might be nothing. You might not have an edge. Decomposition forces you to confront that possibility honestly.

But if you do have an edge, if the residual is consistently positive across years and regimes, then decomposition tells you something equally important: what that edge actually is. It lets you isolate the specific, replicable skill that generates your returns, so you can focus on it, refine it, and protect it from decay.

The Provider and the Hunter

This decomposition logic leads to a profound realization about why trades happen at all.

When I sell you a stock, one of us must be wrong, right?

Not necessarily. We might be playing different games. We might have different pricing kernels, different ways of weighting future states of the world.

Consider: I sell you shares of a small-cap biotech. To me, this is a risk I don't want: illiquidity, binary outcomes, sector concentration. I'm willing to accept a lower price to get rid of it.

To you, this is exactly the risk you're paid to take. You specialize in biotech. You have information I don't have. You're willing to pay a premium (relative to my valuation) to acquire the position.

We're both rational. We're just different kinds of participants.

Providers are in the business of warehousing risk. Market makers, value investors, volatility sellers: they get paid a premium for holding positions that others don't want. They're harvesting factors.

Hunters are in the business of information. They have a specific view, a specific thesis, a specific piece of knowledge that the marginal participant lacks. They're generating alpha.

This maps to the four sources of edge from Chapter 7.

The trade is rational for both of us. The market clears because we're playing complementary roles.

The amateur looks at the price and asks: "Is it going up?"

The professional looks at the price and asks: "Who is on the other side, and what game are they playing?"

What Decomposition Can't Do

Measurement is noisy. Over a small sample of trades, you might show positive alpha purely by luck; the confidence intervals around regression coefficients are wide. Factors are unstable; what explains returns in one regime may not explain them in the next. And alpha decays: today's unique insight becomes tomorrow's crowded factor as the market adapts.

Use decomposition to challenge your P&L, not to certify your genius.

The Humility It Demands

In his book *The Laws of Trading*, Agustin Lebron offers a test: *If you can't explain your edge in five minutes, you don't have one.*

Your edge comes from understanding something about the market that the marginal participant doesn't understand or being able to act on something they can't act on. That's it. If you can't articulate exactly what that is, in plain language, without hand-waving, then you're probably harvesting factor exposure and calling it skill.

Decomposition demands humility. It asks you to accept that most of what happens in your P&L is not about you. The market is bigger than you are. The tides are stronger than your swimming.

But within that humility lies power. If you know which part of your return is actually yours, if you can isolate the residual, the alpha, the specific skill you bring, then you can nurture it. You can focus your energy where it matters. You can stop wasting time on factors you can't control and concentrate on the narrow domain where you might actually be good.

That's the gift decomposition offers: not a flattering mirror, but an accurate one. Not a story about your genius, but the truth about your edge, or the absence of it.

The basketball player who knows their hot hand is real but small can make better decisions than the one who thinks every streak is destiny. The trader who knows their alpha is 2%, not 35%, can size positions appropriately, hedge factor exposure intentionally, and survive long enough to compound what little edge they have.

That's how you build a career. Not by believing your own mythology, but by knowing, precisely, what's actually yours.

The hot hand might be real. But it's probably smaller than you think.

We've built the mental models. Now we use them.

Notes

Hot Hand Study. Gilovich, Thomas, Robert Vallone, and Amos Tversky. "The Hot Hand in Basketball: On the Misperception of Random Sequences." *Cognitive Psychology* 17, no. 3 (1985): 295–314.

Hot Hand Correction. Miller, Joshua B., and Adam Sanjurjo. "Surprised by the Hot Hand Fallacy? A Truth in the Law of Small Numbers." *Econometrica* 86, no. 6 (2018): 2019–2047.

Kahneman on Hot Hand. Kahneman, Daniel. *Thinking, Fast and Slow.* Farrar, Straus and Giroux, 2011. Chapter 10: The Law of Small Numbers.

Factor Models. Fama, Eugene F., and Kenneth R. French. "The Cross-section of Expected Stock Returns." *The Journal of Finance* 47, no. 2 (1992): 427–465.

Momentum Factor. Jegadeesh, Narasimhan, and Sheridan Titman. "Returns to Buying Winners and Selling Losers: Implications for Stock Market Efficiency." *The Journal of Finance* 48, no. 1 (1993): 65–91.

Momentum Crashes. Daniel, Kent, and Tobias J. Moskowitz. "Momentum Crashes." *Journal of Financial Economics* 122, no. 2 (2016): 221–247.

Archegos Collapse. Contemporary reporting from the *Wall Street Journal, Financial Times*, and Bloomberg, March–April 2021. For the legal outcome, see Department of Justice press release, July 2024.

Total Return Swaps. For background on synthetic equity exposure and disclosure requirements, see SEC Staff Bulletin on beneficial ownership reporting.

Mutual Fund Underperformance. SPIVA (S&P Indices Versus Active) annual reports consistently show the majority of active managers underperform their benchmarks over 10+ year periods.

Edge Articulation. Lebron, Agustin. *The Laws of Trading*. Wiley, 2019. Law 1: "If you can't explain your edge in five minutes, you don't have one."

PART III
The Professional's Edge

CHAPTER 12

Second-order Thinking

We've built the toolkit. Now we use it.

The Cut That Killed the Rally

It's 2:00 p.m. on September 18, 2024. You're watching the screens like everyone else.

The FOMC announcement drops: 50 basis points. A jumbo cut. The Fed's first rate reduction since the early COVID days, and they went big—double the 25 basis points most analysts expected just two weeks earlier.

ES futures explode. The S&P 500 rips 1% in 10 minutes. Your Twitter feed lights up with celebration. "The Fed put is back." "Soft landing confirmed." "Risk on." You feel the familiar dopamine rush of being on the right side of history. You're already long. This is it.

For 10 minutes, you feel like a genius.

Then something strange happens.

Treasury yields aren't falling. They're rising. The 10-year ticks up 6 basis points in the hours after the announcement. That's backward. If the Fed is easing and the economy is fine, long-term rates should drop. Instead, the bond market is sending a different signal entirely.

You pull up the Fed's Summary of Economic Projections. The unemployment forecast was just revised upward, from 4.0 to 4.4%. The statement acknowledges that "downside risks to employment have increased." During the press conference, Powell uses the phrase "recalibrating policy" repeatedly. He insists, multiple times, that this is not an emergency measure.

When someone insists that they aren't panicking, they are.

By 2:45 p.m., the initial euphoria has cracked. ES gives back half the move. By the close, the S&P 500, Dow, and Nasdaq have all finished lower on the day: red candles on a day when the Fed delivered exactly what the market had been begging for.

The headlines the next morning capture the confusion: "Stocks Edge Lower After Fed Announces Half-Point Rate Cut." The cognitive dissonance is palpable. How can a dovish surprise produce a down day?

If you bought the 2:00 p.m. spike, you're underwater. You did what the textbook said: Fed cuts = stocks up. You followed the playbook and lost.

You are the victim of first-order thinking.

The Game Theory of Market Announcements

Look at September 18.

The first-order thinkers saw a headline: "Fed Cuts 50bp." They processed it through a simple model: "Rate cuts are bullish. Buy."

The second-order thinkers asked a different question: "*Why* is the Fed cutting 50bp when just four weeks ago, at Jackson Hole, they signaled 25bp?"

The answer reveals the trap.

The Fed doesn't cut 50bp because everything is fine. They cut 50bp because they're worried. A 25bp cut says, "We're normalizing after inflation cooled." A 50bp cut says, "We're front-loading because we see something in the labor data that concerns us." The size of the cut itself was information, and that information was bearish.

But there's a deeper layer.

By September 18, the market had already priced in significant easing. In the week before the announcement, Fed funds futures shifted from 75% odds of 25bp to more than 60% odds of 50bp. When the 50bp cut was announced, it wasn't a surprise; it was a confirmation. And confirmation of something already priced in doesn't move markets up. It moves money out.

This is the game theory of market announcements. By the time you read the headline, the trade is already crowded. The sophisticated participants, the ones who move markets, have already positioned. When you buy the announcement, you're buying from them. You're their exit.

The Wall Street adage captures it perfectly: "Buy the rumor, sell the news." (This is Bayesian updating in practice, as we discussed in Chapter 5: the market updates its probability before the event, leaving no surprise for the event itself.)

But the principle here isn't about interest rates. It's about the structure of information flow in any market-moving event. Earnings surprises, economic data releases, geopolitical shocks, they all follow the same game-theoretic logic. The announcement is the least important moment. What matters is the positioning before and the reassessment after.

The Definition of Second-order Thinking

This happens everywhere.

Howard Marks, billionaire founder of Oaktree Capital, has built a career explaining why smart people lose money. His diagnosis is almost always the same: they're trapped in first-level thinking.

> **First-level thinking** is simplistic, superficial, reactive. The crowd's thinking. "The outlook is bad, so the stock will go down." "The earnings were good, so the stock will go up." "The Fed cut rates, so I should buy."
>
> **Second-level thinking** is deep, complex, and layered. It takes into account the fact that the other participants in the market also have brains, and they have already reacted to the first-level data.
>
>> "The outlook is bad, but everyone knows it's bad. The panic is already priced in. If the news is merely 'bad' instead of 'apocalyptic,' the stock will actually rally because the sellers are exhausted."
>>
>> "The earnings were good, but they missed the whisper number, and the guidance was weak. The stock is priced for perfection, so 'good' isn't good enough. It will crash."
>>
>> "The Fed cut 50bp, but the cut itself signals labor market weakness. The bond market is selling off, not rallying. The 'bullish' cut is actually a recession warning."

Marks puts it bluntly: "First-level thinking says, 'It's a good company; let's buy the stock.' Second-level thinking says, 'It's a good company, but everyone thinks it's a great company, and it's not. So, the stock's overrated and overpriced; let's sell.'"

You aren't paid for being right. You're paid for being right when the consensus is wrong.

If you buy a stock because it's a "good company," and everyone else agrees it's a good company, the price already reflects that goodness. There is no edge in a consensus observation. To generate alpha—returns above the market—you need a view that's different from consensus and correct.

First-order thinking leads to average results. In markets, average results (after fees and slippage) are losses. First-order thinking leads to ruin.

The Keynesian Beauty Contest

Marks gives us a practical framework. But Keynes got there a century earlier.

John Maynard Keynes wasn't just an economist—he was a speculator. Markets aren't about value. They're about perception of value.

He described the stock market using a metaphor from the newspapers of his day: the beauty contest.

Imagine a newspaper runs a competition. They print photos of 100 faces. Readers are asked to choose the six "prettiest" faces. The winner of the competition is not the person who picks the prettiest faces; it is the person whose picks most closely match the average preferences of all other competitors.

Think about the strategy here.

- **At Level 1,** you pick the faces you find prettiest. "I like blondes, so I'll pick the blondes." This is the naive investor who buys a stock because they like the product. They assume their taste is universal. They usually lose.
- **At Level 2,** you ask: "Who will the average reader find prettiest?" You prefer brunettes, but you know the public prefers blondes. So you pick the blondes. This is the momentum trader. They don't care about the asset; they care about what the crowd likes. They are trying to predict the consensus.
- **At Level 3,** you ask: "Who will the average reader *think* the average reader will find prettiest?" You know the public likes blondes. But you also know the other competitors know that. They're all gaming the system, picking the obvious beauty. Maybe the obvious choice is too crowded.

Keynes wrote: "It is not a case of choosing those [faces] that, to the best of one's judgment, are really the prettiest, nor even those that average opinion genuinely thinks the prettiest. We have reached the third degree where we devote our intelligences to anticipating what average opinion expects the average opinion to be."

The loop is infinite.

When you look at a chart, you're not looking at a stock. You're looking at a visual representation of thousands of other traders looking at the stock.

You see a support level at $100. You know that they see the support level at $100. You know that they know that you see the support level at $100.

If everyone sees the support, is it strong? Or is it weak because everyone has already bought, and there's no one left to buy?

The Crowded Trade Paradox

The beauty contest leads to a counterintuitive truth: *the more obvious a trade, the less likely it works.*

If a setup is "perfect"—fundamentals great, technicals clean, macro aligned—then everyone's already seen it. If everyone has seen it, everyone has already bought. If everyone has already bought, who is left to buy?

The buying power is exhausted. The trade is "crowded."

In a crowded trade, the price is vulnerable to even the slightest disappointment. If 10,000 traders are long and the news is merely "okay," the price will drop because there are no new buyers, and the existing buyers are impatient.

Second-order thinking seeks the uncomfortable trade. Chart looks terrible, news is bad, but the selling has stopped. Why? If the news is bad and price isn't dropping, there are no sellers left. The marginal transaction has shifted to the buy side.

The Sparrow Problem

First-order thinking doesn't just cost you money.

In 1958, Mao Zedong launched the Four Pests Campaign. The targets were mosquitoes, flies, rats, and sparrows. Sparrows, the reasoning went, ate grain that Chinese farmers needed. Eliminate the sparrows, increase the harvest.

The campaign was devastatingly effective. Citizens were encouraged to bang pots and pans to keep sparrows from landing. Nests were destroyed. Fledglings killed. Estimates suggest over a billion sparrows were eliminated in a single year.

> **First-order thinking:** Sparrows eat grain. Kill sparrows. More grain.
> **Second-order thinking:** What *else* do sparrows eat?

The answer, which Chinese scientists discovered through autopsies too late, was insects. Sparrows ate far more locusts than grain. With their only natural predator eliminated, locust populations exploded. The insects swarmed the fields and devoured the crops the campaign was designed to protect.

The result was the Great Chinese Famine. Thirty million dead. A policy designed to increase food production caused mass starvation.

Mao eventually replaced sparrows on the pest list with bedbugs. But the locusts had already won.

> **Every intervention has consequences beyond the intended effect.**
> First-order thinkers see the direct impact. Second-order thinkers ask, "And then what?"

Reflexivity

The Sparrow Problem shows second-order effects in a static system. But markets aren't static. They're reflexive—the act of observing and participating changes the system itself.

George Soros built his fortune on this concept.

Classical economics assumes markets tend toward equilibrium—prices settle at fair value like water finding its level. Participants are passive observers. Their buying and selling doesn't change fundamental value.

Soros called this nonsense. He argued that market prices affect the fundamentals.

The relationship is two-way (reflexive). The **cognitive function** flows from fundamentals to price: we observe reality and form expectations, which drive prices. But the **manipulative function** flows from price back to fundamentals: prices, once established, change the reality we're observing.

Black Wednesday. September 16, 1992.

Second-order Thinking

Britain had joined the European Exchange Rate Mechanism, pegging the pound to the German mark at a rate Soros believed was unsustainably high. British inflation ran triple Germany's. Interest rates were crushing asset prices. The fundamentals didn't support the peg.

Soros didn't just bet on this. He understood the reflexive dynamics: if enough participants believed the pound would fall, their selling would force it to fall. Perception becomes reality.

He built a $10 billion short position. On September 15, the Bundesbank president made an offhand comment suggesting "one or two currencies could come under pressure." The market interpreted this as a signal. Other hedge funds piled in behind Soros.

The Bank of England spent an estimated 40% of its foreign exchange reserves in a futile effort to prop up the pound. They raised interest rates from 10% to 12%, then announced a further rise to 15%. Nothing worked. By evening, Britain withdrew from the ERM. The pound collapsed.

Soros made more than $1 billion in a single day.

First-order thinker: currency trading at the official rate, central bank will maintain it.

Second-order thinker: a reflexive loop. The more people doubt the peg, the more expensive to defend, the more likely to break. The perception of unsustainability created unsustainability.

Soros didn't just predict the outcome—he understood that his own actions, combined with others who shared his view, would cause it. In markets, the observer and the observed aren't separate.

The "and Then What?" Test

How do you practice this in the heat of a trade decision? Shane Parrish of Farnam Street offers a simple heuristic: "And then what?"
This is the universal acid for dissolving bad ideas.

> **Consider a scenario:** The Fed cuts interest rates. First-order thinking says "Rates down → Stocks up. Buy everything." Second-order: *Why* is the Fed cutting? They usually cut when the economy is weakening. If the economy weakens, earnings decline. If earnings decline, stocks could fall even with lower rates. *And then what?*

Consider a another scenario: Your position is profitable. First-order: "It's working. Add more." Second-order: If I add here and it reverses, my average cost is worse. I watch my winner become a loser. Will I panic-sell the whole position? Third-order: Adding to winners sounds disciplined, but the asymmetry cuts against you. If it keeps working, you feel smart. If it reverses, you lose on the add and damage your psychology around the original position.

You must play the movie forward: Most traders pause the movie at the scene where they feel good—the entry, the risk reduction. Force yourself to watch the rest.

The Pre-mortem: A Practical Tool

You can't just "think harder." You need a process.

The best tool for second-order thinking is the **pre-mortem**, a concept championed by psychologist Gary Klein and popularized by Daniel Kahneman.

In a standard post-mortem, a doctor examines a body to find out why the patient died. In a pre-mortem, you do the examination before the patient dies.

Before you place a trade—when you're most optimistic, most confident, most sure of your thesis—you stop. Close your eyes.

You tell yourself: *"It's next week. This trade was a disaster. I lost the maximum. The stop was hit with slippage. My thesis was completely wrong."*

Then you ask two questions: *What happened?* And *who took the other side, and why were they right?*

(This inverts the risk audit from Chapter 10. Instead of "What risks am I taking?" you ask "Which risk killed me?")

Your brain shifts gears—from confirmation mode (looking for reasons to buy) to failure analysis mode (looking for threats).

"Well, if it failed, it's probably because the correlation with the dollar broke down." "It failed because the earnings report was actually tomorrow, not next week." "It failed because the liquidity was too thin, and I couldn't get out." "The institution on the other side saw flow data I didn't have access to."

You'll be shocked how obvious the risks become once you assume failure has already happened. The "hidden" risks were never hidden—you were ignoring them because you wanted the trade to work.

The pre-mortem forces you to invert. Instead of "How do I win?" you ask "How did I lose?"

Man muss immer umkehren—invert, always invert.

The Midwit Trap

A warning: second-order thinking can be dangerous.

There's a famous internet meme—the "Midwit" curve—that maps the U-shape of wisdom.

On the left: the Simpleton: "Stock go up. I buy." They make money.

In the middle: the Midwit. "RSI overbought, macro bearish, yield curve inverted, gamma suggests reversal." They short the top, get run over, lose money.

On the right: the Expert: "The flow is too strong. Stock go up. I buy." They make money.

Sometimes, the first-order move is the right move.

In a raging bull market, the "dumb" money wins because they just buy. The "smart" money outsmarts themselves. They see traps that aren't there. They anticipate reversals that never come. Analysis paralysis.

You're seeing factors that aren't there.

"I know that he knows that I know that he knows …" The loop goes forever.

The antidote? **Occam's razor.**

The simplest explanation is usually right unless there is a compelling reason to believe otherwise.

Use second-order thinking to *check* your first-order impulse, not necessarily to override it.

Impulse: "Buy the breakout." Second-order check: "Is this a liquidity trap? Is the volume confirming? Who is selling to me here?" Decision: "The volume is massive, the sellers are being absorbed, and there is no resistance overhead. The first-order move is correct. Buy."

Second-order thinking is a filter, not a mandate to be contrarian. Contrarianism for its own sake is just first-order thinking in a costume.

Liquidity Mapping

How do you apply this to the chart in front of you?

Stop looking for "patterns." Start looking for **liquidity**.

A note: technical analysis is an execution tool, not an idea generator. The trade idea comes from macro, positioning, narrative. What follows is about execution.

Larry Harris, in his seminal book *Trading and Exchanges*, categorizes traders by their motivation. One of the most predatory categories is what he calls Order Anticipators: traders who don't care about fundamental value. They care only about the mechanical necessity of other traders to transact.

The Stop Hunt Is Not a Conspiracy—It's a Business Model

Retail traders love to complain about "stop hunting." They imagine some guy in a dark room pressing a button to steal their shares. The truth is more boring and more ruthless: it's just liquidity provision.

Here's the setup: support is obvious at $100. A "triple bottom" everyone can see. Thousands of retail traders are long. They have placed protective sell stops at $99.90, $99.80, $99.50.

To a sophisticated participant, those stops represent guaranteed liquidity. A sell stop, when triggered, becomes a market sell order.

If I'm a large institution needing to buy 500,000 shares, I have a problem. If I start buying at $100, I push the price to $105 before I'm filled. Massive slippage.

Where can I find 500,000 shares of forced selling? Below $100.

When the price breaks $99.90 (either through natural volatility or aggressive selling), it triggers the first wave of stops. Those market sell orders hit the book. I sit there with passive buy limit orders, absorbing all that panicked selling. I'm buying from people who are forced to sell, not because fundamentals changed, but because their arbitrary line on a chart was crossed.

Once the stops clear, the selling pressure vanishes. There are no more sellers. The price floats back to $100, then $101. I'm now long 500,000 shares at an average of $99.80, and the stock is trading at $101.

How to Map Liquidity

Look at a chart and ask: "Where is the pain?"

Don't ask "Where will it bounce?" Ask "Where will the maximum number of participants be forced to puke their positions?"

The more times a support level has held, the more stops clustered below it. A "triple bottom" isn't strong support—it's a target-rich environment. Humans are lazy: they put stops at round numbers like $100, $150, $200. The 50-day and 200-day moving averages are widely watched, so stops cluster just below them.

The Second-order Trade

Instead of buying at support (first-order), wait for the break. Wait for the flush. Watch the tape.

Does the selling accelerate and then hit a wall? Does volume spike on the breakdown? (Capitulation.) Does price snap back above the level quickly?

If yes, that was a liquidity event. The stops are gone. The weak hands are out. The "strong hands" are now long. *That* is the time to buy.

You are buying the wreckage of first-order thinking.

The September 18 Replay

Replay the FOMC day.

It's 1:55 p.m. You're watching ES futures. The announcement is five minutes away.

> **First-order expectation:** "50bp cut = bullish. Go long."
>
> **Second-order pause:** "Wait. The market has repriced dramatically. Futures already show 60%+ odds of 50bp. If 50bp is delivered, is that news or confirmation?"

You check the cross-asset signals. Treasury yields have been drifting up, not down, in the days before the meeting. That's telling you the bond market isn't celebrating the impending cut; it's worried about what the cut signals.

> **Hypothesis:** "A 50bp cut when the Fed signaled 25bp four weeks ago is an admission. They're worried about employment. The size of the cut is information—and that information is bearish. If yields rise instead of falling, the equity rally will fade."
>
> **New plan:** "I won't chase the 2:00 p.m. spike. I'll wait for confirmation from bonds."

2:00 p.m.—50bp announced. ES rips 50 handles. Your first-order brain screams to get long.

2:05 p.m.—You check the 10-year yield. It's rising. That's not how a "bullish" cut should work.

2:30 p.m.—Euphoria fading. ES has given back half the move. Powell keeps saying "recalibrating policy," trying to frame this as routine when his own projections say unemployment is rising.

3:00 p.m.—You short ES at 5,650. Thesis: the credit market sees what equity traders don't. This cut is a warning, not a gift.

By 4:00 p.m., S&P down 0.29%. Dow down 0.25%. Nasdaq down 0.30%. The "bullish" 50bp cut produced red candles.

Same announcement. Same data. Different outcome.

The difference wasn't in the event—it was in the framework.

The Discipline It Demands

Second-order thinking is uncomfortable. You resist the crowd when every instinct screams to join it. You question your own excitement, asking at the moment of maximum confidence: "What am I missing?"

But discomfort is the source of edge. Comfort is expensive.

The comfortable trade (the one where the thesis is obvious, the chart is clean, and everyone agrees) is the trade where you're the exit liquidity.

The uncomfortable trade (the one where you're buying when others are panicking, selling when others are euphoric, fading the "obvious" move) is where alpha lives.

The standard advice for major decisions: project yourself to age 80 and ask which choice you'd regret not taking. In trading, invert it: project yourself to next week and ask which choice you'd regret making.

First-order thinker: "What do I want to happen?"

Second-order thinker: "What happens if everyone wants the same thing?"

That single question—applied consistently, rigorously, uncomfortably—separates the professionals from the liquidity.

Man muss immer umkehren.

Invert, always invert.

Notes

September 18, 2024, FOMC. Federal Reserve press release and Summary of Economic Projections, September 18, 2024. Market data from Bloomberg and Reuters contemporaneous reporting.

Second-level Thinking. Marks, Howard. *The Most Important Thing: Uncommon Sense for the Thoughtful Investor.* Columbia Business School Publishing, 2011. Chapter 1: "Second-level thinking."

Keynesian Beauty Contest. Keynes, John Maynard. *The General Theory of Employment, Interest and Money.* Macmillan, 1936. Chapter 12: "The state of long-term expectation."

Four Pests Campaign. Dikötter, Frank. *Mao's Great Famine: The History of China's Most Devastating Catastrophe, 1958–1962.* Walker & Company, 2010.

Reflexivity. Soros, George. *The Alchemy of Finance.* Simon & Schuster, 1987. Also, *The New Paradigm for Financial Markets.* PublicAffairs, 2008.

Black Wednesday. Contemporary reporting from the *Financial Times* and *The Economist*, September 1992. For Soros's account, see his various interviews and autobiographical writings.

And Then What? Parrish, Shane. *The Great Mental Models Volume 1: General Thinking Concepts.* Latticework Publishing, 2019.

Pre-mortem. Klein, Gary. "Performing a Project Premortem." *Harvard Business Review*, September 2007. Also discussed in Kahneman, *Thinking, Fast and Slow*, Chapter 24.

Order Anticipators. Harris, Larry. *Trading and Exchanges: Market Microstructure for Practitioners.* Oxford University Press, 2003.

Man muss immer umkehren. Attributed to Carl Gustav Jacob Jacobi, the nineteenth-century mathematician. Popularized in investing by Charlie Munger.

CHAPTER 13

Mathematics of Survival

The market can remain irrational longer than you can remain solvent.
—*Attributed to John Maynard Keynes*

P erfect analysis means nothing if you don't survive long enough to be proven right.

The Physics of Ruin

A trader doesn't operate in a vacuum. You operate within a physical system—a rigid mathematical environment governed by laws as immutable as gravity.

You can master your psychology. You can have an edge that prints money in a backtest. But if your capital management violates the physics of the market, you will die. Not "if"—"when."

Mathematics in trading isn't descriptive. It's prescriptive—a survival manual. It tells you what will kill you and how fast. Why do brilliant, disciplined traders go broke? They confuse the ensemble with the time series.

The concept is **ergodicity**. Borrowed from statistical mechanics, it's the most important idea for your bank account.

(Chapters 2 and 4 touched on this. Now for the full mathematics.)

The Ensemble Average

Imagine you're sitting in a bar in downtown Chicago. Ten other people—mostly struggling day traders complaining about the Fed. You poll everyone for net worth. The average net worth is perhaps $50,000. This number represents the central tendency of the group and is a useful statistic. It tells you something about the demographic reality of the people in that room.

Suddenly, the door opens. The room goes quiet. Elon Musk walks in and orders a drink.

Eleven people now. Recalculate the mean: billions per person. Does this reflect reality? Did you, the struggling trader in the corner, suddenly become a billionaire? Did your purchasing power change? Did your risk of blowing up your account decrease?

No.

The ensemble average claims that everyone in the bar is fabulously wealthy, but the time series of *your* life remains unchanged. You are still struggling. That's **skew**—the first way averages lie. A single outlier distorts the metric for the entire population. In trading, this shows up when you look at a strategy's average return. If a strategy made 1,000% in one lucky year and flatlined for the next ten, the average return looks fantastic. But if you start trading it in year two, you starve. You don't eat the average. You eat the returns of your specific time horizon.

The Coin Flip Illusion

But there's a darker way averages lie.

A hundred traders each start with $100,000. Simple rules: each month, flip a coin. Heads, you gain 50%. Tails, you lose 40%. The game runs 20 months.

Ensemble probability—the math of the backtest—says this is a good game.

Run a Monte Carlo simulation. Some traders get lucky streaks and end up with millions. Others get destroyed early and limp along with a few thousand. The average terminal wealth across all traders? Impressive. Expected value is positive. The average trader made money.

A standard financial risk model—the kind used by banks and taught in MBA programs—would conclude: "Positive expected value. On average, traders profit. We should play."

Now switch to **time probability**—the math of the individual. You're not the average. You're one trader. Your path:

Month 1: Heads. Your $100,000 → $150,000.
Month 2: Tails. $150,000 → $90,000.
Month 3: Heads. $90,000 → $135,000.
Month 4: Tails. $135,000 → $81,000.
Month 5: Tails again. $81,000 → $48,600.

Notice what's happening. Even with a fair coin—equal probability of heads and tails—you're slowly bleeding. After five months, you've lost more than half your capital despite "winning" 40% of the time. Run this out. After 20 flips with equal heads and tails—the most likely outcome—your $100,000 has become approximately $13,000. You've lost 87% of your money in a game with "positive expected value."

Where did the money go? *The ensemble kept it.* The traders who got seven heads in a row (the lottery winners) absorbed the wealth that the median traders lost. The average across the group is positive, but the median outcome is ruin.

The ensemble looks green. The backtest passes. But you don't get to average your wealth with the lucky guy. You eat your own returns. You live your own path.

Markets are Nonergodic

When you trade, you're not the ensemble. You're one trajectory. If you blow up your account—lose 100% of your capital—you don't get to participate in the recovery. If the S&P 500 drops 50% and then rallies 100%, the market is back to highs. But if you were leveraged 2:1 at the top, you were liquidated at the bottom. The market recovered. You didn't.

The first law of market physics: the absorbing barrier.

The Absorbing Barrier

In probability theory, an absorbing barrier is a state that, once entered, cannot be left. A black hole. Once a particle crosses the event horizon, it never returns. In Russian roulette, the barrier is death. In trading, liquidation.

(This is the "ruin" scenario from Chapter 10. Now we see why it's an active force pulling you toward it.)

Traders assume their capital is fluid—it can go up and down indefinitely, and if they just "stick to the strategy," the law of large numbers works in their favor. This is only true if you have infinite capital or infinite time. You have neither.

The absorbing barrier is the wall that stops you from reaching the long run. For the active trader, it's almost never zero.

The Broker Barrier

The hard deck. If you're trading futures (ES, NQ, CL) or Forex, you're using leverage. If your account equity drops below maintenance margin, the broker doesn't ask nicely. Their algorithm market-sells your position instantly. This usually happens at the point of maximum pain—the absolute bottom. You're liquidated, your capital is gone, and five minutes later the market reverses and goes to your target. The market was ergodic. Your account was not.

The Prop Firm Barrier

The trailing drawdown. Many traders go through prop firms. Prop firms have weaponized the absorbing barrier. Common rule: "If your equity drops $2,000 from its high-water mark, you fail." A moving absorbing barrier. It follows you up. This changes everything.

A trade that's "correct" over a week might be a "failure" over an hour if volatility triggers the drawdown limit. You're no longer trading the asset's natural volatility—you're trading the firm's artificial envelope. Your thesis must be right fast enough and smooth enough to survive it. (This is why Chapter 10 treated prop firm rules as hard constraints, not guidelines.)

The Psychological Barrier

The most dangerous barrier because it's invisible. Every trader has a number—a specific dollar amount of loss—the rational prefrontal cortex shuts down and the amygdala takes over. Once you cross this threshold, you're no longer trading your system. You're gambling to get back to even. Maximize leverage. Abandon stops. Enter the revenge loop. Mathematically, once you cross the tilt point, your time-average growth rate turns negative. You're effectively absorbed.

The Volatility Tax

If the absorbing barrier is the cliff, volatility is the slope dragging you toward it.

Most traders have an emotional relationship with volatility—the excitement, the dopamine hit, the reason they got into this instead of accounting. Strip that away. View volatility through pure mathematics.

Something disturbing emerges: *volatility is a tax.*

Not metaphorically. A literal, mathematical deduction from your compounded returns. Money that vanishes from your account not because you made bad trades, but because your equity curve moved around too much while getting there.

(Chapter 9 introduced this. Now for the mechanics.)

Two types of returns sound similar but behave very differently: **arithmetic** and **geometric**.

Arithmetic return is the simple average. Add up your returns, divide by periods, done. It's the number people use at cocktail parties. It's the number the guy at the bar uses when he tells you he's up 40% this year.

Geometric return—CAGR, compound annual growth rate—is the compounded reality. It's what you actually get to spend. The number that shows up in your brokerage account when you withdraw.

Here's where it gets uncomfortable.

The Smooth Path vs. The Turbulent Path

You have $100. Two days, two scenarios. Watch the money.

> **Scenario A (smooth path):** 10% on Day 1 brings you to $110. Another 10% on Day 2. You have $121. Total gain: $21.
>
> **Scenario B (turbulent path):** You crush it on Day 1, up 50%. Balance rockets to $150. Day 2 is rough—you lose 30%. Balance drops to $105. Total gain: $5.

The question: *what was the average return in each scenario?*
Scenario B: (50 − 30) / 2 = +10%. Scenario A: (10 + 10) / 2 = +10%.
Identical average returns. *But the smooth path produced more than four times the profit.*

Where did the money go in Scenario B? You didn't pay it in commissions. You didn't lose it to some counterparty. It just vanished—disappeared into the ether, consumed by the volatility tax.

This reveals something brutal: *negative returns are a stronger force than positive returns.* The math is asymmetric and not in your favor.

Lose 10%, you need 11.1% to get back to even. Lose 20%, you need 25%. Lose 50%, you need to double your money. Lose 90%? You need a 900% return. You need to 10× what's left.

The relationship is exponential. As your drawdown deepens, as volatility increases, the gravitational pull toward the absorbing barrier strengthens. The hole gets deeper and the walls get steeper at the same time.

The approximation every quant knows by heart:

$$R_{Geometric} \approx R_{Arithmetic} - \frac{\sigma^2}{2}$$

That second term—negative sigma-squared over two—is the **volatility drag**. (σ is the standard deviation of your returns—how much your equity curve bounces around.)

This term is always subtracted. Always negative. There's no scenario where volatility adds to your compounded returns. The more your equity curve oscillates, the more money is subtracted from your terminal wealth. Not because you're a bad trader. Because of the physics of multiplication.

The second law of market physics: *smoothness is speed.*

It sounds backward. We associate speed with aggression, big moves, dramatic swings. But in compounding, the opposite is true. A trader making steady 1% per week with low volatility will crush a trader making 10% one week and losing 8% the next—even though the volatile trader has more exciting returns and better stories for the bar.

The steady trader pays almost no volatility tax—compounding on a paved highway. The volatile trader is driving through sand, engine screaming, burning fuel just to maintain position.

Shannon's Demon: Harvesting the Tax

So volatility is always destructive? Minimize at all costs? Not exactly.

Not exactly. And this is where things get interesting. If you truly understand the mathematics (not just fear it, but understand it), you can actually turn the volatility tax into a rebate. You can make volatility pay you.

In the 1940s, Claude Shannon proposed a thought experiment now called Shannon's demon. (Shannon essentially invented Information Theory. The man was operating on a different level.)

Shannon asked: can you profit from a stock that goes absolutely nowhere?

Imagine a stock that doubles one year and halves the next. Year 1: $100 → $200. Year 2: $200 → $100. Perfectly flat over two years. Buy-and-hold made exactly zero.

Shannon proposed a rebalancing strategy: split your $100 between stock and cash, 50/50. At the end of each year, rebalance back to 50/50, no matter what happened.

Here is what happens.

Year 1: Stock doubles. Your $50 in stock becomes $100. Cash still $50. Total: $150. Rebalance: sell $25 of stock. New allocation: $75 stock, $75 cash.

Year 2: Stock halves. Your $75 in stock drops to $37.50. Cash still $75. Total: $112.50.

Wait. The stock went nowhere—ended exactly where it started. But you have $112.50. *You made 12.5% on an asset with zero return.*

Where did that money come from? *You harvested the volatility.* The rebalancing process forced you to systematically sell high (taking profits when the stock was up) and buy low (adding exposure when the stock was down). The very thing that destroys the buy-and-hold investor became your source of return.

The only way to beat the volatility tax: actively harvest it through disciplined rebalancing. But notice the prerequisite: you must survive the drawdown to execute the rebalance. If you hit the absorbing barrier in Year 2—if your broker liquidates you when the stock drops—the demon dies with you. The strategy requires you stay in the game. Which brings us back to survival.

The Leverage Privilege

The most misunderstood concept in trading: **leverage**.

Retail traders are taught leverage is dangerous. Regulators slap warning labels on futures accounts: "You can lose more than your initial investment." Financial advisors wag their fingers. For the amateur—the trader with a jagged, high-variance equity curve—they're right. Leverage is a death sentence.

Here is why. When you apply leverage to a volatile strategy, you magnify the oscillations. You increase the σ^2 term in that equation we just discussed. Which means you're paying a massively amplified volatility tax while simultaneously accelerating your velocity toward the absorbing barrier. You are making both problems worse at the same time.

(This is the math behind the leverage trap from Chapter 11—gap risk, path dependence, the XIV collapse.)

But for the professional, leverage is something else. Not a danger to be avoided—a tool to be earned. I call this the **leverage privilege**.

If you can engineer a strategy that's genuinely smooth—modest returns, near-zero volatility—you've earned the right to apply leverage. And when you do, something remarkable happens.

The Gunslinger and the Surgeon

Two traders:

> **Trader A (the gunslinger):** 5% risk per trade. Swings big—wins huge, loses huge. Year-end numbers: 30% return, 40% max drawdown, Sharpe 0.5.
>
> **Trader B (the surgeon):** 0.5% risk per trade. Small, boring wins. Equity curve almost flat. Year-end numbers: 10% return, 3% max drawdown, Sharpe 2.0.

The amateur gravitates toward the gunslinger. Thirty percent returns! Three times what the surgeon made!

The professional sees something different: *Trader B has earned the leverage privilege.*

Because Trader B's curve is smooth—because he pays almost no volatility tax—he can safely apply leverage. Say 4×.

Levered return: roughly 40% (10% × 4, minus some drag). Levered drawdown: roughly 12% (3% × 4).

Gunslinger: 30% return, 40% drawdown. For every dollar of return, $1.33 of drawdown pain.

Levered surgeon: 40% return, 12% drawdown. For every dollar of return, $0.30 of drawdown pain.

The Surgeon makes more money with a fraction of the risk. Not luck. Not secret information. Mathematics.

This is the secret hiding in plain sight in the hedge fund industry. The best funds don't hunt for high-return trades. They hunt for high-stability trades—strategies that produce consistent, boring, small gains with minimal variance. And then they lever those strategies until the return is attractive to their investors. The return comes from the leverage. The edge comes from the smoothness.

For the intraday trader, this translates directly to position sizing. *You don't earn the right to trade five contracts until you can trade one without turbulence.*

If you're trading one lot and your P&L swings wildly—up $2,000 one day, down $1,500 the next—and you decide to size up to recover faster, you're violating the laws of physics. Adding weight to a crumbling bridge. Increasing σ while moving closer to the barrier.

You must earn the leverage privilege through demonstrated smoothness. Reduce the drag. Prove you can trade small with consistency. Get that equity curve flat while still making money.

Then, and only then, add the horsepower.

The Geometry of Survival

We've established the environment (nonergodic), the cost (volatility tax), the tool (leverage). Now for the timeline.

In the ensemble (standard mathematical analysis), the order of returns doesn't matter. Multiplication is commutative: $1.5 \times 0.5 \times 1.2$ produces the same result as $1.2 \times 0.5 \times 1.5$.

In the time series—your actual account—*sequence is fate.* Path dependency.

Two traders, both with a strategy that generates 20% over 100 trades.

Trader A gets her winning streak first. Doubles her account in the first 50 trades. Then hits a losing streak. Because she's trading with house money—has built a buffer from the absorbing barrier—she survives the drawdown and finishes profitable.

Trader B gets the losing streak first. Loses 40% in the first 50 trades. Hits the tilt point. Loses confidence. His broker reduces his leverage. Even though the winning streak comes later, he can't capitalize. He's quit, been fired, or blown up.

Same strategy. Same edge. Different sequence. Different life.

You can't control the sequence. The market shuffles the deck. You might get the aces first, or you might get the 2–7 offsuit first. It's random. If you trade as if sequence doesn't matter—assuming the long run will save you—you're gambling on a lucky shuffle.

The Kelly Solution

If you can't control the order of the cards, what can you control? *How much you bet.* Kelly Criterion (covered in Chapter 9) gives us the optimal bet size. But "optimal" is a dangerous word.

$$\text{Size} = \text{Edge}/\text{Odds}$$

The full formula is in Chapter 9. The intuition: bet size should be proportional to your edge and inversely proportional to the odds.

Kelly mathematically guarantees the fastest possible geometric growth. Bet exactly the Kelly fraction and you maximize long-term compound growth—over infinite time.

But there's a catch. Kelly assumes you have infinite time, perfect knowledge of your odds (you don't—your edge is an estimate), and a robot's psychology.

Full Kelly is insanely volatile. It accepts 80% or 90% drawdowns as "optimal" because it knows it will bounce back. But you're human. You have an absorbing barrier—panic, margin call. Bet full Kelly and you'll hit the barrier long before you realize the geometric growth.

The professional standard: **fractional Kelly**, typically half. If the formula says "Risk 4%," you risk 2%.

Why size down?

- **Safety margin.** You might be wrong about your edge. What if your win rate is 45%, not 50%? Assume your parameters are worse than measured.
- **Volatility reduction.** Half-Kelly reduces variance by 75% but only reduces growth by 25%. You give up a quarter of your profit to gain massive smoothness.
- **Sequence protection.** By betting smaller, you ensure that a "bad shuffle" (a losing streak at the start) doesn't push you into the absorbing barrier. You're buying time. Paying a premium to stay in the game until the winning streak arrives.

The Physics Checklist

Before you place your next trade, run this checklist.

- **Where Is the Zero?** Calculate your liquidation level or max drawdown limit. Ensure your stop is miles away.

Am I Paying the Volatility Tax? Is this position size going to cause turbulence I can't handle? If I lose this trade, will I be emotionally compromised?

Have I Earned the Leverage? Is my equity curve smooth enough to justify this multiplier? Or am I using leverage to gamble?

Is My Sizing Survival-based? Am I betting full Kelly (greed) or quarter-Kelly (survival)? Could five losses kill me? If yes, size down.

The Great Filter

Amateurs are obsessed with prediction. They focus on the entry, believing that if they can just guess where price is going, the math takes care of itself.

Professionals are obsessed with structure. They focus on size. They accept that prediction is difficult and fragile. They know they'll be wrong often. They know the sequence will be cruel. So they build a structure that can withstand being wrong.

They optimize for geometric return, not arithmetic return—respect the absorbing barrier as the ultimate enemy. Volatility is a tax to minimize, not a thrill to chase. Leverage is a reward for stability. And they size their positions not for the best-case scenario, but for the worst-case scenario.

The market is a great filter. It filters out those who play the ensemble game—the gamblers, the optimists, the tourists who believe in averages. It leaves the survivors: the pragmatists who understand that in a nonergodic world, you must survive the path to claim the prize.

You are not an average. You are a single, fragile trajectory through time. Protect the trajectory. *Survival is the only alpha.*

Notes

Ergodicity. Peters, Ole. "The Ergodicity Problem in Economics." *Nature Physics* 15 (2019): 1216–1221. Also, Peters, Ole, and Murray Gell-Mann. "Evaluating Gambles Using Dynamics." *Chaos* 26 (2016).

Non-ergodicity in Finance. Taleb, Nassim Nicholas. *Skin in the Game: Hidden Asymmetries in Daily Life*. Random House, 2018. Chapter 19: "The logic of risk taking."

Absorbing Barriers. Feller, William. *An Introduction to Probability Theory and Its Applications*. Wiley, 1950.

Volatility Drag. The approximation is derived from the properties of log-normal returns. See Luenberger, David. *Investment Science.* Oxford University Press, 1997.

Shannon's Demon. Poundstone, William. *Fortune's Formula: The Untold Story of the Scientific Betting System That Beat the Casinos and Wall Street.* Hill and Wang, 2005.

The Kelly Criterion. Kelly, John L. Jr. "A New Interpretation of Information Rate." *Bell System Technical Journal* 35 (1956): 917–926.

Fractional Kelly. MacLean, Leonard C., Edward O. Thorp, and William T. Ziemba. *The Kelly Capital Growth Investment Criterion: Theory and Practice.* World Scientific, 2011.

Path Dependency in Finance. Mandelbrot, Benoit, and Richard L. Hudson. *The (Mis)behavior of Markets: A Fractal View of Financial Turbulence.* Basic Books, 2004.

Leverage and Risk. Carver, Robert. *Leveraged Trading: A Professional Approach to Trading FX, Stocks on Margin, CFDs, Spread Bets and Futures for All Traders.* Harriman House, 2019.

CHAPTER 14

Regime Awareness

"The same basic principles of mutation, competition, and natural selection that determine the life history of a herd of antelope also apply to the banking industry, albeit with somewhat different population dynamics."
—Andrew Lo, *Adaptive Markets: Financial Evolution at the Speed of Thought*

*T*he physics of survival operate within an environment that is itself unstable. The parameters that define "optimal" today may define "extinction" tomorrow. This chapter is about reading the weather—recognizing that the strategy that thrives in one season becomes the liability of the next.

The 551-day Silence

In January 1977, the rain stopped falling on Daphne Major.

If you have never been to the Galápagos, you might imagine a lush, tropical paradise. Daphne Major is nothing like that. It is a tiny, hostile volcanic crater rising out of the Pacific: a rock kiln. Under normal conditions, the island receives modest rainfall each year, enough to sustain a carpet of green vines and, crucially, the Portulaca plants that produce small, soft seeds. These seeds are the staple diet of the island's residents, the Medium Ground Finch (*Geospiza fortis*).

But in 1977, the sky turned a seamless, mocking blue and stayed that way for 551 days. The rainfall dropped to a mist. Barely 24 mm fell for the entire year. The island browned, then blackened. The Portulaca withered and vanished.

For the finches, this wasn't just a weather event; it was an economic collapse. The "easy calories" were gone. As the drought dragged on, the only food source remaining on the island was the seed of the *Tribulus cistoides*, the Puncture Vine. The Tribulus seed is a fortress: encased in a hard, spiny, woody shell that requires approximately 55 Newtons of force to crack. To a small bird, it is a biological bank vault.

As the weeks turned into months, a ruthless, silent sorting mechanism began to engage. The finches with smaller beaks (the ones that were agile, efficient, and genetically "superior" during the easy years of 1976) found themselves pecking uselessly at the armor-plated seeds. They lacked the torque. They lacked the leverage. Surrounded by food they could not access, they died by the hundreds, their emaciated bodies littering the volcanic ash.

But the clumsy birds—the outliers with deeper, wider beaks—suddenly possessed the only technology that mattered. They could crack the Tribulus. They survived.

By the time the rain returned in 1978, the population had collapsed by 85%. However, if you looked at the survivors, you saw something terrifyingly precise: *the average beak depth of the population had increased by 3–4%*. Evolution had not occurred over millions of years of gradual drift; it had happened in a single trading season.

Then came the ultimate cruelty. *The regime flipped.*

In 1983, a massive El Niño system parked over the Pacific. It didn't just rain; it poured. The system dumped 1,359 mm of water on Daphne Major, 10 times the previously recorded wet season maximum. It rained for eight months straight. The island exploded with life. Green vines grew so thick they choked out the Tribulus cactus. The large, hard seeds vanished, replaced by a superabundance of tiny, soft seeds.

The large-beaked birds, the winners of 1977, were now overspecialized. Their heavy mandibles were too clumsy to efficiently manipulate the tiny seeds. They were outcompeted by the surviving small-beaked runts. The "superior" hardware of the drought became the liability of the flood.

This is the nightmare of the market participant. It is the story of every trader who survives a crash only to bleed to death in a bull market. We spend our careers optimizing our beaks for the drought, convinced that "hard seeds" are the permanent reality. We build strategies that survive high volatility and tight liquidity. Then, overnight, the rain starts. The volatility vanishes. The liquidity floods in. And we starve. Not because we are wrong, but because we are *extinct*.

In nature, when the regime changes, the maladapted organism starves slowly. In financial markets, the starvation is immediate, and the extinction event is total. There is no starker example of a strategy optimized for a specific season, and obliterated by the changing of the weather, than the events of February 2018.

The Death of XIV

On the morning of February 5, 2018, the VIX (the CBOE Volatility Index, often called the market's "fear gauge") opened at 18.44, having closed the prior session at 17.31. It surged to 37.32 by the close. A single-day increase of +115%. In the after-hours session, it spiked above 50, its highest level since the August 2015 flash crash.

In Those Hours, An Entire Category of Financial Products Ceased to Exist

The VelocityShares Daily Inverse VIX Short-Term ETN (Exchange-Traded Note), trading under the ticker XIV, lost 96% of its value in a single day. Credit Suisse, the product's issuer, announced termination the following morning. Investors who held shares at the close on Friday, February 2, when XIV traded at $115.55, received liquidation proceeds of $5.99 per share. ProShares' SVXY, a similar product, lost 91%. Billions of dollars in notional value, representing years of accumulated gains, evaporated in hours.

For those unfamiliar: an ETN is a debt instrument issued by a bank, not a fund holding assets. "Inverse VIX" meant the product went up when volatility went down. When volatility spiked, these products imploded.

The Mechanism Was Reflexive, Precisely as Soros Would Have Predicted

XIV and similar products were designed to deliver the inverse daily return of short-term VIX futures. When volatility fell, they rose. When volatility rose, they fell. To maintain this inverse exposure, the products needed to rebalance at the end of each trading day. If VIX futures rose significantly, the products' assets under management declined, forcing them to buy VIX futures at the close to maintain target leverage. Those purchases pushed VIX futures higher, which caused the products to decline further, which required additional purchases.

The feedback loop was documented in the prospectus. Credit Suisse explicitly disclosed that an acceleration event (forced liquidation) would be triggered if the product's value declined by more than 80% in a single day. Sophisticated traders understood this. Academic papers had analyzed the potential for catastrophic losses. The risk was known, public, and priced into the products' design.

None of That Mattered to Investors Experiencing Three Years of Consistent Profits

From 2015 through 2017, volatility stayed suppressed. VIX futures maintained persistent contango, a term structure where near-term contracts are priced below far-term contracts, creating positive roll yield for short-volatility strategies. (When you're short volatility in contango, you're essentially collecting a premium as the expensive far-dated contracts you sold roll down to cheaper near-dated prices.) Month after month, XIV rose. Social media filled with posts about "free money." Forum threads debated optimal leverage ratios for harvesting volatility premium. Some investors borrowed to buy more, treating the strategy as a bond replacement with enhanced yield.

The edge was real. It was structural, arising from the term structure of VIX futures and the hedging behavior of market makers. It worked for years.

The Edge Was Also Conditional on a Regime That Could Not Persist Forever

On February 5, the combination of rising rate expectations, an unexpected wage growth report, and a sudden unwind in crowded positions created a feedback cascade. Stocks fell. Volatility rose. Short-volatility products declined. Their mandatory rebalancing amplified the volatility spike. The amplification triggered more selling. Within hours, what began as a routine market correction had destroyed products that had been profitable for a thousand consecutive trading days.

This was not a black swan, an unpredictable, unprecedented event outside all reasonable models. This was the inevitable consequence of optimizing for a specific regime while ignoring the certainty that regimes change. The XIV prospectus disclosed the termination trigger. The physics of the feedback loop were mathematically derivable from the product's structure. Anyone with sufficient sophistication could have calculated the scenario that would cause catastrophic failure.

The failure was not informational. It was epistemological. Investors operated as though past performance, even three years of consistent, documented, structurally explained performance, constituted proof that future performance would continue. They were turkeys at peak confidence, certain that tomorrow would resemble today because all their tomorrows had resembled their todays so far.

Maximum certainty preceded maximum surprise by exactly one trading session.

The Static Fallacy

The finch story and the XIV collapse share a common root cause. Why does this happen? Why do smart people (engineers, doctors, people who can solve differential equations) blow up in the market?

It usually isn't a lack of discipline, and it certainly isn't a lack of intelligence. It is a fundamental error in how we map the territory. Most of us view the market through the lens of stationarity.

Stationarity is a statistical concept: the parameters of a system—the mean and variance—stay constant over time. Think of a casino. In roulette, the odds of hitting red are 47.4%. That number is a physical constant. It doesn't matter if it is raining outside, if the casino is bankrupt, or if the player next to you is screaming. The physics of the wheel are closed. If markets were like roulette, you could "solve" them. You could find the "optimal strategy," leverage it up, and retire.

But markets are not mechanical; they are biological. They are **nonstationary**.

The "edge" you found in your backtest isn't a law of physics like gravity. It is a temporary behavioral agreement between participants. Unlike gravity, that agreement can be broken in an instant.

(This is the epistemological foundation we built in Chapter 4: the distinction between risk and uncertainty. Stationarity assumes you're drawing from Urn A, where the distribution is known. Markets are Urn B. The distribution itself is uncertain, and it changes.)

We saw this play out with the "buy the dip" strategy over the last decade. From 2010 to 2019, buying every 5% drawdown in the S&P 500 wasn't just a good idea; it was a dominant strategy. It felt like a law of nature. But that "law" was contingent on a specific regime: low inflation and a supportive Federal Reserve. In 2022, when the regime shifted to high inflation, that same strategy hemorrhaged money. The strategy didn't change. The operator didn't change. The physics of the room changed.

During the low-volatility years of the 2010s, many short volatility funds looked like geniuses. They were printing money every month. In reality, they were simply harvesting a risk premium that had not yet been called due. When the regime shifted in 2018 (the "Volmageddon" event we discussed in Chapter 7), that Alpha was revealed to be nothing more than leveraged Beta masquerading as competence.

The Problem of Ergodicity

This vulnerability connects to **ergodicity** from Chapter 13. Markets are nonergodic: your individual path can hit ruin before the long-run average materializes. What matters isn't the ensemble average—it's whether you survive the sequence.

If you lose 100%, you cannot play the next round. The game stops. This is why "average returns" are a lie. If a strategy makes +50% in Year 1 and –50% in Year 2, the "average return" is 0%. But your actual money has gone from $100 to $150, then down to $75. You have lost 25% of your wealth.

This matters for regime awareness because optimization assumes ergodicity. When you optimize a strategy for the last 10 years, you're assuming that you can survive the "path" of the market. But if the regime shifts (if the volatility creates a drawdown deep enough to hit your absorbing barrier, whether that's a margin call or an emotional break), you don't get to realize the long-term average. You are the finch that starved before the rain came back.

Survival is not just about "staying in the game." It is about ensuring that your time average never hits zero. You cannot be an "average" participant. You must be a surviving participant.

The Taxonomy of Strategies

If we stop treating the market like a math problem and start treating it like an ecology, the first thing we notice is that not all participants are trying to eat the same food.

If you examine the strategies traded by systematic funds, CTAs, and professional discretionary traders, they cluster into distinct families. Each has its own native habitat, its own feeding mechanism, and its own extinction risk. This is the practical application of the "structural edge" introduced in Chapter 7.

Academic literature and practitioner research (notably from AQR, Moskowitz-Pedersen, and Robert Carver) have converged on a robust taxonomy. The core strategy families are trend/momentum, mean reversion, carry, value, and volatility premium. For intraday and swing traders, there is a sixth category that bridges technical and systematic approaches: breakout/range strategies. Each of these strategies is regime-dependent; they don't work everywhere, all the time.

Trend-following and Momentum

Trend-following buys assets that are going up and sells assets that are going down. The logic is persistence: strength begets strength, and weakness begets weakness. The strategy ignores "value" or "fair price" to focus exclusively on motion.

There are two primary implementations. **Time-series momentum** asks, "Is this asset doing better than its own past?" The trader goes long if the asset's recent return is positive and short if negative. This is the dominant approach in CTA trend-following, trading futures across equities, bonds, commodities, and currencies. **Cross-sectional momentum** asks, "Is this asset outperforming its peers?" The trader buys the relative winners and shorts the relative losers within a universe (such as sectors or country indices).

Moskowitz, Ooi, and Pedersen's seminal 2012 paper demonstrated that time-series momentum generated significant risk-adjusted returns across 58 futures markets over multiple decades. The returns are driven by autocorrelation: past winners tend to keep winning, at least for a while.

The native habitat is directional markets with persistence: high-volatility environments and crisis periods. Trend-following historically generates "crisis alpha" because it tends to be short when markets crash.

The kill zone is range-bound, choppy markets. When the Hurst exponent is low ($H < 0.5$), every breakout fails. The strategy churns through capital, buying tops and selling bottoms. Trend strategies can lose money for months or years waiting for a trend that never materializes.

The characteristic profile is a low win rate (often 30–40%), but winners are much larger than losers. This requires psychological resilience to endure losing streaks. Transaction costs are relatively low due to longer holding periods.

Mean Reversion

Mean reversion operates on the opposite premise: prices that deviate from their historical average will snap back. The strategy buys when prices stretch "too far" below the mean (oversold) and sells when prices stretch "too far" above (overbought).

Implementations span a wide range. **Statistical arbitrage and pairs trading** identify two correlated assets that have temporarily diverged and bets on convergence. **Technical mean reversion** uses indicators like RSI, Bollinger Bands, or VWAP to identify overextension: when RSI drops below 30, buy; when it rises above 70, sell. **Fundamental value investing** buys assets that are "cheap" relative to intrinsic value metrics (P/E, P/B) and waits for the market to correct the mispricing.

The native habitat is range-bound markets with defined boundaries: low-volatility environments where structure is stable and "fair value" is identifiable.

What kills it: trending markets where "oversold" keeps getting more oversold. If you keep fading a move that has fundamentally broken the old structure (a parabolic run or a liquidation cascade), you drown. The 2022 bond market taught this lesson violently. Traders who kept buying "cheap" bonds as yields rose were applying a mean-reversion heuristic to a regime that had structurally shifted.

The characteristic profile is a high win rate (often 70–85%), but losers are larger than winners. This requires discipline to hold through drawdowns, as the edge often improves as the position moves against you. Stop-losses must be wide, which creates uncomfortable P&L swings.

Carry

Carry exploits yield differentials. The strategy borrows in low-yielding assets and invests in high-yielding assets to capture the spread.

Currency carry borrows Japanese yen (low interest rates) and invests in Australian dollars or emerging market currencies (high interest rates). **Fixed income carry** captures the yield premium of longer-duration bonds over short-term rates (the term premium). **Commodity carry** exploits the roll yield when futures curves are in backwardation (spot price higher than futures).

Carry has been called "picking up pennies in front of a steamroller." The returns are steady and predictable in calm markets, but the strategy is exposed to sudden, violent reversals when risk sentiment shifts.

The native habitat is low-volatility, "risk-on" environments: periods of monetary policy stability when the VIX is low and correlations are muted.

What kills it: risk-off events. When carry unwinds, it unwinds violently. The yen carry trade unwound spectacularly in August 2024, just as it did in 2008. High-yielding assets get sold en masse, and the "safe haven" currencies spike. Carry strategies have negative skewness: they make money most of the time and lose catastrophically on occasion.

The characteristic profile is a high win rate, small consistent gains, and large infrequent losses. Carry correlates negatively with volatility and requires careful tail-risk management.

Volatility Premium

Volatility selling harvests the gap between implied volatility (what options cost) and realized volatility (what actually happens). Because market participants systematically overpay for insurance, there is a persistent premium to be earned by selling that insurance via short puts, short straddles, or short VIX futures. Research consistently shows that implied volatility exceeds realized volatility by 2–4% points on average. Sellers of volatility capture this premium day after day, month after month.

The native habitat is "normal" market conditions where fear exceeds reality: periods when implied volatility is elevated but realized volatility is contained.

The hostile regime is tail events. When the fear becomes reality (when realized volatility explodes through implied), the short volatility seller is crushed. Volmageddon (February 2018) wiped out years of accumulated gains in a single day. The XIV ETN lost over 90% of its value overnight. The return distribution is the mirror image of trend-following: many small gains, occasional catastrophic losses.

The characteristic profile is a very high win rate (can exceed 90%), but losses are severe when they occur. Negative skewness. This requires rigorous risk management and the discipline to survive tail events.

Breakout and Range

These strategies sit at the intersection of trend and mean reversion, but they focus on structural boundaries: support, resistance, and the transition between regimes.

Range trading trades within a defined range, buying at support and selling at resistance. The trader assumes the boundaries will hold. **Breakout trading** trades the violation of a range. When price breaks above resistance or below support, enter in the direction of the break and ride the new trend.

These approaches are the bread and butter of technical analysis. The opening range breakout (ORB), where traders mark the high and low of the first 15–30 minutes and trade the breakout, is a classic intraday implementation.

The critical question is regime detection. Is the market in a range (fade the extremes) or transitioning to a trend (ride the breakout)? Getting this wrong is fatal. If you range-trade a breakout, you sell into strength that keeps running. If you breakout-trade a range, you buy every false breakout and get chopped to pieces.

The native habitat for range strategies is consolidation periods: low-volatility environments with clear structural boundaries.

The native habitat for breakout strategies is transitional periods: when ranges compress (volatility contraction), breakouts often follow, particularly around news events or structural shifts that invalidate old boundaries.

The extinction risk: mistiming the transition. Breakout strategies suffer in choppy, range-bound markets (false breakouts). Range strategies suffer when the range breaks and trends emerge.

The Regime Dependency Matrix

Now we can map where strategies live and where they die.

In trending, high-volatility markets (think March 2020 or late 2022), trend-following thrives while mean reversion dies. The momentum trader rides the wave; the value trader catches falling knives.

In range-bound, low-volatility markets (think 2017 or early 2019), mean reversion thrives while trend-following bleeds. The range trader fades every move back to the mean; the trend trader gets whipsawed on every false breakout.

In calm, "risk-on" environments, carry and volatility selling thrive. The pennies accumulate. But when the environment shifts to risk-off crisis, those same strategies face catastrophic losses: the steamroller arrives.

In transitional periods (range compression followed by expansion), breakout strategies shine. But in established trends or ranges, they suffer false signals and chop.

AQR's research on alternative risk premia found that combining these strategies (because they have low or negative correlations) produces significantly better risk-adjusted returns than any single strategy in isolation. Momentum and value, in particular, have a correlation of approximately –0.6, meaning they tend to perform well at different times.

This is the ecological insight: *Diversification across regimes is more powerful than optimization within a regime.* The finch that can eat both hard seeds and soft seeds survives the drought *and* the flood.

The Strategy Audit

Before you can apply regime awareness, you must conduct an honest audit of your own strategy.

- **Identify your core edge.** Are you betting on persistence (momentum) or reversion (mean reversion)? Harvesting a premium (carry, volatility) or capturing a structural transition (breakout)?
- **Define your native habitat.** What market conditions favor your approach? Do you need volatility? A range? A trend?
- **Understand what kills your strategy.** Trend-followers die in chop. Mean-reversion traders die in trends. Volatility sellers die in tail events.
- **Develop a plan for hostile regimes.** Can you recognize when the environment has shifted against you? Do you have a throttle—a mechanism to reduce exposure when conditions deteriorate?

The amateur trades as if conditions are permanent. The professional trades as if conditions are temporary, because they are. The rain always comes. And then it stops.

The Sensors

To read the regime, we need a few specific measurements.

Memory: The Hurst Exponent

The first thing we need to measure is memory. Most academic finance assumes price is a "random walk," a drunkard stumbling down the street where the next step is independent of the last. But we know that is not always true. Sometimes the drunkard has a destination.

We measure this using the **Hurst exponent**. The question Hurst answers is simple: *does the market have a memory?*

If the Hurst value is low (H < 0.5), the market is fighting itself. It is mean-reverting. Every step forward is likely to be followed by a step back. This is paradise for the range trader.

But if the Hurst value spikes (H > 0.5), the market is locking into a trend. Strength begets strength. In this regime, your "overbought" oscillator is a lie. The market isn't overbought; it is just getting started.

Note that Hurst is an estimation, not a magic number. It is noisy. But it is the only tool that distinguishes "choppy" from "trending" without lagging price.

Cohesion: Cross-asset Correlation

The second sensor is cohesion. In a healthy market, assets move independently. Apple moves because of iPhone sales; Exxon moves because of oil prices. This implies a market of diverse opinions.

But in a liquidity crisis, that diversity vanishes. The correlation between assets goes to 1.0. If you look at your screen and see "good news" on a specific stock being ignored while everything moves in lockstep, you're in a liquidity regime. In this environment, stock picking is dead. You are not holding a diversified portfolio; you're holding a single, leveraged bet on the market's plumbing.

When correlations tighten, your realized risk is exponentially higher than your theoretical risk. (This is why the "correlation caps" in the risk architecture from Chapter 9 exist—they're not just belt-and-suspenders; they're regime sensors.)

Fear: The VIX Term Structure

Finally, look at fear, but not the way the media looks at it. The VIX is useful, but the price of the VIX matters less than its shape: the term structure.

Normally, the VIX is in "**contango**," meaning future volatility is more expensive than today's volatility. That is healthy. It means people are worried about the unknown future.

But when the regime breaks, the curve flips into "**backwardation**." Spot volatility rips higher than future volatility. This is the market screaming for immediate cash. When you see this inversion, value investing is suicide for the leveraged trader. The floor is gone.

The Autopsy of 60/40

The 2022 bond crash is a textbook case.

For 40 years, the entire investment industry relied on a single correlation: Stocks and Bonds move in opposite directions. This was the bedrock of the "60/40 Portfolio." The logic was that if stocks crashed (due to recession), the Fed would cut rates, and bonds would go up. You were hedged.

But that correlation was not a law of physics. It was a byproduct of a low-inflation regime.

In 2022, inflation broke the ceiling. Suddenly, the Fed could not cut rates to save the stock market; they had to raise rates to kill inflation. The correlation flipped. The hedge became an amplifier. When stocks crashed 18%, bonds did not save the day; they crashed 13% right alongside them.

Traders who kept buying bonds in 2022 thinking "they have to bounce" were exactly like the large-beaked finches in the rainy season. They were applying a heuristic that was no longer physically possible in the new atmosphere. They thought they were taking duration risk in isolation. They were taking inflation regime risk—a completely different animal.

The Throttle

So, what do we do with this? We cannot predict when the regime will change. We cannot predict when the rain will start.

We adapt by using the only thing we actually control: the **throttle**.

Amateurs think in binary terms: "long" or "short." Professionals think in continuous terms: "How much?"

When your sensors align (when the Hurst is high, correlations are low, and the VIX is stable) and you're a trend follower, you press the gas. You take your full risk allocation. You don't hesitate because this is your native habitat. The seeds are everywhere.

But when the signals get mixed (when the price is trending, but volatility is screaming, or when correlations start to tighten), you don't just "hope." You lift your foot off the gas. You cut your size. You acknowledge that the environment is becoming hostile.

And then there is the third state. The **red light**. The regime is directly opposed to your survival.

In this state, you go to **cash**.

I know how painful that sounds. For an active trader, sitting in cash feels like failure. It feels like "doing nothing." But you must reframe that immediately. Cash is not "nothing." Cash is a position. It has zero duration, zero convexity, and maximum optionality.

When you're in a trade, your mental capital is hostage. You are biased. You are defending your P&L. But when you're in cash, you are pure potential energy. You are preserving your capital while the rest of the flock suffocates trying to breathe underwater.

Don't starve trying to force a trade the physics of the room won't sustain. *Wait for the rain.*

Notes

Daphne Major Finches. Grant, Peter R., and B. Rosemary Grant. *How and Why Species Multiply: The Radiation of Darwin's Finches.* Princeton University Press, 2008. Also, Weiner, Jonathan. *The Beak of the Finch: A Story of Evolution in Our Time.* Vintage, 1994.

Adaptive Markets Hypothesis. Lo, Andrew W. *Adaptive Markets: Financial Evolution at the Speed of Thought.* Princeton University Press, 2017.

Non-stationarity in Finance. Mandelbrot, Benoit, and Richard L. Hudson. *The (Mis)behavior of Markets: A Fractal View of Financial Turbulence.* Basic Books, 2004.

Time-series Momentum. Moskowitz, Tobias J., Yao Hua Ooi, and Lasse Heje Pedersen. "Time Series Momentum." *Journal of Financial Economics* 104, no. 2 (2012): 228–250.

Cross-sectional Momentum. Jegadeesh, Narasimhan, and Sheridan Titman. "Returns to Buying Winners and Selling Losers." *Journal of Finance* 48, no. 1 (1993): 65–91.

Alternative Risk Premia. Ilmanen, Antti. *Expected Returns: An Investor's Guide to Harvesting Market Rewards.* Wiley, 2011.

Carry Trade Dynamics. Brunnermeier, Markus K., Stefan Nagel, and Lasse H. Pedersen. "Carry Trades and Currency Crashes." *NBER Macroeconomics Annual* 23 (2008): 313–347.

Volatility Risk Premium. Carr, Peter, and Liuren Wu. "Variance Risk Premiums." *Review of Financial Studies* 22, no. 3 (2009): 1311–1341.

The Hurst Exponent. Hurst, H.E. "Long-term Storage Capacity of Reservoirs." *Transactions of the American Society of Civil Engineers* 116 (1951): 770–799.

Correlation Regimes. Longin, François, and Bruno Solnik. "Extreme Correlation of International Equity Markets." *Journal of Finance* 56, no. 2 (2001): 649–676.

VIX Term Structure. Mixon, Scott. "The Implied Volatility Term Structure of Stock Index Options." *Journal of Empirical Finance* 14, no. 3 (2007): 333–354.

2022 Stock-bond Correlation. Asness, Clifford. *The 60/40 Obituary.* AQR, 2022.

Strategy Diversification. Carver, Robert. *Systematic Trading: A Unique New Method for Designing Trading and Investing Systems.* Harriman House, 2015.

CHAPTER

Operating System

"Experience is inevitable. Learning is not."
—*Paul Shoemaker*

Chapter 14 showed us that the market is not a machine with fixed rules but an ecosystem that evolves. We learned to read regimes, to identify when the environment favors our strategy and when it threatens extinction. But regime awareness is useless if you can't translate it into consistent action.

The Wicked Environment

If you play tennis and hit the ball into the net, you know immediately that you made a mistake. The feedback is instant, clear, and accurate. If you play chess and leave your queen exposed, your opponent punishes you. The feedback is logical. You learn not to do it again.

Trading Isn't Tennis or Chess

In trading, you can do everything wrong—chase a breakout, ignore your stop, size up to get back to even—and make money. The market rewards your stupidity with a dopamine hit. Conversely, you can do everything right—wait for the setup, size correctly, execute perfectly—and lose money. The market punishes your discipline with pain.

Psychologists call this a **wicked environment**. The term comes from Robin Hogarth's work on learning environments. A "kind" environment, like chess, gives you reliable feedback. A "wicked" one, like medicine or markets, doesn't. In a wicked environment, feedback is noisy, delayed, and often inverted. Experience doesn't guarantee expertise. In fact, if you learn the wrong lessons from the wrong feedback, experience just makes you more confident in your bad habits.

The trader with 10 years of experience who's still losing money doesn't have 10 years of experience. *He has one year of bad habits repeated ten times.*

To survive, you need a system.

The Checklist: The B-17 Insight

The necessity of an operating system was written in fire and wreckage long before algorithmic trading existed.

In 1935, the US Army Air Corps held a competition for its next-generation bomber. Boeing's entry, the Model 299, was a marvel—faster, bigger, and more complex than any aircraft before it. It was the future of aviation. During a flight demonstration with the Army's top test pilot at the controls, the plane climbed steeply, stalled, and crashed in a fiery explosion. Two crew members died.

The investigation found no mechanical failure. The cause was "pilot error." The aircraft was simply too complex for one man's memory. The pilot had forgotten to release a simple locking mechanism on the rudder. The press declared the plane "too much airplane for one man to fly."

Boeing didn't redesign the plane. *They redesigned the pilot's process.* They created a simple index card with a list of steps for takeoff, flight, landing, and taxiing. With this tool, the Model 299 became the B-17 Flying Fortress—the backbone of the Allied air campaign.

The checklist was not a sign of incompetence. It was an admission that complexity outstrips memory.

Trading is your B-17. It is too complex to fly on memory. You need an external prosthetic for your discipline.

The Execution Loop

Checklists provide structure before the trade. But what about the chaotic moments in between, when the market is moving fast and you have seconds to decide?

Enter John Boyd. A fighter pilot, Korean War veteran, and military theorist, Boyd realized that victory wasn't about having the fastest plane—it was about having the fastest mind. He codified this as the OODA loop: Observe, Orient, Decide, Act. Whoever cycles through the loop faster gains a compounding advantage.

The loop has four stages. You **observe**—take in raw data. Price, volume, the order book, news flow. Then you **orient**—and this is the critical step. Orientation means filtering the data through your mental models. "Is this a trend pullback or a reversal?" "Is this news priced in or a surprise?" Third, you **decide**—you select the predefined tactic from your playbook that matches the orientation. And fourth, you **act**—you execute without hesitation.

The amateur gets stuck in observe, paralyzed by too much data, too many indicators, too many opinions. Or they skip orient entirely, reacting impulsively to price movement without understanding the context, like a fighter pilot who fires without acquiring a target lock.

The professional uses the OODA loop to create "**tempo**." By cycling through observe-orient-decide-act faster than their opponent—and in trading, your opponent is the market's consensus—they act before the consensus has finished reacting. They are positioned before the crowd recognizes what is happening.

The Feedback Loop

The Most Dangerous Trade Is the Bad Win

Imagine you're driving home drunk. You weave through traffic, run a red light, and park safely in your driveway. Your brain says: "I am a great driver. I can handle my liquor." You are a statistical ticking time bomb. You just got lucky.

In decision science, judging a decision by its outcome is called **resulting**. The term comes from Annie Duke's work on poker and decision-making. It is the cardinal sin of probability.

If you buy a stock because you "had a feeling," and it goes up 20%, your brain wires that "feeling" as a valid strategy. You feel like a genius. You size up on the next "feeling." Eventually, the luck runs out, and because you have no actual edge, you're destroyed.

I use what I call the **debrief matrix**:

	Good Outcome	Bad Outcome
Good Process	Deserved Success (Reinforce)	Bad Luck (Variance) (Resilience)
Bad Process	Dumb Luck (Correct!)	Poetic Justice (Learn)

Deserved success is the easy one—you followed your plan, you made money. Reinforce what you did. **Poetic justice** is also straightforward—you broke your rules and lost. You paid tuition. Learn the lesson.

The tricky quadrants are the off-diagonals. **Bad luck** is when you did everything right and still lost money. This is the cost of doing business in a probabilistic game. *Do not change the plan.* The worst thing you can do is abandon a sound strategy because of variance. If you do, you're just chasing outcomes.

And then there is **dumb luck**—you broke the rules and made money. *This is toxic alpha.* You must treat this as a failure. That profit is poisoned. It will cost you 10 times more down the road when you try to replicate a "success" that was never real.

You must learn to hate bad profits.

The Four Pillars of Review

When you debrief a trade, don't just look at P&L. Audit the four pillars of the operation.

> **Plan Adherence**—Did I follow the checklist? Did I wait for the setup? The metric: How much money did lack of discipline cost me this session?
>
> **Execution Quality**—Did I get a good fill? Did I slide? This is the gap between your theoretical model price and where you actually got executed.
>
> **Thesis Quality**—Was my orientation correct? Did the market behave as I anticipated? Track your win rate by setup type. You might discover that your breakout trades win 60% but your mean-reversion trades only win 35%. That's actionable intelligence.

Operator State—Was I in my A-game? Or was I tilted, bored, distracted, trading angry? Score yourself from 1 to 10. If your biggest losses always happen when you're at a 7 or higher on the tilt scale, you've found a leak. You don't need a better strategy; you need a rule that says, "If tilt >5, walk away."

Single-loop vs. Double-loop Learning

Finally, you need to distinguish how you fix problems because there are two fundamentally different types of failure.

Single-loop asks: "Are we doing things right?" The problem is operator error. I missed my entry because I was getting coffee. Fix: don't leave the desk at 9:30 a.m.

Double-loop asks: "Are we doing the right things?" The problem is system failure. I followed the plan perfectly, but this strategy has lost money for three months. Fix: retire or re-engineer. The edge has decayed.

Single-loop is like a thermostat adjusting temperature. Double-loop is asking whether you should be using a thermostat at all.

The critical mistake is confusing the two. If you change your strategy (double-loop) because you lacked discipline (operator failure), you're just pivoting from one failure to another. You are treating a behavioral problem with a structural solution. And you'll carry your bad habits right into the new strategy.

The Wall Around Your Worst Self

Here is the uncomfortable truth about everything in this chapter: *knowing what to do is not the same as doing it.*

Most traders stop at "I need to be more disciplined." That is a weak hypothesis. It cannot be tested, and more importantly, it relies on willpower—a finite resource that depletes throughout the trading day.

The professionals don't rely on willpower. They rely on **mechanism design**. They build walls around their bad habits so they physically cannot repeat them.

If you keep widening stops, you ask your broker to set a hard max-loss limit on your account that you cannot override during the session. If you overtrade when you're bored, you install a website blocker that locks you out of the trading platform after your predefined session ends. If you revenge trade after losses, you have a partner who changes your platform password after any day that exceeds your loss limit.

> *This isn't a sign of weakness. It's the opposite.* It's recognizing that you have predictable failure modes, and the right response isn't shame—it's architecture.
> *Do not rely on discipline. Rely on design.*

Build the wall before you need it, because in the heat of the moment—when the market is moving against you, when the tilt is rising, when every instinct screams at you to do the wrong thing—willpower will not save you.
Only the system will.

Notes

Wicked Environment. Hogarth, Robin. *Educating Intuition.* University of Chicago Press, 2001. Also, Epstein, David. *Range: Why Generalists Triumph in a Specialized World.* Riverhead Books, 2019.

B-17 Checklist Story. Gawande, Atul. *The Checklist Manifesto: How to Get Things Right.* Metropolitan Books, 2009.

OODA Loop. Boyd, John. *A Discourse on Winning and Losing.* The OODA Loop (Observe-Orient-Decide-Act) is central to Boyd's theory of maneuver warfare.

Resulting. Duke, Annie. *Thinking in Bets: Making Smarter Decisions When You Don't Have All the Facts.* Portfolio, 2018.

Single vs. Double Loop Learning. Argyris, Chris. *Reasoning, Learning, and Action: Individual and Organizational.* Jossey-Bass, 1982.

PART IV
The Business of Trading

CHAPTER 16

Tactical Protocols

"Amateurs have goals. Professionals have processes."

The Manual

This chapter closes the gap between philosophy and execution.

Translating Theory into Protocols

Brent Donnelly describes every trader as "a steaming hot bowl of bias stew." These biases aren't occasional visitors—they're permanent residents of your psyche, waiting for the moment when stress or boredom or greed cracks open the door.

The only defense is process. Not willpower. Not discipline in the abstract. Written, executable procedures that force your rational brain to engage before your amygdala takes the wheel.

Mark Douglas identified what he called the "**profit gap**"—the difference between what your strategy could make and what you actually make. Most traders assume this gap comes from analytical errors: wrong entries, bad reads, poor timing. Douglas argued the opposite. The gap comes from **execution failures**. From the moments when you abandon your process because you *feel* something.

The protocols in this chapter are designed to close that gap. They're not suggestions. They're not "best practices." In a high-stress environment, you don't rise to the occasion—you sink to the level of your training.

Print them. Laminate them. Tape them to your monitor.

Protocol 1: The Daily Decision Journal

Purpose: To force System 2 (slow, deliberative) thinking before you engage System 1 (fast, intuitive) execution. This document must be completed before every significant trade.

This is the preflight ritual from Chapter 8, formalized into a written record. The act of writing activates different cognitive processes than thinking. It slows you down. It exposes gaps. It creates accountability.

The Thesis

Every trade begins with a thesis. If you cannot articulate your thesis in writing, you don't have a trade—you have a feeling. Feelings are not edge.

The Narrative. Write one sentence explaining the fundamental or macro story. You need to know why the market should move, not just that it might. Example: "OPEC+ production cuts are holding, inventory data shows tightening, and geopolitical risk premium is returning to crude." If you cannot write this sentence, you're trading noise, not signal.

The Trigger. Write one sentence explaining the technical setup that confirms entry timing. The narrative tells you *what* to trade. The trigger tells you *when*. Example: "Price reclaimed the 200-day moving average on expanding volume, establishing a higher low above the previous swing point." This is where your chart work earns its keep—not as prophecy, but as timing mechanism.

The Invalidation. Write the specific price level where your thesis dies. Not a dollar amount. A structural level. Example: "If price closes below yesterday's low at $75.50, the higher-low structure is broken and the thesis is invalid." This is your stop loss framed correctly—as the point where you're wrong, not the point where you've lost enough money.

The Math

Position sizing isn't a feeling. It's arithmetic. Complete this section with a calculator, not your intuition.

Start with your **free capital base**—capital available after subtracting locked positions and required buffers. Write this number down. Update it daily.

Select your **risk percentage**—the fraction of free capital you're risking on this trade. For most trades, this is 0.5–1.0%. For Type II setups with fusion alignment, you may go to 1.5–3.0%. For Type III asymmetric bets, up to 5%. Multiply your free capital base by this percentage to get your **dollar risk budget**.

Calculate **stop distance**—the number of ticks, cents, or pips between your entry and your invalidation level. Add a **gap/slippage buffer** of 10–20% for volatile assets. Stops exist only in continuous price space. Reality is discontinuous.

Finally, divide your dollar risk budget by (Stop Distance + Buffer) to get your **position size**. This is the exact number of contracts, shares, or units you will trade. Not approximately. Exactly.

Write all these numbers down. If you cannot complete this math, you're not ready to trade.

The Pre-mortem

Before you click "Buy," imagine it is tomorrow. You lost maximum risk. The trade was a disaster. What happened?

This is the pre-mortem from Chapter 12, but now we formalize it into a checklist. For each item, answer honestly. If any answer is "Yes," the trade requires reconsideration—or outright rejection.

- **The "B" Setup Trap.** Is this really an A+ trade, or am I just bored and chasing action? Most trades that blow up are trades that should never have been entered—trades where the setup was "good enough" but not compelling.
- **The Tilt Check.** Am I trying to make back yesterday's losses? If yes, stop. Revenge trading is the single most reliable way to turn a bad day into a catastrophic week.
- **The Event Risk.** Is there a Fed speaker, earnings release, or data print in the next two hours that could invalidate my thesis regardless of technicals? If you're holding through an event, know what uncertainty you're accepting.
- **The Liquidity Trap.** Is the spread wide? Is volume thin? Am I the sucker at the table? If you're trading thin markets with obvious stop levels, you're donating liquidity to professionals.

The Correlation Blind Spot. Is this trade actually different from my other positions, or am I doubling down on the same directional bet with a different ticker? If you're long crude, long the Canadian dollar, and long energy stocks, you don't have three positions—you have one position with triple the risk.

After completing the pre-mortem, make a **go/no-go** decision. Execute if the thesis is sound, the math is complete, and the pre-mortem is clean. Abort if any element fails. There's no shame in aborting. The trade you don't take can't hurt you.

Protocol 2: The Post-trade Review

Purpose: To extract maximum learning from every trade, whether win or loss. Complete this within 24 hours of closing any significant position.

Most traders review only their losses. This is a mistake. Winning trades can be just as instructive—especially when you win for the wrong reasons. A trade that made money despite violating your process is a trap. It reinforces bad behavior. The post-trade review catches both.

Execution Analysis

Entry Quality. Did you enter at the level you planned? If not, how much slippage and why? Did you chase? Did you hesitate and miss the initial entry, then panic-buy higher? Write the planned entry, the actual entry, and the difference in dollars.

Stop Discipline. If stopped out, did your stop hold at the planned level? Or did you move it—widening to "give the trade room" or tightening to "lock in gains"? Moving stops is one of the most reliable predictors of future blow-ups. Track it.

Exit Quality. If you hit your target, did you take profit at the planned level? Or did you get greedy and hold for more, then watch profits evaporate? Conversely, did you exit too early out of fear, leaving significant profit on the table? Write the planned exit, the actual exit, and the difference.

Thesis Validation

- **Narrative Accuracy.** Did the market move for the reasons you expected? If you were bullish because of tight supply, did the move come from supply dynamics—or from an unrelated macro catalyst? A trade can be right for the wrong reasons. This is lucky, not good. Track the distinction.
- **Technical Accuracy.** Did the technical setup behave as expected? Did the support hold? Did the breakout follow through? If the technicals failed, was the failure predictable in hindsight (a lesson to incorporate) or truly random (noise to ignore)?
- **Sizing Appropriateness.** In retrospect, was your position size appropriate for the volatility and the outcome? If you lost maximum risk and it caused emotional distress, you sized too big—regardless of what the formula said. If you won but the profit felt trivial, you may have sized too small for the quality of the setup. Calibrate for next time.

The Honest Scorecard

Rate the trade on two separate dimensions.

- **Process Score (1–10):** Did you follow your plan? Did you complete the Daily Decision Journal? Did you enter at the right size, hold through the noise, exit at the right level? This score measures *you*—your execution of the system.
- **Outcome Score (1–10):** Did the trade make money? How much relative to risk? This score measures the *result*—which you don't fully control.

Over time, track the relationship between these scores. This maps directly to the debrief matrix from Chapter 15—the four quadrants of process versus outcome. You already know how to interpret these combinations.

Protocol 3: The Monthly Risk Audit

Purpose: To detect "risk creep" and "strategy drift" before they become solvency issues. Perform this audit on the first weekend of every month.

Risk creep is the gradual, unconscious expansion of size when markets are calm. Strategy drift is the slow mutation of your approach—taking trades you wouldn't have taken six months ago, holding through levels you would have exited. Both are invisible in real time. The audit makes them visible.

Exposure and Sizing Check

Calculate your average risk per trade over the past month. Compare it to your target risk per trade (typically 0.5–1.0%). If your average exceeds your target by more than 20%, you're sizing too big. Reduce your base unit by 25% for the next month and monitor.

Calculate your maximum single-day exposure over the past month. Compare it to your maximum acceptable exposure. If you exceeded your daily stop at any point, investigate why. Was it intentional (a high-conviction bet)? Or did positions accumulate without you noticing?

Calculate your maximum correlated exposure. What was the largest concentration of risk in a single direction or theme? Were you ever, unknowingly, "all-in" on a single macro thesis? Don't unknowingly become 100% long a single thesis across your salary, home, and investment portfolio.

The Leakage Audit

Compare your "Model P&L" (what you would have made if every trade filled at your decision price) with your "Actual P&L" (what you actually made after fills, fees, and errors).

- **Slippage Cost:** Total dollars lost to bad fills. This includes entries that chased, stops that gapped through, and exits that suffered from thin liquidity. Sum it for the month.
- **Commission Cost:** Total fees paid to your broker. This is straightforward arithmetic but often ignored.
- **Error Cost:** Total dollars lost to fat-finger mistakes, missed order cancellations, and operational failures. Every trader has these. Track them ruthlessly.

Add these three numbers to get your **total friction**. Subtract total friction from your gross profit to get your **net edge**.

Diagnostic: If your total friction exceeds 20% of your gross profit, you have a problem. Either your strategy is too active (too many trades, each carrying friction) or your execution is poor (bad fills, operational errors). The fix is usually one of two things: trade less frequently (move to higher time frames) or use limit orders more aggressively (accept the risk of missing fills in exchange for better prices when you do get filled).

The Correlation Stress Test

Look at your current open positions or your typical daily book. Run a simple thought experiment: What happens if the US dollar spikes 1% tomorrow?

If you're long gold, you're likely down. If you're long the S&P 500, you are likely down. If you are short EUR/USD, you are likely up.

Net these exposures. Are you diversified? Or are you, effectively, just "short the dollar" across five different instruments that feel independent but move together in stress?

Repeat the exercise for other macro shocks: What if the 10-year Treasury yield jumps 25 basis points? What if the VIX spikes to 30? What if crude oil gaps down 10%?

You're not just taking individual positions—you're constructing a portfolio with embedded factor exposures. Know what they are before the market shows you.

Protocol 4: The Weekly Regime Check

Purpose: To objectively classify the market environment before you trade in it. Strategies that work in "quiet bull" will kill you in "volatile chop." Update this assessment every Sunday.

You can't adapt to regimes if you don't explicitly identify them.

The Indicators

Trend Strength. Is the asset above or below its 50-day and 200-day moving averages? Is it making higher highs and higher lows (uptrend), lower highs and lower lows (downtrend), or neither (range)? The Hurst exponent, if you calculate it, gives a more precise measure: below 0.5 is mean-reverting, above 0.5 is trending.

- **Volatility Level.** Is the VIX (or your asset's equivalent volatility measure) high, normal, or low relative to its historical range? Below 15 is quiet; 15–25 is normal; above 25 is elevated; and above 35 is crisis.
- **Volatility Structure.** Is the VIX term structure in contango (normal—future volatility more expensive than spot) or backwardation (crisis—spot volatility spiking above futures)? Backwardation is a warning sign that the market is under stress.
- **Correlation Regime.** Are assets moving independently (normal—diverse opinions) or in lockstep (crisis—liquidity driving everything)? When correlations spike toward 1.0, your diversification disappears.

Regime Classification

Based on these indicators, classify the current regime into one of four categories.

Quiet trend describes a market with strong directional movement and low volatility—the "easy mode" environment where trend-following thrives. If this is your regime, take full size on trend trades and avoid mean-reversion plays.

Volatile trend describes strong directional movement with high volatility—the environment of crashes and parabolic rallies. Trend trades work, but sizing must be reduced to survive the swings. Cut your base unit by 25–50%. Expect slippage. Expect gaps.

Quiet range describes a market with no clear direction and low volatility—the "chop zone" where mean-reversion strategies shine and trend strategies bleed. Fade extremes. Reduce trend exposure. Be patient.

Volatile chop describes no clear direction with high volatility—the worst possible environment for any directional strategy. Every breakout fails. Every fade gets run over. This is the regime where the best trade is often no trade. Reduce exposure to 25–50% of normal. Consider sitting in cash until the regime clarifies.

Write down your current regime classification and the sizing multiplier you'll apply for the coming week. This is not optional. Match your strategy to the regime.

Protocol 5: The Sizing Matrix

Purpose: To remove emotion from position sizing decisions. Print this and tape it to your monitor.

Tactical Protocols   237

This is Chapter 9's position sizing framework, compressed into a quick reference. When you're staring at a setup and feeling the urge to "size up," consult the matrix. It doesn't negotiate.

The Framework

Start with your **base unit**—typically 1% of your free capital. This is your default risk per trade. All sizing decisions are multipliers of this base.

Assess your **setup quality** using the Fusion Analysis framework. A **Type I setup (3-star)** has technical alignment only—the chart looks good, but the narrative is unclear or absent. A **Type II setup (4-star)** has technical and narrative alignment—the chart confirms a story you understand fundamentally. A **Type III setup (5-star)** has full fusion—technicals, narrative, sentiment, positioning, and intermarket signals all pointing the same direction. These are rare.

Assess your **performance state**. You are in a **cold state** if you're in a drawdown exceeding 3% from your equity peak or if you have lost three or more of your last five trades. You are in a **hot state** if you're within 1% of your equity peak *and* you have won three or more of your last five trades. Otherwise, you are **neutral**.

The Decision Rules

When in a cold state, take only Type II and Type III setups. Size at 0.5 × base unit. You are in capital preservation mode. Your job is not to make money—it is to stop the bleeding and rebuild confidence through small wins.

When neutral, take all setup types. Size Type I setups at 0.75 × base unit, Type II setups at 1.0 × base unit, and Type III setups at 1.5 × base unit.

When in a hot state, you have earned the right to press. Size Type I setups at 1.0 × base unit, Type II setups at 1.5 × base unit, and Type III setups at 2.0 × base unit. Smoothness earns leverage.

> **Absolute Rules.** Never exceed 2.0 × base unit, no matter how good the setup looks. Never trade Type I setups when in a cold state—they're not worth the risk to your psychology. If in doubt, size down. You can always add to a winning position. You can't untake a loss.

Protocol 6: The Pre-execution Kill List

Purpose: A rapid mental checklist to run in the seconds before you click "Buy" or "Sell." If you answer "yes" to any question, step away from the keyboard.

Five questions you can run in 10 seconds. The pre-mortem (Protocol 1) is for before you decide. The kill list is for the moment before you click. It's not a substitute for the full Daily Decision Journal—it's a final safety check.

Am I bored? Trading for entertainment is a losing proposition. The market charges admission for excitement. If you're clicking because you're understimulated, close the platform and take a walk.

Am I angry? Revenge trading after a loss is the most predictable path to ruin. Anger narrows cognition and increases risk-taking. If you're trading to "get back" at the market, you've already lost.

Am I rushing? Fear of missing out isn't a trading strategy. If you're chasing a candle that already moved, you're paying a premium for the right to be late. The market will still be here tomorrow. The setup that "got away" will recur. Wait.

Did I move my stop? If you've already widened your stop on an existing position, you're in bargaining mode. You're negotiating with reality instead of accepting it. Don't compound the error by adding to the position or taking new trades in the same mindset.

Is this money I can't afford to lose? Scared money never wins. If the dollar amount at risk would cause genuine hardship if lost, you're over-risked. Reduce size until the potential loss is genuinely acceptable—not just theoretically, but emotionally.

Protocol 7: The Weekly Review

Purpose: To zoom out from individual trades and assess your performance at the system level. Complete this every Sunday before the new week begins.

Individual trades are noisy. A week of trades begins to show patterns. A month of weeks reveals your true edge—or its absence.

The Numbers

Calculate your weekly P&L, both in dollars and in R-multiples. A week where you made $2,000 risking $500 per trade is a +4R week. A week where you made $2,000 risking $2,000 per trade is a +1R week. The R-multiple is more informative than the dollar amount.

Calculate your win rate for the week. What percentage of trades were profitable? How does this compare to your historical average?

Calculate your average winner and average loser. Is your payoff ratio (average win divided by average loss) holding at the level your strategy requires?

Calculate your trade frequency. How many trades did you take? Is this more or less than your target frequency? Over-trading and under-trading are both symptoms—of boredom and fear, respectively.

The Patterns

- **Time-of-day Analysis.** When did your best and worst trades occur? Some traders are sharp in the morning and sloppy in the afternoon. One trader I know discovered his results collapsed after 11 a.m. and built a rule to square up by then. Others are the opposite. Track your P&L by time of day and adapt.
- **Asset Analysis.** Which instruments made you money and which cost you? You may discover you are consistently profitable in crude and consistently unprofitable in the Nasdaq. Stop trading the Nasdaq. Specialize in what works.
- **Setup Analysis.** Which setup types performed best? Your Type II setups may have a 70%-win rate while your Type I setups are coin flips. Weight your trading toward the setups with demonstrated edge.

The Lessons

- **What did I do well this week?** Identify specific behaviors to repeat. "I held my winners longer" is vague. "I let the crude trade run to target on Wednesday despite wanting to take profit early" is specific and reinforceable.
- **What did I do poorly this week?** Identify specific behaviors to eliminate. "I over-traded" is vague. "I took three Type I setups on Monday when I should have waited for confirmation" is specific and correctable.

What will I do differently next week? Commit to one change. Not five changes. One. "I will not take any trades in the first 30 minutes." "I will reduce my base unit by 25% until I have three winning days in a row." Make it concrete. Make it measurable. Review it next Sunday.

The Commitment

These protocols are useless if they remain on the page. They must become habit—patterns you execute without thinking, because when the market is moving and the adrenaline is flowing, you won't have time to think.

The research on habit formation is clear: it takes 66 days, on average, for a new behavior to become automatic. For the next 66 trading days, commit to completing these protocols religiously. No shortcuts. No exceptions. No "I'll do it later."

The Daily Decision Journal before every trade. The Post-trade Review after every close. The Weekly Review every Sunday. The Monthly Audit every first weekend. The Regime Check whenever conditions shift.

At first, this will feel tedious. Bureaucratic. Slow. You will resent the friction. You will want to skip steps "just this once."

Do Not Skip

The friction is the point. The slowness is the feature. Every second you spend writing out your thesis, calculating your size, and running the pre-mortem is a second your System 2 has to override your System 1. Every moment of deliberation is a moment you are not impulsive.

Amateurs have goals. Professionals have processes.
Execute the process.

CHAPTER 17

Building a Professional Future

Over the past 16 chapters, I've given you everything I know about how professional trading actually works. Not the YouTube version. Not the Discord pump-and-dump version. The real thing—the epistemology, the risk architecture, the psychology, the regime awareness.

If you've made it this far, you're serious.

But here's the part most trading books skip: they teach you how to trade, then leave you at the door of the market with a vague wish of good luck, as if knowing how to read a chart or size a position answers the question of what you're actually building toward. It doesn't. The structure of your trading career—how you capitalize it, how you scale it, how you eventually professionalize it—is as important as any entry signal or risk parameter. Get the structure wrong, and even exceptional trading skill fails to compound into anything meaningful.

So, this final chapter is about what comes next. The terrain ahead. The major pathways available to you: trading your own capital, joining a proprietary trading firm, and—for those with the ambition and the track record—building toward institutional capital allocation. These aren't mutually exclusive. For many traders, they're sequential stages of the same journey.

Let's map it out.

The Fork in the Road

You have the software. The question is how to deploy it.
What does your trading life look like in a year? In five? In ten?

Path 1: Trading Your Own Capital

The most common starting point is also the most difficult: trading your own money.

Self-funded trading is honest. Every dollar you risk is a dollar you earned elsewhere—from your job, your savings, your family. There is no capital cushion from an institution. There is no mentor looking over your shoulder. There is no one to blame when things go wrong.

This is both the curse and the gift of self-funding. The curse is that the stakes are psychologically real in a way that simulated or funded trading never quite captures. The gift is that you learn, viscerally, what risk actually feels like.

The Education Phase

If you are at this stage, your primary objective is not profit. It is survival while learning. Your capital is tuition. You are paying the market to teach you.

This reframe is critical. If you approach self-funded trading expecting to get rich quickly, you will almost certainly blow up. The statistics are grim: 70–95% of retail traders lose money in any given year. The survivors are not smarter than the casualties—they simply lasted long enough to learn.

(This is the absorbing barrier from Chapter 13 in action. Most traders hit ruin before they accumulate enough sample size for their edge—if they have one—to manifest.)

The practical guidelines for this phase are simple but demanding:

- **Size tiny.** Trade the smallest position size your broker allows. Your goal is repetitions, not returns. You are building pattern recognition and emotional calluses—the "chair flying" we discussed in Chapter 8, but with real money.
- **Protect your capital ruthlessly.** If you lose 20% of your stake, stop trading live. Return to simulation. Diagnose what went wrong. This is not weakness—it's survival. The circuit breaker rules from Chapter 8 apply to your entire trading career, not just individual sessions.

- **Track everything.** Your journal is your most valuable asset. Every trade, every emotion, every deviation from your plan. The patterns in that data will teach you more than any book. This is the deliberate practice framework we established—you cannot improve what you don't measure.
- **Set a time horizon.** Give yourself a defined period—six months, a year—to achieve consistency. If you are not consistently profitable by then, reassess. Not everyone is suited to trading, and discovering that early is a gift, not a failure.

The Compounding Phase

If you survive the education phase—if you achieve genuine consistency over a meaningful sample size (100+ trades minimum)—you enter the compounding phase. Here, your objective shifts from survival to growth.

This is where the mathematics of Chapter 13 become practical reality. Your edge, however small, begins to compound. You can cautiously increase position size as your equity grows. You reinvest profits rather than withdrawing them.

- **The danger at this stage is impatience.** You have proven you can trade profitably, and the temptation to "size up" aggressively is overwhelming. Resist it. The traders who blow up at this stage are not the ones who couldn't find edge—they are the ones who found edge and then over-leveraged it. (Remember the leverage privilege from Chapter 13: you must earn the right to apply leverage through demonstrated smoothness.) Stay within your risk parameters. Let the curve compound.

Path 2: Joining a Proprietary Trading Firm

For many traders, the fastest path runs through a proprietary trading firm.

A prop firm provides what self-funded trading cannot: capital, infrastructure, and structure. Instead of risking your own savings, you trade the firm's capital. Instead of cobbling together retail tools, you access institutional-grade platforms. Instead of learning alone, you operate within a community of professionals.

The prop firm industry has bifurcated dramatically in recent years. Understanding the distinction is critical.

Retail "Funded Trader" Programs

The explosion of funded trader programs (FTMO, TopStep, and dozens of imitators) has created a new category in the market. These programs charge traders a fee to take an "evaluation," and those who pass receive access to a funded account with profit splits (typically 70–90% to the trader).

These programs serve a purpose. If you have skill but lack capital, they offer a path to trading real size without personal financial risk. But understand what they are. The evaluation process—typically requiring consistent profitability with strict drawdown limits—does filter for some baseline competence.

- **However, understand the business model.** Most funded trader programs make the majority of their revenue from evaluation fees, not from trading profits. Their incentive is to attract as many paying evaluators as possible, not necessarily to develop world-class traders. The failure rates on evaluations are high by design.
- **And understand the rule structures.** Most programs are riddled with "gotcha rules" buried in thousands of lines of terms and conditions. Trailing drawdowns that follow your equity curve upward punish exactly the asymmetric winners you should be seeking. Consistency rules that cap daily profit percentages actively encourage cutting winners short—the precise opposite of what professionals do. News trading restrictions eliminate some of the highest-edge opportunities in the market. Do your research before committing.

Here's the deeper irony: the trading style that gets you through these evaluations is often fundamentally incompatible with long-term professional success. The habits that get you through an evaluation—playing small, taking quick profits, avoiding volatility—are the exact habits you'll need to unlearn at a real firm or in a properly capitalized account.

Use funded programs strategically: as a capital source once you've already proven consistency, not as a substitute for developing genuine edge. And recognize what you're optimizing for.

Institutional Proprietary Trading Firms

A different category entirely is the institutional prop firm—firms like Jane Street, Optiver, DRW, Susquehanna, Jump Trading, and others. These firms recruit traders (typically from top universities), provide intensive training, and deploy significant capital behind proven performers. Compensation is substantial, but so are expectations. The hiring bar is exceptionally high, the culture is intensely competitive, and most entrants don't survive their first few years.

For most readers of this book, the institutional prop path is not directly accessible. These firms recruit from specific pipelines (quantitative degrees, elite universities, competitive programming backgrounds) and rarely hire experienced retail traders.

Beyond Traditional Gatekeeping

When I left the Navy, I applied to over 40 prop firms. Not one said yes. My background wasn't quantitative enough. I didn't have the pedigree. I didn't know the right people. Every door was closed.

So I built my own door.

Raen Trading, where I serve as CEO, takes a different approach than the firms that rejected me. We're a principal trading firm with institutional infrastructure—same execution platforms, same capital commitment, same profit-sharing economics as the established shops. The difference is how we find traders.

Alongside standard recruiting, we run an open assessment program. A global tryout. If you can trade, you can compete for a seat. No pedigree required.

This isn't charity. It's not a funded trader program in different clothing. The firm's economics are built entirely on trading performance—we make money when traders make money, period. We're looking for future professionals, not evaluation fees.

Less than 2% of people who attempt the assessment pass. The bar is high precisely because the opportunity is real. But the path exists.

For everyone who gets told no because they didn't go to Wharton or work at Citadel or know the right people—that was me. I built this because I wish it had existed for me.

Several firms are beginning to explore similar models. In a field where performance is measurable, meritocracy shouldn't be optional.

What to Look for in a Prop Firm

If you're evaluating prop firms, ask these questions:

- **How does the firm make money?** If the primary revenue source is evaluation fees, be cautious. A firm that profits when you profit has a fundamentally different relationship with you than one that profits when you fail and pay again.
- **What are your actual trading costs?** Many funded trader programs charge upward of $4 per round turn in commissions—costs that compound relentlessly and erode edge. Legitimate prop firms typically access exchange member rates, often a quarter of that or less depending on the product. Over thousands of trades, this difference alone can determine whether a marginally profitable strategy survives or bleeds out. Ask for the actual fee schedule, not marketing language.
- **What infrastructure do you access?** Institutional-grade platforms versus retail tools matter for execution quality. The difference in fill quality, latency, and order types can meaningfully impact your P&L. This is part of the "operational edge" we discussed in Chapter 7.
- **What is the path to scale?** Can you grow your allocation as you prove yourself? What does the trajectory from junior trader to senior trader look like? A firm with no upward mobility is a dead end, not a career.
- **Who are the other traders?** The quality of your peers matters. You will learn faster surrounded by experienced professionals than by other retail traders finding their way. The mentorship and culture of a firm compound over time.
- **What happens if you fail?** Understand the downside. Some firms charge fees on failure; others simply terminate the relationship. Know the terms. The absorbing barrier exists at the firm level too—understand where it is.

Path 3: Building Toward Institutional Capital

For traders with ambition beyond personal wealth, the ultimate destination is managing institutional capital—whether as a fund manager, a CTA, or through a separately managed account (SMA) structure.

This path is long, demanding, and not for everyone. But for those who pursue it, the rewards are substantial: the ability to scale your edge across significant capital, the professionalization of your trading business, and the potential for meaningful wealth creation.

The Track Record Requirement

> **The single most important asset for attracting institutional capital is a verified track record.** Everything else—your strategy, your pitch, your credentials—matters, but nothing matters more than demonstrable, audited performance.

Institutional allocators—family offices, funds of funds, endowments—are professional skeptics. They have seen thousands of traders with compelling stories and backtests. What they cannot ignore is a live track record showing consistent risk-adjusted returns over multiple years.

This is why the decomposition framework from Chapter 11 matters so much. Allocators will strip away your beta and factor exposures. They want to see genuine alpha—the residual that remains after the tide and currents are removed. If your returns are just leveraged market exposure, sophisticated capital will see through it immediately.

The standard requirements vary by allocator type. Family offices and high-net-worth individuals are often willing to consider shorter track records (12–18 months) if the strategy is compelling and the trader has relevant professional experience. Funds of funds typically require two to three years of audited performance. Institutional allocators (pensions, endowments) generally require three to five years of track record and minimum AUM thresholds ($100M+).

Research from AIMA (Alternative Investment Management Association) found that half of surveyed investors would consider allocating to managers with less than one year of track record—but this typically requires either exceptional performance or strong prior institutional experience.

Building a Verifiable Track Record

> **If institutional capital is your goal, start building your track record now.** Every day you trade without documentation is a day wasted.

The most straightforward approach is to trade real capital in a segregated account. Even small amounts ($10,000–$50,000) establish a live trading history. Keep meticulous records. Brokerage statements provide contemporaneous evidence that cannot be fabricated retroactively.

Alternatively, third-party verification platforms like Darwinex, FundSeeder, and others allow traders to establish verified track records that can be presented to potential allocators. Darwinex's DarwinIA program provides seed capital allocations to top-performing traders—up to €375,000 for DarwinIA SILVER and up to €500,000 for DarwinIA GOLD—with 15% performance fees on profits. These allocations are cumulative and can be held simultaneously, meaning consistent top performers can manage several million euros in notional capital. These platforms solve the chicken-and-egg problem of needing capital to build a track record.

For more formal verification, you can pursue an independent audit. Hiring an independent accountant to audit your trading records can cost $10,000–$50,000+ depending on complexity, but it provides the credibility required for serious fundraising.

If you intend to raise institutional capital, consider GIPS compliance from day one. GIPS are the gold standard for performance reporting, and compliance signals professionalism and eliminates questions about performance calculation methodology. It is more work upfront, but it removes friction later.

The SMA Path

For emerging managers, SMAs have become an increasingly attractive path to institutional capital.

In an SMA structure, the investor creates their own investment vehicle and appoints the trader as an investment advisor. The trader manages the capital, but the investor retains beneficial ownership of the underlying positions. This structure offers advantages for both parties.

For allocators, SMAs provide greater transparency into positions and risk, direct control over custody and operations, the ability to customize mandates (leverage, instruments, ESG constraints), and lower minimum investments than seeding a new fund.

For managers, SMAs provide access to institutional capital without the overhead of launching a fund. The operational burden—compliance, administration, audit—is handled by the platform, allowing you to focus on trading rather than business operations. Most importantly, SMAs create a pathway to larger allocations as your track record develops.

The SMA space has grown substantially. J.P. Morgan research found that 56% of hedge fund managers have at least one SMA or "fund of one," with this percentage increasing substantially for larger firms. The average minimum allocation for an SMA is approximately $73 million, though platforms serving emerging managers may accept lower amounts. More recent data suggest accelerating adoption: J.P. Morgan expects 58% of new fund launches to use SMA structures, and Goldman Sachs projects the space to grow by more than $400 billion by 2027.

For traders aspiring to institutional capital, the SMA path offers a more accessible entry point than launching a standalone fund. Various prime broker managed account platforms and specialist emerging manager platforms can provide the infrastructure. If you have a track record and want to explore the SMA path, reach out directly. We facilitate these opportunities at Raen, and I'm always happy to talk with traders who've done the work.

The Fund Launch

Traditionally, the most capital-intensive path has been launching your own hedge fund. The barriers to entry are historically high, requiring complex global infrastructure: legal formation (typically Cayman Islands or Delaware), a web of service providers (administrators, auditors, prime brokers), and strict regulatory compliance.

In the past, the economics were prohibitive. Many emerging managers cited $100 million AUM as the threshold for a sustainable business—enough to generate management fees that cover operating expenses. Below that level, the fund may operate at a loss for years while building a track record. For the individual trader, this path was often premature.

However, the landscape has shifted.

Technology has bridged the gap between retail trading and institutional structure. Through specialized infrastructure providers—such as ARB and its integration of the 4Alt platform—the operational heavy lifting of fund formation has been streamlined. These modern solutions provide the structural support that allows managers to bypass the traditional, costly barriers of fund formation.

You no longer need to wait for massive institutional scale to start building your business properly. By leveraging these platforms, a trader with a verified track record can set up a professional fund structure efficiently, turning performance history into a marketable investment vehicle.

The Career Arc

Let me offer a stylized version of how these paths might sequence over a trading career.

The Foundation years (Years 1–2) Survival, not success. Most traders approach this phase with capital appreciation in mind—they're trying to make money. This is exactly wrong. Your focus should be reps and capital preservation, in that order. If you can put the idea of making money out of your head entirely during this period, you'll be in a far better position than those chasing returns from day one. Trade personal capital in small size, focusing on process rather than profits. Your objective is to achieve consistency over 100+ trades while building the journal and documentation habits that will serve you for decades.

From years of working with traders, I can tell you the most common mistake I see: people believe they just need to learn more, read more, study more. It's not that. You can read every book on trading ever written and still blow up your first account. What you actually need is time in the seat—the accumulated experience of placing orders, managing risk in real-time, and making the thousands of small decisions that can't be learned from a page. Most traders never leave this phase—either because they blow up or because they never achieve genuine consistency.

> **The Capitalization years (roughly Years 2–4)** are about accessing larger capital. This might mean joining a prop firm to trade institutional size or continuing to self-fund with a now-proven edge. Either way, you begin establishing a verified track record that can be presented to future allocators. You also develop specialization—the specific instrument, strategy, and timeframe where your edge is sharpest.
>
> **The Professionalization years (roughly Years 4–7)** are about building infrastructure around your trading. You achieve meaningful AUM ($1–10 million under management), consider

an SMA platform or small fund structure, build relationships with potential allocators, and refine your operations (risk management, compliance, reporting). Trading becomes less about individual trades and more about systems.

The Scale years (Year 7 and beyond) are about compounding everything you've built. You attract institutional capital, launch a standalone fund or expand SMA relationships, build a team (analysts, operations, risk), and compound both capital and reputation. At this stage, your trading business has become a business in the fullest sense.

A word on expectations. Everyone believes they're the exception to the timeline. They're usually not.

The worst mistake aspiring traders make is treating this as a supplement to their income—a side hustle, the new dropshipping. It isn't. You might string together some winners, but over any meaningful sample size, part-time attention produces full-time losses. If someone is pitching you trading as a side business, they're selling you something other than reality.

This doesn't mean the statistics should discourage you from trying. The failure rates in trading are brutal, but so are the failure rates in entrepreneurship. If we refused to attempt anything with long odds, we'd have no founders, no artists, no breakthroughs. The path is worth walking. But walk it with open eyes.

If you enter thinking you'll be profitable in three months or six months, you're setting yourself up for disappointment—not because you lack talent, but because you haven't yet encountered the mistakes you can't foresee. You'll leave orders in overnight. You'll have the wrong product window up and execute in the wrong market. News will hit while you're offside and wipe out a month of progress. These aren't failures of pattern recognition; they're the tuition payments of inexperience. You don't know what you don't know, and you need time in the seat to discover it.

Set the expectations correctly from the beginning. Save capital. Plan for a multi-year journey. And understand what you're building toward: if you make it through, professional trading is one of the most lucrative and intellectually rewarding careers on the planet. The odds are long, but the payoff—both financial and personal—justifies the attempt for those willing to do it properly.

This is not the only path, and timelines vary enormously based on skill, luck, and market conditions. Some traders achieve institutional backing in three years; others take 15. The key is to have a direction—to understand what you are building toward and to make decisions that compound in that direction.

The Infinite Game

James Carse wrote about the difference between finite and infinite games in 1986 (Simon Sinek later popularized the concept). A finite game has fixed rules, known players, and a definitive end point. An infinite game has evolving rules, changing players, and no end—the objective is simply to keep playing.

Trading Is an Infinite Game

There is no "winning" in the conventional sense. There is no final boss to defeat, no championship to claim. The market will be here tomorrow, and the day after, and the decade after that. Your objective is not to win a single trade or even a single year. Your objective is to stay in the game long enough for your edge to compound.

Everything in this book has been in service of that objective—keeping you in the game long enough for your edge to compound.

A Final Word

When I started trading years ago, I had none of the frameworks in this book. I learned them the hard way—through blown accounts, sleepless nights, and the kind of drawdowns that test everything you believe about yourself.

I wrote this book because I wish someone had written it for me.

The path from retail trader to professional is longer and harder than the trading influencers would have you believe. Most people who attempt it will fail. The market is a negative-sum game played against the most intelligent, well-resourced adversaries on the planet. The only way to survive is to be genuinely better—not luckier, not more leveraged, but better.

But if you have made it this far—if you have absorbed these concepts, built your operating system, and committed to the deliberate practice that mastery requires—you have a chance. Not a guarantee, but a chance. That is all anyone can offer.

The market doesn't care about your dreams, your background, or your circumstances. It cares only about your decisions.

And remember Chapter 1: if you don't know who the marginal trader is, it's you.

I'll see you on the other side.

—Ryan Wright
Founder & CEO, Raen Trading
Palma de Mallorca, 2026

Connect with Ryan Wright:
Website: ryanwright.co
Substack: ryanwright.substack.com
X (Twitter): @baynkr

Glossary

A

Absorbing Barrier A condition (such as bankruptcy, liquidation, or psychological break) from which a trader cannot recover. In a non-ergodic system, hitting an absorbing barrier terminates the game, making the long-run average return irrelevant. The barrier can be hard (margin call) or soft (tilt point).

Adverse Selection The phenomenon where one party in a transaction possesses information the other lacks, causing the uninformed party to systematically receive worse terms. In trading, if someone is eager to sell to you at your price, they may know something you don't. This is the "winner's curse" applied to markets.

Alpha The portion of a return not explained by the market's general movement (beta) or systematic factor exposures. It represents the genuine skill component of trading performance—what remains after stripping away tide and currents.

B

Backtest Tax The discount applied to backtested parameters (win rate, payoff ratio) to account for overfitting, survivorship bias, and the difference between historical and future conditions. Typically, 10–15% on win rate and 20–30% on payoff ratio.

Backwardation A market condition where near-term futures prices are higher than far-term prices. In volatility markets, backwardation signals crisis (spot volatility spiking above futures). Opposite of contango.

Bayesian Updating A statistical framework where probabilities are not fixed frequencies but degrees of belief that are continuously updated as new information arrives. In trading, this means adjusting position sizing and conviction as the trade develops.

Beta The return attributable to baseline market exposure—the "tide" that lifts all boats. A portfolio with beta of 1.2 moves 1.2% for every 1% the market moves. Beta is not edge; it's available to anyone who buys an index fund.

C

Carry A strategy that exploits yield differentials by borrowing in low-yielding assets and investing in high-yielding assets. Examples include currency carry (borrowing yen, investing in AUD) and fixed income carry (capturing term premium).

256 Glossary

Contango A market condition where far-term futures prices are higher than near-term prices. In volatility markets, contango is the normal state. Creates positive roll yield for short-volatility strategies.

Correlation Risk The risk that seemingly distinct positions or strategies will move in tandem during periods of market stress, effectively concentrating risk precisely when diversification is needed most. Correlations measured in backtests often differ from correlations in drawdowns.

D

Decomposition The discipline of separating trading returns into their component parts—market beta, factor exposures, and residual alpha—to determine what portion of P&L represents genuine skill versus luck or systematic risk harvesting.

Drawdown The peak-to-trough decline in an investment's value, typically expressed as a percentage. Managing drawdown depth is critical for both psychological stability and mathematical recovery, as losses require disproportionately larger gains to recover.

E

Edge A structural, informational, or behavioral advantage that allows a trader to generate positive expected value over a large sample of trades. Edge is not a feeling; it's a quantifiable asymmetry that can be articulated and measured.

Ensemble Average The average outcome across a population of participants at a single point in time. In an ergodic system, the ensemble average equals the time average for any individual. Markets are nonergodic, so ensemble averages can be misleading for individual traders.

Ergodicity A property of a system where the time average of a single trajectory equals the ensemble average of the population. Financial markets are nonergodic because an individual can go bust (hit an absorbing barrier), preventing them from achieving the market's long-term average return.

Expectancy The average amount a trader expects to win or lose per dollar risked over many trades. Calculated as: (Win Rate × Average Win) − (Loss Rate × Average Loss). Positive expectancy is necessary but not sufficient for profitability; survival is also required.

F

Factor Exposure Systematic sources of return beyond market beta, including momentum, value, carry, volatility risk premium, and size. Factor returns are compensation for bearing specific risks and are distinct from alpha, which cannot be explained by any known factor.

Fat Tails A property of probability distributions (like financial markets) where extreme events occur more frequently than predicted by a normal (Gaussian) distribution. Fat tails make value at risk models systematically underestimate true risk.

Fractional Kelly   A risk management strategy where a trader bets a fraction (typically half or quarter) of the theoretically optimal Kelly size to account for parameter uncertainty, reduce volatility, and improve psychological sustainability.

Free Capital   The portion of total equity that a trader designates as available for trading risk, adjusted for year-to-date P&L. Risk is calculated as a percentage of free capital, not total equity, to maintain appropriate position sizing through drawdowns and profits.

Friction   The total cost of executing a trade, including commissions, spreads, slippage, and market impact. Friction reduces gross edge to net edge and can turn a profitable strategy into a losing one if not carefully managed.

Fusion Analysis   A multi-lens approach to trade idea generation that synthesizes five pillars: narrative (fundamental story), technicals (price action), fundamentals (quantitative data), sentiment and positioning (market psychology), and intermarket analysis (cross-asset signals).

G

Gap Risk   The risk that price will move discontinuously from one level to another without trading in between, typically occurring when markets are closed (overnight or weekends). Stop losses Don't protect against gap risk; they exist only in continuous price space.

Geometric Return   The compound rate of growth of an investment, accounting for the sequence of returns. Geometric return is always lower than arithmetic average return due to volatility drag. It represents what you actually keep.

Grossman-Stiglitz Paradox   The economic theorem stating that if markets were perfectly informationally efficient, there would be no incentive to gather information, leading to inefficiency. Therefore, markets must be inefficient enough to compensate informed traders for their costs.

H

Hurst Exponent   A measure of market "memory" ranging from 0 to 1. Values below 0.5 indicate mean-reverting behavior; values above 0.5 indicate trending behavior. Used to detect regime characteristics and adjust strategy selection.

Hurdle Rate   The minimum rate of return required to justify the risk and effort of a trading strategy. The hurdle includes the risk-free rate, opportunity cost of capital, and a premium for the stress and uncertainty of active trading.

I

Inversion   A problem-solving technique (popularized by mathematician Carl Jacobi and investor Charlie Munger) where one addresses a problem backward. Instead of asking, "How do I succeed?" one asks, "How do I fail?" and systematically avoids those conditions.

K

Kelly Criterion A formula for determining the optimal theoretical bet size to maximize the logarithm of wealth (geometric growth) over the long run, assuming known probabilities and payoffs. Full Kelly is too volatile for human psychology; fractional Kelly is the professional standard.

Knightian Uncertainty A state where the distribution of outcomes is unknown or unmeasurable, as opposed to risk, where the distribution is known. Most trading situations involve Knightian uncertainty, not merely quantifiable risk. The distinction is epistemologically fundamental.

L

Leverage Privilege The principle that leverage is not inherently dangerous—it is a tool that must be earned through demonstrated smoothness of returns. A smooth equity curve can be safely leveraged; a volatile curve becomes more dangerous with leverage.

Liquidity Risk The risk that a trader cannot exit a position at or near the current market price due to a lack of buyers or sellers. Liquidity is conditional—it evaporates precisely when you need it most, during market stress.

M

Marginal Participant The specific buyer or seller who sets the current market price at any given moment. Understanding the constraints and motivations of the marginal participant is key to identifying edge and anticipating price movement.

Mean Reversion A strategy premised on the idea that prices deviate temporarily from fair value and will snap back. Implementations include statistical arbitrage, pairs trading, and technical oversold/overbought systems.

N

Negative-sum Game A game where the total winnings are less than the total losses due to transaction costs (friction). Trading is a negative-sum game for the aggregate participants; the house always extracts value.

Nonergodicity The property of a system (like financial markets) where the time average of an individual trajectory differs from the ensemble average of the population. An individual can hit an absorbing barrier and exit the game before achieving the population's average outcome.

Nonstationarity The property of a system whose statistical parameters (mean, variance, correlations) change over time. Financial markets are nonstationary; the rules shift as participants adapt. See Chapter 14.

O

OODA Loop Observe-Orient-Decide-Act. A decision framework developed by military strategist John Boyd. In trading, cycling through the loop faster than the market consensus creates a compounding advantage.

Glossary

Operator's Equation The formula defining professional trading performance: Performance = (Expected Value × Optimal Exposure) − Friction. Each component represents a distinct skill: finding edge, sizing appropriately, and minimizing costs.

P

Path Dependence The concept that the sequence of outcomes matters, not just the final result. In trading, the path taken by P&L determines survival; a strategy that is profitable in expectation can still cause ruin if losses cluster at the beginning.

Precautionary Principle A decision-making framework that advocates for caution and risk avoidance when the potential consequences of an action are severe or irreversible, even if the probability is uncertain. In trading, this manifests as fractional Kelly sizing and position limits.

Pre-mortem A prospective failure analysis technique where a trader imagines a trade has already failed, then works backward to identify the causes. This forces consideration of risks that confirmation bias would otherwise hide.

R

Reflexivity A theory (associated with George Soros) stating that market participants' biases affect market prices, which in turn affect the fundamentals, creating a feedback loop. The observer changes the observed; perception creates reality.

Regime A distinct market environment characterized by specific patterns of trend, volatility, and correlation. Strategies that profit in one regime (e.g., low-volatility trending) may hemorrhage in another (e.g., high-volatility choppy). Adaptation requires regime awareness.

Risk Audit A systematic process of identifying all risks associated with a trade—thesis risk, market risk, sector risk, liquidity risk, gap risk, correlation risk—and determining which are compensated (edge) and which should be hedged or eliminated.

R-multiple A unit of measurement expressing trade outcomes in terms of initial risk. A trade where you risked $500 and made $1,500 is a 3R winner. R-multiples allow comparison of trades across different instruments and position sizes.

S

Sharpe Ratio A measure of risk-adjusted return, calculated as excess return divided by standard deviation (volatility). Higher Sharpe ratios indicate smoother equity curves and greater capacity for leverage.

Survivorship Bias The logical error of concentrating on the people or things that "survived" some process while inadvertently overlooking those that did not. In trading, this manifests as studying only successful traders and ignoring the many who failed using identical methods.

T

Time Average   The average outcome for a single participant over time. In nonergodic systems like trading, the time average for an individual differs from the ensemble average across the population.

Trend-following   A strategy that buys assets going up and sells assets going down, betting on persistence. Time-series momentum compares an asset to its own past; cross-sectional momentum compares assets to peers.

Type I/II/III Allocation   A tiered position sizing framework based on conviction level. Type I (3-star) is standard size for technical-only setups; Type II (4-star) is increased size for fusion alignment; Type III (5-star) is maximum size for rare asymmetric opportunities with full confluence.

U

Urn A/Urn B   A framework (from the Ellsberg paradox) distinguishing between measurable risk (Urn A, where you know the distribution) and unmeasurable uncertainty (Urn B, where the distribution itself is unknown). Trading primarily involves Urn B.

V

Variance   A statistical measurement of the spread between numbers in a data set. In trading, variance represents volatility of returns. High variance reduces geometric growth through volatility drag and taxes the equity curve mathematically.

Volatility Drag   The mathematical reduction in compound returns caused by volatility. Approximated as: Geometric Return ≈ Arithmetic Return − $(\sigma^2/2)$. The higher the volatility, the greater the drag on long-term wealth accumulation.

Volatility Tax   The asymmetric nature of percentage losses—a larger percentage gain is required to recover from any loss. A 50% loss requires a 100% gain to recover; a 90% loss requires 900%. This asymmetry is why drawdown management is existential.

W

Wicked environment   A learning environment (per Robin Hogarth) where feedback is noisy, delayed, or inverted, making it difficult to learn correct lessons from experience. Trading is a wicked environment; chess is a "kind" one. See Chapter 15.

Winner's Curse   The tendency for the winning bid in an auction to exceed the intrinsic value, or for the winner to be the one who most overestimated value. In trading, buying often means you were the most optimistic person in the market—a warning signal.

Z

Zero-sum Game   A situation where one person's gain is exactly balanced by another's loss. Trading before costs is zero-sum; after costs (friction), it is negative-sum. Your profit must come from someone else's loss.

Index

absorbing barrier, 195–203, 210, 242, 246
adverse selection, 17–18, 37–48
alpha (*vs.* beta), 99, 108–109, 165, 167, 168, 170, 170–175, 210, 211
ambiguity aversion, 152
Archegos Capital, 167–169

backtest tax, 133–134, 146
Bayesian updating, 75, 85–87, 181
beta (market exposure), 165–166, 168, 170, 172
Black Wednesday (1992), 184
buffer (stop loss), 139

capacity to act, 69
carry strategies, 212–213
Challenger disaster, 79–80
circuit breaker (Rule of Three), 123–124
confirmation bias, 72
correlation risk, 150, 154, 158
counterparty analysis, 20–21, 44–48

Daphne Major finches, 205, 206
decision hygiene, 116–117
decomposition (return attribution), 163–175
diversification, 156–157, 160, 215
Donnelly, Brent, 122, 125, 141, 156, 229
dopamine trap, 121
drawdown management, 135–136, 145, 196, 200

edge (sources of), 54–57, 59, 62, 80–83, 85–92, 97–111
efficient market hypothesis, 14–15
Ellsberg paradox, 151–152
ensemble *vs.* time average, 194
ergodicity, 193, 210
Everest Disaster (1996), 149–151
expectancy, 67–77, 80–81

factor exposures, 168
falsification, 71, 72, 77, 79
fat tails, 62, 122, 159
Feynman, Richard, 125
flaw audit, 122–123
FOMC (September 2024), 179
fractional Kelly, 136, 146, 202
free capital (adjusted), 139, 141–142
friction, 82, 88–90, 92
fusion analysis, 237

gap risk, 144–145, 151, 154, 158, 160
geometric return, 74, 197, 203
give-back protocols, 122
Grossman-Stiglitz paradox, 14

hot hand fallacy, 164
hurdle rate, 88–89
Hurst exponent, 216

infinite game, 252
information theory, 98, 132, 199
inversion (*Man muss immer umkehren*), 187, 190